Negation and Clausal Structure

OXFORD STUDIES IN COMPARATIVE SYNTAX
Richard Kayne, *General Editor*

NEGATION AND CLAUSAL STRUCTURE

A Comparative Study of
Romance Languages

Raffaella Zanuttini

New York   Oxford
Oxford University Press
1997

Oxford University Press

Oxford   New York

Athens   Auckland   Bangkok   Bogota   Bombay   Buenos Aires
Calcutta   Cape Town   Dar es Salaam   Delhi   Florence   Hong Kong
Istanbul   Karachi   Kuala Lumpur   Madras   Madrid   Melbourne
Mexico City   Nairobi   Paris   Singapore   Taipei   Tokyo   Toronto

and associated companies in
Berlin   Ibadan

Copyright © 1997 by Raffaella Zanuttini

Published by Oxford University Press, Inc.
198 Madison Avenue, New York, New York 10016

Oxford is a registered trademark of Oxford University Press

Library of Congress Cataloguing-in-Publication Data
Zanuttini, Raffaella.
Negation and clausal structure : a comparative study of Romance
languages / Raffaella Zanuttini.
p.   cm. — (Oxford studies in comparative syntax)
Includes bibliographical references and index.
ISBN 0-19-508054-8; 0-19-508055-6 (pbk.)
1. Romance languages — Negatives. 2. Romance languages — Grammar,
Comparative. 3. Romance languages — Clauses. 4. Italian language —
Dialects. I. Title. II. Series.
PC119.Z36   1997
440 — dc20   96-18432

1 3 5 7 9 8 6 4 2

Printed in the United States of America
on acid-free paper

A Bob

PREFACE

This book offers a systematic investigation of negative markers in several languages within the Romance family, focusing in particular on less widely known varieties, often called "dialects." It can be considered a dialectological study cast in modern terms — that is, one that aims not only at uncovering patterns and generalizations but also at raising questions and seeking answers to further our understanding of the abstract structure of language.

Given that my ultimate goal is that of characterizing not only the properties of a particular language but also the properties of universal grammar, one might wonder why I begin with the study of a particular language family (i.e., Romance) instead of comparing the expression of sentential negation in languages that are representative of different families (e.g., Italian, German, Japanese, and Turkish). The advantage of starting from the examination of closely related languages has emerged most clearly in recent years from the work of such linguists as Richard Kayne, Paola Benincà, Christer Platzack, and Anders Holmberg, among others, who have been working within the paradigm of comparative syntax. Their work shows that conducting research on a set of languages that differ from one another only minimally allows us to perform experiments in which we have controlled for external factors (i.e., gross variation among languages) and we can therefore observe the effect of changing a single variable on a battery of tests. In this case, the variable is the different syntactic realizations of sentential negation. From this perspective, the Romance languages provide an excellent testing ground for the purposes of this study, since it is possible to find varieties that differ only minimally and precisely with respect to those properties related to the expression of sentential negation.

I have been able to gather a new and rich collection of data concerning the syntactic expression of sentential negation, thanks mainly to the resources of the Center for

Dialectology of the University of Padua, Italy. These data show minimal differences in controlled environments (provided by closely related languages), thus giving us insights into otherwise impenetrable aspects of syntactic structure. They also provide a precious data base for syntacticians who study phenomenona other than sentential negation, as they come from languages that are not easily accessible for investigation, having small numbers of native speakers and relatively few grammatical descriptions. The data come from different sources: in addition to scholarly articles, I relied on linguistic atlases, grammar books, dissertations, and investigations conducted with informants.

Alongside the richness in empirical data, this book offers precise proposals concerning the structure of negative clauses and the properties of the negative markers under investigation. The study of negative markers leads me to examine several aspects of clausal structure. In particular, I investigate their distribution with respect to both subject and object clitics, as well as with certain classes of adverbs. This requires a reevaluation of the proper syntactic representation of all these classes of elements. I also discuss at length the interaction of negative markers and verb movement, focusing especially on yes/no questions and WH-questions, exclamative clauses and imperative clauses. Movement of non-finite verbal forms will also play a role in this discussion, in particular the comparison between infinitives and past participles. Therefore, this book can also be viewed as a study of clausal structure through the magnifying glass that negative markers provide.

Though the investigation is based on a comparison of Romance languages, the results are of interest beyond the boundaries of this language family. They represent a study of the possible range of variation of the syntactic means for the expression of sentential negation and shed light on the interaction of negative markers with other aspects of sentential structure. For example, I identify the possible structural positions negative markers can occupy in Romance, thus providing a basis against which to compare the structural position of these elements across languages. I also analyze the role of the negative marker in questions, arguing that, given the proper configuration, a negative marker is attracted to $C°$ to check an interrogative feature. The generality of this proposal will have to be evaluated by examining other languages which also exhibit interrogative features in $C°$ and negative markers which count as the (non-nominal) element structurally closest to $C°$. In general, I believe that this work can be viewed as a step toward defining how sentential negation can be realized in natural language generally and how it interacts with other syntactic manifestations of sentential properties, most of which are present across languages and are not peculiar to Romance. As I am emphasizing that this analysis can provide a basis on which to conduct the study of other language families, I should also add that it was itself informed by studies on sentential negation conducted on languages outside Romance. Such interaction is pervasive and hard to make precise, but should become obvious throughout the book.

Baltimore, Maryland   R. Z.
February 1996

ACKNOWLEDGMENTS

My interest in the syntactic properties of sentential negation started while I was in graduate school at the University of Pennsylvania. My 1991 dissertation reflects my thinking on these issues at that time, and I am grateful to my committee members — Tony Kroch, Richie Kayne, Rich Campbell, and Jack Hoeksema — for their guidance in that work. Since then, my thinking has changed in some fundamental ways, due both to an expansion in the empirical domain and to related developments in syntactic theory, though of course some of the guiding questions remain the same.

Kayne was the one who first suggested that I write a book on this topic. Throughout the evolution of this project, he has been my main source of inspiration and encouragement. I am deeply grateful to him for being a model of intellectual rigor and creativity, for his warm and gentle support, and for his unfailing trust that this book would eventually see the light of day.

The general plan of the book was conceived during a wonderful year spent as a postdoctoral fellow in the department of cognitive science at Johns Hopkins University. I would like to thank Steve Anderson, Luigi Burzio, and Alfonso Caramazza for granting me the opportunity to spend a year in such a rich intellectual environment. I am particularly indebted to Steve and Luigi for their inspiring classes and discussions, for being rigorous scholars and warm and generous friends, and for allowing me to remain part of the department even after my postdoctoral year was through. They cannot possibly realize just how much I treasure the richness of their knowledge, the depth of their thought, and their friendship.

Work on this book continued during my first few years as a faculty member at the linguistics department at Georgetown University. I would like to thank two senior colleagues who served as department chair during these years, Solomon Sara and Ralph Fasold, for their support in helping me bring this project to completion. I am grateful to them for their trust and their encouragement, and for their aid in procuring financial support from Georgetown in the form of a summer faculty research grant and leave time to devote to my research. My thanks also go to Marisa Jiménez for her help as a research assistant.

The empirical coverage of this book would not be nearly so rich were it not for the two semesters I spent in the linguistics department of the University of Padua, Italy. I am immensely grateful to Paola Benincà and Laura Vanelli for helping me obtain a research fellowship, which allowed me to spend several productive months there. While in Padua, I benefited greatly from their expertise on Romance dialectology and linguistics in general, from the department's rich resources, as well as from some much appreciated peaceful time devoted to this work. All of this contributed to making my stay in Padua rich and satisfying on both intellectual and personal levels. I am also deeply indebted to Cecilia Poletto for innumerable fascinating discussions on linguistic matters and for her energizing friendship and companionship. Guglielmo Cinque also greatly contributed to making my time in Italy so fruitful, and I would like to thank him for his kindness, for putting at my disposal his vast knowledge of the linguistic literature, and for his incisive comments during discussions that were always most inspiring.

My heartfelt thanks go to Paola Benincà, Guglielmo Cinque, Bob Frank, Richie Kayne, Nicola Munaro, and Cecilia Poletto for their insightful and extensive comments on (sometimes more than one version of) each chapter of this book. They helped me see the strengths and weaknesses of my proposals, discussed with me possible implications I had missed, and brought to my attention many relevant data and bibliographical references. I am deeply grateful to them for their time and patience; this book could not have been written without their help and support. I am also indebted to Judy Bernstein, Paul Portner, and Beatrice Santorini, each of whom read a preliminary version of the entire manuscript and provided me with extremely valuable comments on matters of both form and content. I have also benefited from discussions with Héctor Campos, Giuliana Giusti, Giorgio Graffi, Bill Ladusaw, Andrea Moro, Mair Parry, Jean-Yves Pollock, Paul Portner, Marisa Rivero, Arhonto Terzi, and Massimo Vai. Finally, I would like to express my personal and intellectual debt to Liliane Haegeman, who has helped me throughout these years with her friendship, her support and encouragement, her crucial role during our collaborations, and her own work on negation.

This work would not have been possible without the kind assistance of Lucia Belli, Carla Broglino, Rosanna Buttier, Ida Cossavella, Valeria Figini, Donatella Jeantet, Andrea Moro, Nicola Munaro, Massimo Vai, and Giorgio Vassoney. They patiently provided the data from a number of the northern Italian varieties discussed in this book.

During the past few year, I have had the good fortune of making a number of short visits to the linguistics departments of several academic institutions. I am grateful to Bill Ladusaw and Jim McCloskey for inviting me to discuss my work at the University of California at Santa Cruz, to Sten Vikner for a similar opportunity at the University of Stuttgart, and to Guglielmo Cinque and Charlotte Galves for providing me the opportunity to teach short courses on this material at the University of Venice and the University of Campinas, Brazil, respectively. I greatly valued these opportunities and am grateful to all those who discussed these issues with me. I have also benefitted from comments and questions I received during presentations I made over the past few years. In particular, parts of chapter 3 were presented at the Workshop on Negation held in Ottawa in May 1995, and the joint work with Paul Portner discussed in chapter 2 was presented at the 1995 annual meeting of the North East Linguistic Society (NELS) in Boston. Parts of chapter 4 were presented at the colloquium series of the linguistics department of the University of Padua and of the University of Ottawa. I thank the members of those audiences and apologize for not having been able to take more of their comments into account.

Finally, I would like to thank those people who made this book possible through their love and support. My parents, Maria Stella and Rino, constantly remind me of all that's wonderful in life. I would never have acquired the perseverance, humility, and good humor that are necessary to write a book if I hadn't had them by my side all these years. The existence and example of my siblings — Roberto, Riccardo, and Rosy — have helped me keep things in perspective and face with serenity life's many difficult choices. I am also in debt to my friends, my aunts and uncles, and the rest of my extended family, spread over two continents, who so generously provide me with everything I could possibly need, from delicious food to good laughter, to love and trust and acceptance. Among them, I would like to mention Ginny, a wonderful Zia, and my nephew Edoardo, in my opinion the sweetest child in the world. Finally, I owe more than I could possibly express in words to Bob, whose remarkable intellectual talents combined with an incredibly generous and loving nature have made my life better than any dream.

Contents

Negation and Clausal Structure

1

Issues in the Syntax of Sentential Negation

1.1. Negative markers and clausal structure

The discussion in this book is organized around a distinction that has both empirical and theoretical relevance: the distinction between pre- and post-verbal negative markers. I introduce this distinction now, as it will help me outline the organization of the book.

The distribution of negative markers in Romance falls into two broad classes, which give rise to three main strategies for negating a clause:

1. *Negative markers in pre-verbal position.* Some Romance languages negate the clause by employing only a pre-verbal negative marker; among these are standard Italian, Spanish, Catalan, Portuguese, Romanian, Galician, all of the dialects of central and southern Italy, the northern Italian dialects spoken in the eastern part of northern Italy, and varieties of Eastern Rhaeto-Romantsch spoken in Upper Engadine, Lower Engadine, and Val Müstair. This strategy is exemplified in the following examples:

(1) a. Gianni *non* ha telefonato a sua madre. (Italian)
    b. Juan *no* ha llamado a su madre. (Spanish)
    c. El Joan *no* a trucat a sa mare. (Catalan)
    d. João *não* ligou para sua mãe. (Portuguese)
    e. Jon *nu*-i telefona mamei lui. (Romanian)

    'John hasn't called his mother.'

(2) *Non* quero xantar. (Galician)
    neg want to-sing
    'I don't want to sing.'

3

As shown by the examples in (3), the negative marker always precedes the main verb, whether it is finite (as in (3)a) or non-finite (as in (3)b and (3)c) and whether it is a simple form or a compound form consisting of the auxiliary plus the past participle (as in (3)d). Though these examples are from standard Italian, analogous patterns are found in the other Romance languages in this group:

(3) a. Gianni *non* legge articoli di sintassi. (Italian)
        Gianni neg reads articles of syntax
        'Gianni doesn't read syntax articles.'

     b. *Non* leggere articoli di sintassi è un vero peccato.
        neg to-read articles of syntax is a real shame
        'Not to read syntax articles is a real pity.'

     c. *Non* leggendo articoli di sintassi, Gianni non conosce il   minimalismo.
        neg reading articles of syntax, Gianni neg knows   the minimalism
        'Not reading syntax articles, Gianni is not familiar with minimalism.'

     d. Gianni *non* avrebbe   mai letto articoli di sintassi.
        Gianni neg had(cond.) never read articles of syntax
        'Gianni would never have read syntax articles.'

   2. *Negative markers in post-verbal position.* Other Romance languages negate the clause by employing only a post-verbal negative marker; among these are varieties of Occitan, Valdotain, Piedmontese, Sursilvan, and Surmeiran.[1] These languages are geographically contiguous, covering the area of southeastern France, the Romance part of Switzerland, and the western part and central part of northern Italy. The defining property of this class of negative markers is that they always follow the main verb when it is finite and in a simple form, as illustrated in the following examples:[2]

(4) Maria a   mangia *nen*. (Piedmontese)
     Mary s.cl eats   neg
     'Mary doesn't eat.'

(5) Lo film l'ëra   *pa* dzen.   (Valdotain)
     the movie s.cl'was neg beautiful
     'The movie wasn't good.'

(6) Il parle *pas* jamais. (Quebecois)
     he talks neg never
     'He never talks.'

(7) a. Vôl *pas* venir.   (Occitan)
        wants neg to-come
        'He doesn't want to come.'

     b. Troberon *pas* digun.
        will-find neg nobody
        'They won't find anyone.'

When the verbal form consists of an auxiliary and a past participle, some post-verbal negative markers occur in a position immediately following the auxiliary, while others can follow both the auxiliary and the past participle. Piedmontese *nen*, for example, follows the auxiliary and obligatorily precedes the past participle (cf. (8)a); similarly Valdotain *pa* (cf. (8)b), Milanese *minga* (cf. (8)c), and Sursilvan *buca* (cf. (8)d):[3]

(8) a. Maria a   l'ha   *nen* parlà tant. (Piedmontese)
Mary s.cl s.cl'has neg talked much
'Mary hasn't talked much.'

  b. Dz'i   *pa* mindzà. (Valdotain)
s.cl'have neg eaten
'I haven't eaten.'

  c. El l'ha   *minga* scrivuu. (Milanese)
he s.cl'has neg   written
'He hasn't written.'

  d. El ha *buca* fatg ils pensums. (Sursilvan)
he has neg done the exercises
'He hasn't done the exercises.'

In contrast, Milanese *no* obligatorily follows the past participle, as illustrated in (9):

(9) a. El l'ha   scrivuu *no*. (Milanese)
he s.cl'has written neg
'He hasn't written.'

  b. *El l'ha *no* scrivuu.

3. *Co-occurrence of a pre-verbal and a post-verbal negative marker.* Some Romance languages employ two negative markers. Standard French is probably the best known such case; an example is given here:

(10) Je *n*'ai   *pas* parlé de toi. (French)
I neg'have neg spoken of you
'I didn't talk about you.'

Other Romance languages that employ the same strategy are the variety of Piedmontese spoken in Cairo Montenotte (*n . . . nent*), some Rhaeto-Romantsch languages, e.g., Surmeiran (*na . . . betg*), and Walloon, spoken in Belgium (*nu/ni . . . nin*). Some examples follow:[4]

(11) a. U *n* li   sent *nent*. (Cairese)
s.cl neg him hears neg
'He can't hear him.'

  b. Igl bab   *na* lavoura *betg*. (Surmeiran)
the father neg works   neg
'The father doesn't work.'

  c. Po *n*'mu   *nin* tromper. (Walloon)
for neg'me neg to-err
'So that I don't make a mistake.'

In this book I generally set aside the case of French, which is rather complex and would require me to draw not only dialectal distinctions among the varieties spoken in different geographical areas but also genre distinctions between formal and non-formal registers.[5] With the exception of French and Walloon, the pre-verbal negative marker in these languages does not appear with a non-finite verb. That is, it cannot occur with infinitives, imperatives, gerunds, and past participles.[6]

These differences are relevant both empirically and theoretically, as the pre-verbal negative markers exhibit different properties from the the post-verbal negative markers; moreover, the pre-verbal negative markers that negate a clause by themselves have different properties from those that must co-occur with another negative element.

In Chapter 2, I examine the syntactic properties of pre-verbal negative markers and the contrast between those pre-verbal elements that can negate a clause by themselves and those that cannot. This will lead me to discuss their interaction with both complement and subject clitics — that is, the pronominal elements that occur in pre-verbal position. We will see that the pre-verbal negative markers that can negate a clause by themselves always precede all complement clitics in linear order, whereas those that cannot do not necessarily do so. I take this to constitute a first piece of evidence that the two types of negative markers differ syntactically, in addition to differing in their contribution to the interpretation of the clause. Further evidence in the same direction comes from an examination of the interaction of negative markers and subject clitics. Although the data seem extremely complicated at first sight, a closer observation reveals a systematic pattern, in which the negative markers that can negate a clause by themselves exhibit a different distribution from those that cannot. To see this difference, I need to discuss in some detail certain differences among subject clitics: it is only through the characterization of different classes of subject clitics that we can see the pattern underlying the behavior of the negative markers. Simplifying grossly, my investigation of this part of the clause reveals that the negative markers that can negate the clause by themselves are structurally higher than those that cannot, thus confirming my previous finding and making it more precise. Note that such a detailed investigation of the differences between these two types of negative markers is possible only because I am comparing languages that differ in the variable under investigation while keeping other properties constant; that is, it is made possible by the fact that the languages examined here are the same in all relevant respects (both having finite verbs that raise to the same extent, both having subject clitics, both allowing the same options for the position of the subject) and differ only in the one being examined — namely, in the syntax of the pre-verbal negative marker. Finally, negative markers that can negate a clause by themselves and those that cannot differ also in the presence of verb movement to a position higher than the one the verb normally occupies in declarative clauses (let's call it C°, for simplicity). In languages where the finite verb precedes the subject clitic in yes/no questions (so-called *subject clitic inversion*), for example, the negative markers that can negate the clause by themselves do not co-occur with this word order, whereas those that cannot do. Whereas lack of co-occurrence with subject clitic inversion is often interpreted as a blocking effect of the negative marker on movement of the verb, I propose to view it differently. I argue that the negative markers that can negate the clause by themselves constitute the closer head which can be attracted to C° to satisfy the interrogative feature that characterizes questions; hence, the verb need not, and thus cannot, move. The negative markers that cannot negate the clause by themselves, in contrast, do not constitute a head, which can be attracted to C°, and thus the verb must move even in their presence. This discussion of the interaction of pre-verbal negative markers and verb movement also leads me to examine exclamative clauses, yes/no questions, and WH-questions that trigger a scalar implicature. We will see that the difference between pre-verbal negative markers that can negate a clause by themselves and those that cannot is not only structural but also related to the semantic features that characterize them.

Chapter 3 is devoted to the identification of the structural position of post-verbal negative markers and to the issue of whether there exists a correspondence between a certain structural position and a given interpretation. Because I define this class of negative markers as those occurring after the finite verb and before the VP-internal complements of the verb, I will study their distribution in relation to that of other elements which occur in the same part of the clause, namely certain classes of adverbs and non-finite forms of the verb (participles and infinitivals). I will first examine the relative position of adverb classes with respect to one another. Then I will show that the negative markers occupy a fixed position with respect to such classes of adverbs and that, moreover, they do not all occupy the same position. Piedmontese *pa*, for example, precedes the adverb *gia* 'already', whereas Piedmontese *nen* follows it. Similar differences can also be seen with respect to the distribution of the past participle and of infinitival verbs. Thus Milanese *minga* precedes the past participle, whereas Milanese *no* obligatorily follows it. Finally, I will argue that the highest of the positions a post-verbal negative marker can occupy is associated with what I will call a "presuppositional reading" — that is, the negation of a proposition assumed in the discourse. In contrast, the other two positions do not share this reading; rather they negate a proposition with no particular discourse status (as is the case for the pre-verbal negative markers).

Chapter 4 is a study of the constraints exhibited by sentential negative markers in imperative clauses. Pre-verbal negative markers that can negate a clause by themselves cannot occur in imperative clauses if the main verb has a morphological form unique to the imperative paradigm. In contrast, they can occur in imperative clauses if the auxiliary verb has a morphological form unique to the imperative or if the verb (main or auxiliary) is a so-called suppletive form, that is, a form borrowed from a verbal paradigm other than the imperative (e.g., indicative, subjunctive, infinitive, or gerund). Post-verbal negative markers do not exhibit such restrictions. The impossibility of a pre-verbal negative marker in an imperative clause has often been attributed to a blocking effect of the pre-verbal negative marker on verb movement to $C°$. I make the novel empirical observation that such a restriction is limited to main verbs and fails to affect auxiliaries. Bearing this fact in mind and building on the properties of pre-verbal negative markers highlighted in the course of the book, I cannot subscribe to a view in terms of a blocking effect of the pre-verbal negative marker. I propose instead that the pre-verbal negative marker is attracted to $C°$ to satisfy the feature that characterizes imperative clauses. This is parallel to what happens in interrogative clauses and has the same consequence of making verb movement unnecessary. In my view, the ungrammaticality that ensues in negative imperative clauses stems from the fact that the pre-verbal negative marker triggers the presence of certain features in the functional projection expressing mood (MoodP). Such features can be checked by the presence of an (overt or abstract) auxiliary or by the abstract mood features associated with verbs in the indicative or the subjunctive; but they fail to be checked when a main verb in the imperative form occurs in the clause. In contrast, no ungrammaticality ensues when an imperative clause is negated by a post-verbal negative marker because such elements do not have any effect on the projection MoodP, as they are not in the head position that takes it as its complement.

1.2.   The distribution of negative constituents

A great many syntactic phenomena related to sentential negation in Romance are not covered in this book. I discuss one in this section, albeit briefly: the constraints that govern the distribution of negative constituents in post-verbal position. By negative constituents I refer to the counterparts of 'nobody', 'nothing', 'never', or 'no + N' (e.g., 'no student', 'no place') in the languages under investigation. The reason I want to point out this phenomenon, even though I will not investigate it in detail in this context, is that there is a correlation between the existence of such constraints and the kind of sentential negative marker the language employs to negate a clause. In particular, the relevant factor seems to be whether the language expresses sentential negation by means of a negative marker in pre-verbal position, which by itself can negate the clause, or by means of a negative marker in post-verbal position.

If a language expresses sentential negation by means of a pre-verbal negative marker that by itself can negate the clause, then it also exhibits certain distributional constraints on negative constituents, which can be described informally as follows. A negative constituent can occur as the only negative element in the clause if it is in a structural position that c-commands the finite verb (e.g., in pre-verbal subject position). If, on the other hand, it is in a structural position that does not c-command the finite verb, it cannot occur as the only negative element in the clause.[7] For example, if a negative constituent occurs in the canonical object position, it cannot be the only negative element in the clause, as shown in (12):

(12)   a. *Ho visto *nessuno*. (Italian)
      b. *He visto *a nadie*. (Spanish)
      c. *He vist *ningú*. (Catalan)
      d. *Vi *ninguem*. (Portuguese)
      e. *Am vazut pe *nimeni*. (Romanian)
        'I haven't seen anybody.'

For the clause to be grammatical, such a VP-internal negative constituent must co-occur with a negative element in a position c-commanding the finite verb. This can be either the negative marker in NegP, as shown in (13), or a negative constituent in pre-verbal subject position, as in (14), or a negative constituent in a topicalized position:

(13)   a. *Non* ho visto *nessuno*. (Italian)
      b. *No* he visto *a nadie*. (Spanish)
      c. *No* he vist *ningú*. (Catalan)
      d. *Não* vi *ninguem*. (Portuguese)
      e. *Nu* am vazut pe *nimeni*. (Romanian)
        'I haven't seen anybody.'

(14)   a. *Nessuno* ha detto *niente*. (Italian)
      b. *Nadie* ha dicho *nada*. (Spanish)

c. *Ningú* (no) ha dit *res*. (Catalan)
d. *Ninguem* (não) disse *nada*. (Portuguese)
e. *Nimeni* nu a zis *nimic*. (Romanian)
   'Nobody said anything.'

Note that the sentence with a negative constituent inside VP would be ungrammatical if another negative element occured in the clause in a position from which it failed to c-command the finite verb. This is exemplified in example (15)a from Italian:

(15) a. *I genitori di *nessuno* dei miei studenti avevano detto *niente*. (Italian)
          the parents of none   of my students had   said nothing
          'The parents of none of my students said anything.'

      b. *Nessuno* dei   genitori dei   miei studenti aveva detto *niente*.
          none   of-the parents of-the my   students had   said nothing
          'None of the parents of my students said anything.'

On the other hand, if a language expresses sentential negation by means of a negative marker in post-verbal position, it does not exhibit any such restriction on the distribution of negative constituents. In such languages, negative constituents can occur in a position structurally lower than the finite verb without requiring the co-occurrence of another negative element in a position c-commanding the finite verb. This is shown in the following examples:

(16) I   l'hai   vist *gnun*. (Piedmontese)
      s.cl s.cl'have seen no one
      'I didn't see anyone.'

(17) Dz'i   *gneuna esperiance*. (Valdotain)
      s.cl'have no   experience
      'I don't have experience.'

(18) a. Hoo vist *nissùn*. (Milanese)
          have seen no one
          'I didn't see anyone.'

      b. L'ha   mangiaa *niént*.
          s.cl'has eaten   nothing
          'He didn't eat anything.'

      c. Gh'è   vegnuu *nissùn*.
          there'is come   no one
          'No one came.'

Though post-verbal negative markers can occur in more than one structural position, as we will see, the relevant contrast seems to be between languages that negate a clause with a pre-verbal negative marker and those that do so with a post-verbal negative marker; other differences do not appear to be significant.

   Note that the phenomenon just described overlaps with the set of cases that go under the name of "negative concord," but it does not coincide with them. Negative concord is a term typically used to refer to the co-occurrence of more than one negative element in the same clause with the interpretation of a single instance of negation. It can refer both to the co-occurrence of a negative marker and a negative constituent, as shown in (19), and to the co-occurrence of negative constituents, as shown in (20):

(19) a. *Non* ha detto *niente.* (Italian)
         neg has said nothing
         'S/he hasn't said anything.'

      b. A l'ha   *pa* dit *gnente.* (Piedmontese)
         s.cl s.cl'has neg said nothing
         'S/he hasn't said anything.'

(20) a. *Nessuno* ha detto *niente.* (Italian)
         nobody has said nothing
         'Nobody has said anything.'

      b. *Gnun* a l'ha   dit *gnente.* (Piedmontese)
         nobody s.cl s.cl'has said nothing
         'Nobody said anything.'

These cases raise interesting questions both on the syntactic and on the semantic level, which can be grouped into two main categories. On the one hand, there is the issue of whether the elements I have referred to as negative constituents are best viewed as negative polarity items, as negative quantifiers or as indefinites licensed by the presence of negation (cf. Laka 1990; Longobardi 1991; Zanuttini 1991; Ladusaw 1992; Acquaviva 1992, 1993, among others). On the other hand, there is the challenge of characterizing the structural and semantic properties that yield the reading of a single instance of sentential negation (cf. Ladusaw 1992; Acquaviva 1994, 1995; Haegeman 1991, 1992a, 1992b, 1994, 1995; Déprez in press; among others).

The phenomenon to which I am drawing attention is somewhat different: it has to do with whether or not a negative constituent can occur in a position structurally lower than the position occupied by the finite verb and yield a grammatical result. We have just seen that in some languages the result is grammatical only if the negative constituent is c-commanded by another negative element, which can either be the negative marker or another negative constituent, whereas in others no such restriction is found. Note that languages that do and do not exhibit such constraints are not distinguished by the possibility of co-occurrence of negative constituents: in both types of languages, negative constituents can co-occur and yield one instance of sentential negation. They are also not distinguished by whether or not the negative constituents can co-occur with the negative markers: among the languages that mark sentential negation with a post-verbal negative marker, some allow the co-occurrence of a negative constituent with the negative marker whereas others do not (as will be discussed in chapter 3).

I think it is particularly interesting to point out that a strictly syntactic distinction is at the basis of the constraints governing the distribution of negative constituents. Though semantic factors are likely to play a role, the structural position of the negative marker seems to be the key element: if the negative marker is structurally higher than the finite verb, then the language exhibits such constraints; if it is lower, it does not. In view of this I believe that the present study, which examines in detail the syntactic properties of the various types of sentential negative markers found in Romance, will help shed light on this phenomenon.

Before I conclude, let me mention one possible way of looking at the phenomenon just described.[8] Anticipating the discussion to come, let me refer to the structural position in which pre-verbal negative markers that can negate the clause by themselves occur as 'NegP-1', to distinguish it from that of other negative markers lower in the clause. Let me also assume that NegP-1 c-commands the position where the finite verb occurs in Romance, which we can call $I°$ here for simplicity. I suggest that the relevant factor in the distribution of negative constituents is not whether they c-command $I°$, the position of the finite verb in Romance, but instead whether they c-command NegP-1, the position where the negative marker occurs.

If parametric variation is to be reduced to properties of functional heads (following Borer 1983 and Chomsky 1991, among others), we can characterize the observed variation in terms of the properties of the head of the functional projection NegP-1. Following Chomsky (1993, 1995) in expressing properties of functional heads in terms of features, we can hypothesize that the head of NegP-1 has 'strong' features in the languages that express sentential negation by means of a pre-verbal negative marker which by itself can negate the clause, and 'weak' features in the languages that express sentential negation by means of a negative marker of another kind. When the features of NegP-1 are strong, they need to be checked in the syntax; when they are weak, they can be checked by movement that takes place at LF. Therefore, in a language with strong features in NegP-1, a negative clause must have a negative marker in NegP-1 or else a negative constituent in a position c-commanding NegP-1.[9] When no negative marker is present and a negative constituent is in a position structurally lower than NegP-1, ungrammaticality will ensue because the strong features of this functional projection are not checked in the syntax. In contrast, in a language with weak features in NegP-1, a negative clause need not have a negative marker in NegP-1 or a negative constituent in a position c-commanding NegP-1 in the syntax. Both a negative marker and a negative constituent in a structurally lower position can raise at LF and check the features of NegP-1 at that level.[10] If this line of reasoning is correct, then the projection NegP-1 has a special status that differentiates it from the other projections where negative markers can occur. That is, NegP-1 is the position where the syntactic feature corresponding to the expression of sentential negation can be found. The other positions, on the other hand, are simply positions where the negative element is generated but which do not carry syntactic features corresponding to sentential negation. I will not pursue this issue any further in this book but leave it for further research.

1.3. Jespersen's cycle

The historical development of sentential negation in Romance reflects rather closely what has come to be known as "Jespersen's cycle." As pointed out in Jespersen (1917, 1924/65), it is quite common in the history of languages to find that they express sentential negation initially by means of only one negative marker, then by the negative marker in combination with an adverb or a noun phrase in complement position, until the second element takes on the function of expressing negation by itself and the original negative marker becomes optional and eventually disappears. Jespersen related the fluctuation between different types of negative markers to phonetic stress: when a negative marker is weakly stressed and becomes clitic in nature, it is strengthened by another element, which then comes to be interpreted as the negative marker proper.[11] Jespersen exemplifies this phenomenon with the case of Latin and French, Scandinavian, German, and English. Latin *ne* was felt to be too weak and strengthened by *oenum* 'one', resulting in *ne-oenum* which gave rise to *non*. Latin *non* then lost its stress and became Old French *nen*, later *ne*. French *ne* is the only negative marker for a certain amount of time (and still survives as the only negative marker in some expressions of literary French), but then is felt to be weak and is strengthened by *pas* (e.g., *Je ne dis pas*). Finally, the weak *ne* disappears leaving *pas* as the main negative marker, e.g., *Je dis pas*, in modern colloquial French. In Scandinavian, the original *ne* was first strengthened by other words and then replaced by those words which acquired the function of negative markers (e.g., Danish *ej, ikke*). In German, the negative marker is at first pre-verbal *ni*, then it weakens, becoming *n-* or *en* and co-occurs with *nicht* in post-verbal position, until *nicht* becomes the only negative marker in the clause. Similar stages can also be found in English, as witnessed by the pre-verbal negative marker in Old English (Ic *ne* secge), then both a pre-verbal and a post-verbal negative marker in Middle English (I *ne* seye *not*) and a post-verbal negative marker only in Early Modern English (I say *not*).

Many languages within the Indo-European family went through a process of diachronic change that can be seen to reflect Jespersen's cycle. Within Romance, all the languages that now express sentential negation by means of a post-verbal negative marker used to have a pre-verbal negative marker and went through a stage in which they marked negation by using both a pre- and a post-verbal element. Schwegler (1983) shows that the same type of diachronic change witnessed for French is also documented in Occitan. In this language, in the 16th century pre-verbal *ne* could still function as the sole negative marker, as shown in (21)a, though it could also be accompanied by a post-verbal emphasizer, as in (21)b and (21)c:[12]

(21)   a. *N'anes de tous grans mots ma Princess eichanta.* (Occitan from the 16th century)
         'Don't go scaring my princess with your big words.'

       b. *Io no parlari pas de la goerra Troiana.*
          'I will not speak of the Trojan war.'

       c. *E ma beutat n'a punt autre mai que Nature.*
          'And my beauty isn't equalled by anything except Nature.'

In the 17th century, post-verbal *pas* was already used as the only negative marker, as shown in (22), and by the 19th century the majority of examples have *pas* as the negative marker, as in (23):

(22)   *Deve pas ieu prendre une corse?* (Occitan from the 17th century)
       'Shouldn't I take a cord?'

(23)   *T'agradon pas li traite?* (Occitan from the 19th century)
       'Don't you like the traitors?'

Posner (1985) provides evidence that the diachronic change has taken place in Sur-silvan, a language of the Romantsch group. She cites the example in (24)a, from the 1684 Bible text, which contrasts with the modern examples, exemplified in (24)b:

(24) a. Mo jou *na* teng quint   da naginna caussa. (Sursilvan from the 17th century)
          now I   neg hold account of no   thing
          'None of these things move me.'

      b. Ils genitors stoppien *buca* pli curclar ils cuosts da studi per lur affons. (present-day
          Sursilvan)

          'Parents are not bound to cover the cost of their children's studies.'

Albin (1984: 25–69) shows that Piedmontese had a pre-verbal negative marker, attested from the 12th to the 18th century (in the forms of *no, ne, non*); the language then employed both a pre- and a post-verbal negative marker (*ne ... nen*) from the 16th through the 19th centuries, and now employs only the post-verbal negative marker in most of its varieties.[13]

The literature on Jespersen's cycle typically addresses the question of the reasons behind such a process of change, either challenging or building on Jespersen's idea that the diachronic change is to be related to phonetic weakening of the pre-verbal negative marker. I cannot do justice to such a debate in this context, but will mention very briefly the gist of some of the different proposals.[14] Focusing on French, Iordan and Manoliu (1972: 373) invoke the redundancy of *ne*, given the presence of *pas*; Lockwood (1968) suggests the influence of German on French. Vennemann (1974) and Harris (1976, 1978a, 1978b) relate the change from pre-verbal to post-verbal negation to more far-reaching typological changes in word order. As Vennemann argues, if negation is an adverb, it is expected to precede the verb in verb-final languages and to follow it in verb-medial languages. Ashby (1981) points out that such an approach cannot account for languages such as Italian and Spanish, which consistently retained the negative marker in pre-verbal position, while being verb-medial. Ramat, Bernini, and Molinelli (1986) also cast doubt on the possibility of relating the diachronic change in the expression of sentential negation to a typology of word order in any simple way. Schwegler (1983) views the diachronic cycle as resulting from a psychological need for negative emphasizers, whereas Schwegler (1988) invokes a variety of different language internal and language external factors as motivations behind the change ("multiple causation"), thus explaining the different forms it has taken in different languages. Posner (1985) introduces the relevance of socio-cultural factors, in particular the influence of other languages. Horn (1989) views the cycle as the result of the opposing tendencies of least effort (which leads to weakening) and of preserving information (which leads to strengthening) — a tension that keeps the cycle in motion. As Jespersen seemed to suggest, a phonetically weak syllable is not apt to express the logically very important notion of negation, hence it is reinforced; but once it is reinforced by another element, it is perceived as redundant.

In this book, I will not address the issue of the possible reasons behind the historical change. I will investigate an area close to Jespersen's cycle, however, since the three different strategies for the expression of sentential negation identified by Jespersen in a diachronic perspective can also be found at the synchronic level, not only across contemporary Romance languages but also in different varieties of the same language. We can take Italian, which employs only a pre-verbal negative marker, to represent the first stage of Jespersen's cycle, standard French, which has both a pre- and a post-verbal negative marker, to represent the second stage, and central Piedmontese, which has only a post-verbal negative marker, to represent the third stage:

(25) a. *Non* abito là.   (Italian: first stage)
         neg live there
         'I don't live there.'

      b. Il *ne* marche *pas*. (French: second stage)
         he neg walks   neg
         'He doesn't walk.'

      c. A tëm *nen* la mort. (Piedmontese: third stage)
         s.cl fears neg death
         'He doesn't fear death.'

But we also find different varieties of the same language showing all three strategies; for example, if we look at the data from Piedmontese on chart 1630 of the linguistics atlas of Jaberg and Jud (1928–40) we see that, while the central and northern varieties of Piedmontese employ only a post-verbal negative marker, the varieties spoken in Calizzano, Sassello, Isola, and Rovegno, towns on the border of Piedmont and Liguria,[15] have a pre-verbal negative marker only; while the variety spoken in the town of Cairo Montenotte (described in Parry 1985) has both a pre- and a post-verbal negative marker. In fact, even within Cairese itself, as noted by Parry (1985: 288–95, 1989), it is possible to find all three strategies:[16]

(26) a. U *n'*importa. (Cairese: first stage)
         s.cl neg matters
         'It doesn't matter.'

      b. U *n*   bugia *nent*. (Cairese: second stage)
         s.cl neg moves neg
         'He doesn't move.'

      c. Renata am   piaz   *nent*. (Cairese: third stage)
         Renata s.cl me pleases neg
         'I don't like Renata.'

This investigation will have as the object of study the syntactic differences that distinguish these three strategies. My goal is to provide a syntactic characterization of the negative markers and of the grammatical system that corresponds to each particular strategy for the expression of sentential negation. Though focusing on synchronic varieties, this work will shed light on the grammatical system of the different diachronic stages as well: since the synchronic stages correspond so closely to the diachronic ones, an investigation of the former will help us better understand the latter. I believe that, as suggested by some of the authors who studied the triggers of Jespersen's cycle, a syntactic analysis of the negative markers is necessary to understand the changes that bring a language from one stage to the other.

2

Pre-verbal Negative Markers

2.1. The range of variation

A question that arises in several domains of syntactic research concerns the syntactic characterization of negative markers that precede the finite verb. The puzzling fact is that such negative markers do not exhibit consistent behavior across languages, or even in different stages of a single language. In some cases they interfere with head-movement processes (such as verb movement), or count as first position in contexts that show second-position effects. Yet, in other cases, they do not interfere with head-movement processes nor do they count as first position. In general, if a syntactic property is systematically present in non-negative clauses and absent in negative clauses, it is legitimate to wonder whether the two types of clauses are subject to different syntactic requirements. For example, if verb movement were present in all non-negative questions and absent in all negative questions, we would explore the possibility that the trigger for verb movement might not apply in the same way in the two contexts. But when a syntactic property that is present in non-negative clauses is absent from negative clauses only in some cases and not in others, then it seems more promising to explore the possibility that the syntactic requirements for that type of clause might be uniform, and that they might be obscured in some cases by (certain properties of) negative clauses, perhaps related to the nature of the negative marker. The questions then arise of whether there exist syntactically different types of negative markers and whether such differences might be at the basis of the observed variation. This chapter will address precisely these questions, within a well-defined empirical domain.

Here I analyze negative markers that obligatorily precede the finite verb[1] in several representative Romance varieties. I refer to this class of elements, pre-theoretically, as "pre-verbal negative markers." As will become clear from the discussion throughout the book, they differ from the negative markers that follow the finite verb in many respects, which are relevant for their syntactic characterization. Moreover, the grammar of a Romance language that negates a clause with a pre-verbal negative marker differs from that of a Romance language that negates a clause with a post-verbal negative marker in several respects, in particular concerning the formation of questions, the kinds of imperative clauses that are possible, and the distribution of negative indefinites. Thus I believe that a precise syntactic character-ization of pre-verbal negative markers constitutes the necessary first step toward a deeper understanding of the grammar of these languages.

The results of my investigation are at first sight startling because of the complexity of the variation exhibited by the data. For example, we see that, whereas some of the pre-verbal negative markers precede all complement clitics, others precede third person but not first and second person complement clitics (simplifying the pattern). Perhaps equally surprisingly, we also observe that, within a given language, the same negative marker may co-occur or fail to co-occur with verb movement, depending on the syntactic environment in which it occurs. My task will thus be twofold: on the one hand, I attempt to provide a precise description of the syntactic variation exhibited in the contexts examined; on the other, I try to understand the observed variation and systematize it, seeking an answer to the underlying questions of what determines it and how it can be learned.

I will show that there are several reasons to believe that pre-verbal negative mark-ers do not constitute a syntactically homogeneous class but rather are syntactically ambiguous. First I show that differences among pre-verbal negative markers appear when we examine their distribution with respect to complement clitics (section 2.2). Then I argue for the need to distinguish two classes of pre-verbal negative markers to account for their distribution with respect to subject clitics (section 2.3). This will lead me to a discussion of the various kinds of subject clitics exhibited by the northern Italian dialects.[2] Finally I examine the effect of the presence of a pre-verbal negative marker on environments which require verb movement around the subject clitic, such as questions and exclamative clauses (section 2.4). The results of this last section also argue for the presence of two syntactically distinct types of negative markers, though whether or not they fully coincide with the classes identified in the previous two sections remains to be established.

In organizing the description of the data, I will find it useful to refer to the following distinction among pre-verbal negative markers: whether they can occur as the only negative element in a negative clause — that is, whether they can negate a clause by themselves — or whether they must co-occur with another negative element. The pre-verbal negative markers of Italian, Spanish, Portuguese, Catalan, Romanian, Sardinian, and the Romance varieties spoken in northeastern, central, and southern Italy can occur as the only negative element in a clause:

(1) a. Maria *non* lavora qui. (Italian)

    b. María *no* trabaja aquí. (Spanish)
      Maria neg works here
      'Maria does not work here.'

    c. Ele *não* escreveu. (Portuguese)
      he neg wrote
      'He didn't write.'

In contrast, the pre-verbal negative markers of French, Wallon, some Rhaeto-Romantsch varieties and certain varieties spoken in northwestern Italy cannot be the only negative element in a negative clause but must co-occur with another negative element. Such an element can be a post-verbal negative marker, as shown in the following examples, or another negative constituent, as we will see later on:[3]

(2) a. Jean *n*'aime *(pas)* la viande. (French)
      Jean neg'likes neg the meat
      'John doesn't like meat.'

    b. La feglia *na* canta *(betg)*. (Surmeiran)
      the daughter neg sings neg
      'The daughter doesn't sing.'

    c. A*n*'s   dis *(brisa)* aksì. (Romagnolo)
      s.cl-neg's.cl say neg like-that
      'One doesn't say it that way.'

    d. A*n* 's dis *(mia)* achsé. (Emiliano)
      s.cl-neg one says neg like-that
      'One doesn't say it that way.'

    e. U *n*i   va *(nent)*. (Cairese)
      s.cl neg-loc.cl goes neg
      'He doesn't go there.'

The pre-verbal negative markers that must co-occur with another negative element differ as to the degree to which their presence is obligatory. French *ne*, for example, while part of the written language, is often missing from less formal styles, though its precise distribution is a rather complex matter (cf. Ashby 1981 and Lemieux 1985, among others). Here I will not address the issue of the degree to which they are obligatory or optional, but limit myself to pointing out the distribution of these elements and contrast it with that of the pre-verbal negative markers that can occur alone in a negative clause.[4]

    The strategy of negating a clause via both a pre-verbal and a post-verbal negative marker is often referred to as "discontinuous negation." Since this label seems to refer to a property of a syntactic constituent, I prefer not to use it at this preliminary stage of the discussion and to adopt instead terminology that is devoid of implications concerning the syntactic representation of the elements under investigation.[5]

2.2.   Pre-verbal negative markers and complement clitics

Examination of the relative position of pre-verbal negative markers and complement clitics reveals the existence of two distinct patterns. Some pre-verbal negative markers precede all complement clitics. These are all the negative markers that can negate a clause by themselves as well as some of the negative markers that must co-occur with another negative element (e.g., French *ne*). Though the relative order of pronominal clitics may vary from language to language, they always follow these negative markers and never undergo reordering with them:

(3)   a. Maria *non glielo* ha dato. (Italian)

    b. Maria *no   se   lo* dió. (Spanish)
       Maria neg him it gave
       'Maria didn't give it to him.'

    c. Ele *não o* comeu. (Portuguese)
       he   neg it ate
       'He didn't eat it.'

In other words, one never finds a complement clitic on the left of a negative marker (i.e., *clitic–neg–(clitic)*) in a language where the negative marker by itself can negate the clause:[6]

(4)   a. *Maria *glielo non* ha dato. (Italian)
       Maria   him-it neg has given

    b. *Maria *gli   non lo* ha dato.
       Maria   him neg it has given

    c. *Maria *lo non gli* ha dato.
       Maria   it neg him has given

This property of the pre-verbal negative markers was already mentioned in Brandi and Cordin (1981, 1989) and Rizzi (1986), works that point out that the negative marker may precede or follow subject clitics but is never found within the cluster of complement clitics. Their observation needs to be qualified, as we will see, since it is true of the pre-verbal negative markers that can negate a clause by themselves but is not always true of the others.[7]

    In contrast with the situation just described, certain pre-verbal negative markers that must co-occur with another negative element fail to precede some of the complement clitics. Among these are the pre-verbal negative elements of a group of Val Bormida dialects (spoken in the Liguria hinterland, in northwestern Italy) described in Parry (in press a).[8] In these varieties, sentential negation is expressed by both a pre-verbal negative element, *n*, and a post-verbal one, *nent*. Pre-verbal *n* precedes the singular and plural third person pronouns, as well as the partitive clitic corresponding to French *en* and Italian *ne* (Cairese *n*) and the locative clitic *i*:[9]

(5)   a. U *n*   **li/la**   sent nent. (Cairese)
       s.cl neg him/her hears neg
       'He doesn't hear him/her.'

    b. U *n*i   sent nent. (Cairese)
       s.cl neg-them hears neg
       'He doesn't hear them.'

    c. U *n*i   va nent. (Cairese)
       s.cl neg-loc.cl goes neg
       'He does not go there.'

    d. A*n*   **li** vug nent. (S. Giulia)
       s.cl-neg him see neg
       'I cannot see him.'

With the clitics of first and second person, singular and plural, though, as well as all the reflexives, the order is the opposite: the pre-verbal negative marker *n* follows them. All the following data are from Parry (in press a):

(6) a. U **mi***n* sent nent. (Cairese)
       s.cl me-neg hears neg
       'He doesn't hear me.'

    b. U **ti***n*   sent nent. (Cairese)
       s.cl you-neg hears neg
       'He doesn't hear you.'

    c. U **ni***n* sent nent. (Cairese)
       s.cl us-neg hears neg
       'He doesn't hear us.'

    d. U **vi***n*   sent nent. (Cairese)
       s.cl you(pl.)-neg hears neg
       'He doesn't hear you (pl.).'

    e. U **si***n*   lava nent. (Cairese)
       s.cl self-neg wash neg
       'He doesn't wash himself.'

(7)   A **ve***n*   vug nent. (S. Giulia)
       s.cl you(pl.)-neg see neg
       'I cannot see you (pl.).'

(8)   A **te***n*   vug nent. (Piana Crixia)
       s.cl you(sg.)-neg see neg
       'I cannot see you (sg.).'

(9)   I **se***n*   taiu nent. (Dego)
       s.cl self-neg cut neg
       'They are not cuttable.'

(10) E **ve***n*   seu dive   niente. (Carcare)
       s.cl you(pl.)-neg know to-tell-you(pl.) nothing
       'I cannot tell you anything.'

When complement clitics of first or second person co-occur with complement clitics of third person, the resulting linear order will have the first/second person complement clitics precede the negative marker *n*, which in turn will precede the third person complement clitics. The following examples illustrate this situation:[10]

(11) a. I **me**n **le** devi nent dumandele. (Cairese)
           s.cl me-neg them must neg to-ask-them
           'You shouldn't ask me for them.'

      b. U **me**n **le** da 'nenta.
           s.cl me-neg it gives neg
           'He doesn't give it to me.'

      c. U **te**n **la** 'kata 'nenta.
           s.cl you-neg it buys neg
           'He won't buy it for you.

      d. U **vi** *n* **i** da 'nenta, i 'sodi.
           s.cl you neg them gives neg, the money
           'As for the money, he won't give it to you.'

The relative ordering of pre-verbal negative markers and pronominal clitics just described is not to be viewed as a peculiarity of the dialects spoken in the Val Bormida. The dialect of Vermes, in the Jura (at the Swiss-French border), described in Butz (1981) and reported in Parry (in press a) shows an identical pattern: the pre-verbal negative marker *n* follows the complement clitics of first and second person, singular and plural, as well as all the reflexives. As far as I can tell, this negative marker must always co-occur with another negative element in the clause; in the examples below, it co-occurs with the counterpart of 'nothing' (cf. (12)a), 'no more' (cf. (12)b) and with the post-verbal negative marker (cf. (12)c). The examples are from Butz (1981:76), cited in Parry (in press a):

(12) a. Soli **no** *n* di rã. (Vermes)
           that us neg says nothing
           'That doesn't tell us anything.'

      b. Mūn ãn **m** ∂*n* tròv pu.
           my husband me-neg finds no more
           'My husband can no longer find me.'

      c. A **s** *n* e p meryè.
           s.cl refl. neg is neg married
           'He hasn't got married.'

Other examples are found in Spiess (1977: 206) from the dialect of Collina d'Oro, near Lugano, Switzerland, and in Jaberg and Jud (1928–40),[11] from Ronco Canavese, north of Turin, in Piedmont, both cited in Parry (in press a):

(13) a. Mi **ma** *n* incali miga. (Collina d'Oro)
           I me neg dare neg
           'I do not dare.'

      b. Ha fena hi i **m**n pyay ñent. (Ronco Canavese)
           this woman here s.cl me-neg pleases neg
           'I do not like this woman.'

Note that in these examples as well the pre-verbal negative marker co-occurs with a post-verbal one.

The difference in the relative position of the complement clitics and the negative marker could be interpreted in a scenario where the position of the negative marker remains constant but the position of the pronominal clitics changes. It has been suggested in Parry (in press a: §4.3) that these data be viewed as a consequence of raising of the pronouns of first and second person, as well as the reflexives, to left-adjoin to the negative marker.[12] The alternative point of view — namely, that the position of the pronominal clitics remain constant and the negative marker lowers to adjoin to the right of the relevant class of pronominal clitics — is excluded on the basis of theoretical considerations that rule out lowering as a possible type of movement.

Another alternative that I will explore is based on different assumptions. Suppose that neither do the clitics raise and adjoin to the negative marker, nor does the negative marker lower and adjoin to the pronominal clitics. Instead, suppose that the pronominal clitics of first and second person and the reflexives occupy a different structural position from the clitics of third person, the locative, and the partitive. In the following table, I group the clitics of first and second person and all the reflexives under the label "CL-1", and the clitics of third person, the locative, and the genitive clitic under the label "CL-2":

(14)

CL-1	CL-2
first person	third person
second person	locative
reflexives	partitive

That clitics may occur in different structural positions is not implausible, given the relative ordering they exhibit in the Romance languages. Notice the case of Italian, for example, where the first and second person clitics and all the reflexives precede third person clitics, the locative *ci*, and the partitive *ne*:[13]

(15) a. *Me/te/ce/ve*   lo ha dato subito.   (Italian)
      me/you(sg)/us/you(pl) it has given right away
      'He has given it to me/you(sg)/us/you(pl) right away.'

      b. *Ti* **ci**   porto domani.
      you there take tomorrow
      'I'll take you there tomorrow.'

      c. *Mi* **ci**   recherò da solo.
      me there go (fut) by self
      'I'll go there alone.'

      d. *Me* **ne**   sono comprati tre.
      me of-them am bought three
      'I bought myself three of them.'

It is then tempting to suggest that pre-verbal negative markers can occur in two different structural positions: One position is before CL-1 (that is, before the clitics of first and second person and all the reflexives); the other is immediately before CL-2 (that is, before the clitics of third person, locative, and genitive), as indicated in (16):

(16)   Positions of pre-verbal negative markers

neg	CL-1	neg	CL-2
	first person		third person
	second person		locative
	reflexives		genitive

The idea that pre-verbal negative markers might occur in two different structural positions is supported by the fact that there are some languages where two negative markers can co-occur in pre-verbal position. In such cases, one occurs before CL-1 — that is, the clitics of first and second person and the reflexives — while the other occurs after CL-1. Examples (17)a and (17)b are from Parry (in press a), (17)c is from ASIS (see Benincà et al. 1990–present):[14]

(17) a. In   **ten**   dan nent u libr. (Cosseria)
         s.cl-neg you-neg give neg the book
         'They do not give you the book.'

      b. E*n*   **ten**   capisc.   (Carcare)
         s.cl-neg you-neg understand
         'I do not understand you.'

      c. U   *n*   **me** *n*'a   vist nisciün. (Carcare)
         s.cl neg me neg'has seen no-one
         'Nobody has seen me.'

If two positions are available for pre-verbal negative markers, we then need to ask what governs their distribution in one or the other position. Since I noted that the pre-verbal negative marker that by itself can negate a clause (that of Italian, Spanish, etc.) always precedes all complement clitics, I am led to conclude that it occurs in the higher of the two positions I am here proposing. I argue that the negative markers that can negate a clause by themselves occur in a functional projection, which can be labeled NegP (for Negative Phrase) or PolP (for Polarity Phrase) and which is structurally higher than the head to which the complement clitics adjoin.[15] The choice of labels is a matter of terminology and is not crucial for the rest of this discussion, which will focus on negative markers only. The label PolP suggests that the projection can contain not only negative elements but also markers of emphatic affirmation, which in some cases can be shown to be in complementary distribution with sentential negative markers (cf. Laka 1990 for Spanish; Belletti 1990 for Italian; Campos 1986 for Gascon, though this work argues against taking complementary distribution as evidence that these elements occupy the same structural position).[16] For theory internal reasons that will become clear in the course of the discussion, I assume that these negative markers are heads in terms of X-bar theory.

If the pre-verbal negative markers that can negate a clause by themselves are in the head of NegP, where are the other negative markers — that is, those that must co-occur with another negative element? Because some of them precede and some follow CL-1 — that is, the clitics of first and second person and the reflexives — they cannot be said to all occur in the same structural position. French *ne*, for example, always precedes all complement clitics, whereas the pre-verbal *n* of Cairese follows the pronominal clitics of first and second person and the reflexives. One apparently simple solution might be to say that French *ne* occurs in the same position as Italian *non* (in the head of NegP), whereas Cairese *n* occurs in a lower structural position. Despite its simplicity, I will not adopt such a solution in exactly these terms, because I do not want to completely assimilate Italian *non* and French *ne*: I want to encode in the syntactic representation of these elements the fact that the former can by itself negate a clause while the latter cannot. In other words, I want to make a three-way distinction: I want to distinguish those pre-verbal negative markers that can negate a clause by themselves from those that cannot; then, among the latter class, I also want to distinguish between those that precede all complements clitics and those that follow CL-1. This could be done exclusively in structural terms; alternatively, it could be done in terms of features, by assuming that negative markers can differ in the strength of their features, and consequently differ in whether or not they can negate a clause by themselves; or through a combination of both these strategies.

I will rely mainly on a structural solution.[17] I express the first of the differences I want to capture by saying that, whereas the negative markers that can negate a clause by themselves (e.g., Italian *non*) are the head of NegP, those that cannot (e.g., French *ne* and Cairese *n*) do not head NegP but rather are left-adjoined to an independently existing functional head. In principle, this could be an abstract functional head, which might be either contentful (for example one expressing negation, tense, or mood) or not; or, alternatively, an overt head (for example, the finite verb or the complement clitic). Note that the functional head to which a negative marker like French *ne* is left-adjoined could be Neg°; in such a case, French *ne* would differ from a negative marker that by itself can negate the clause in that the latter is the true head of NegP, whereas the former is an element adjoined to the head of NegP, hence not the real head.

Unfortunately, the empirical evidence at my disposal does not allow me to determine to which head the pre-verbal negative markers that cannot negate the clause by themselves are adjoined. On purely theoretical grounds, we can exclude the possibility that they might left-adjoin to the finite verb if we adopt Kayne's (1994) proposal that asymmetric c-command maps into linear precedence, and the restriction that follows from it that at most one head can adjoin to another head. Kayne's (1994: §4.6) reasoning goes as follows. Take a finite verb that consists of a prefix, the stem, the thematic vowel, and a (person/number agreement) suffix. Assuming that affixes are always exhaustively dominated by a non-terminal, this leads to the conclusion that this prefix must be adjoined to the stem [prefix stem], the unit thus formed is adjoined to the thematic vowel [[prefix stem] them.vowel], and this unit in turn is adjoined to the suffix [[[prefix stem] them.vowel] suffix]. If a clitic were to be adjoined, it would have to be adjoined to the prefix, a conclusion that is to be rejected in view of the fact that pronominal elements generally cannot occur within words. If the same assumptions and the same reasoning were to be applied in the case of pre-verbal negative markers, the same conclusion would be reached — namely, that a negative marker cannot be adjoined to the verb. Assuming this conclusion to be valid,[18] we are then left with the other options for the adjunction site of pre-verbal negative markers that cannot negate the clause by themselves: that is, they adjoin to an abstract functional head or they adjoin to the pronominal clitics. For the sake of concreteness, in the discussion following the examples in (19) I examine in some detail the latter of these two possibilities; I am not ruling out

for the class of pre-verbal negative markers that cannot negate a clause by themselves, at least to the extent that I argue that, in the position in which they appear, they are adjoined to an independently existing functional head.[21] At the same time, I maintain Laka's (1990) and Zanuttini's (1990, 1991) proposal insofar as the other class of pre-verbal negative markers is concerned — that is, those consisting of elements that can negate the clause by themselves: I argue that they head an independent functional projection higher than Infl, namely NegP-1.[22]

Note that, under this approach, French *ne* is neither identical to Italian *non* nor to Cairese *n*. It is similar to the former, in that it precedes all pronominal clitics, but differs from it in that it does not head NegP; instead it is left-adjoined to a functional head, which might be abstract (e.g., Neg° itself) or overt (e.g., a pronominal clitic). It is also similar to the latter, in being left-adjoined to an independently existing functional head, but differs from it in that it precedes all pronominal clitics. For the sake of concreteness, let me discuss how we could examine, under this view, the pre-verbal negative markers of French and Cairese in the presence of pronominal clitics. For ease of reference, I repeat the Cairese examples (6)a and (11)a:

(19)   a.   U   mi*n*   sent nent. (Cairese)
             s.cl me-neg hears neg
             'He doesn't hear me.'

       b.   I   me*n*   le   devi nent dumandele.
             s.cl me-neg them must neg to-ask-them
             'You shouldn't ask me for them.'

On the model of Pollock's (1989) analysis of French *ne*, Cairese *n* can be taken to originate as the head of the projection of which the post-verbal negative marker *nent* is the specifier, and to raise to pre-verbal position, where it left-adjoins to a syntactic head. Obviously a more precise statement is needed to express to which head exactly it adjoins. The difficulties in making such a statement stem in part from the difficulty in stating clearly how the pronominal clitics are adjoined. Let us assume, following Kayne (1991, 1994), that clitics adjoin to an empty functional head. When more than one pronominal clitic occurs, do they adjoin to the same head or do they each adjoin independently to a different syntactic head? Both options are given (see discussion in Kayne 1994: §3.3). Since I am not in a position to choose between the two (and perhaps it is not even possible to do so abstractly), I will examine them both. Let us take the first option — namely, that the pronominal clitics adjoin to the same head. As I did above, I adopt Kayne's (1994) proposal that multiple adjunction to a given head is not legitimate.[23] The only way in which adjunction of two clitics to the same head is possible is for one clitic to adjoin to the target functional head (call it H), and for the other clitic to adjoin to it:

(20)

How could a pre-verbal negative marker become part of such a cluster? It would first form a unit with a pronominal clitic, either by having the clitic adjoin to the negative marker yielding the order [cl neg] (as in Cairese, e.g., *min* of example (19)a), or else by having the negative marker adjoin to the clitic thus yielding the order [neg cl] (as in French, e.g., *ne me*):

(21)   Cairese: French:

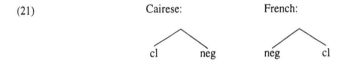

Then such a unit would adjoin to the second pronominal clitic, yielding the sequence [[cl neg] cl] (in Cairese, e.g., *men le* of example (19)b) or [[neg cl] cl] (in French, e.g., *ne me le*); in turn, this cluster would adjoin to the empty head, as indicated in (22):

(22)   Cairese: French:

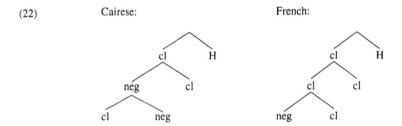

Alternatively, if each clitic were to adjoin to a different empty syntactic head, in a configuration of the sort [cl-1 H-1] [cl-2 H-2], we would say that the negative marker can either adjoin to cl-2 and form a unit with it, giving us the case of Cairese *men le* of example (19)b ([cl-1 H-1] [[neg cl-2] H-2]) or else adjoin to cl-1 and form a unit with it, giving the case of French *ne me le* ([[neg cl-1] H-1] [cl-2 H-2]), as indicated in (23):[24]

(23)   Cairese: French:

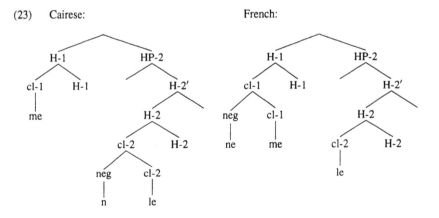

I will leave this discussion at this stage and turn to the examination of other distributional patterns that provide support for the distinction outlined in this section between two distinct classes of pre-verbal negative markers.

2.3. Pre-verbal negative markers and subject clitics

The term "subject clitic" refers to elements that appear exclusively in co-occurrence with finite verbs. They may express person, number, or gender features of the subject and may co-occur with an overt subject, though these properties are not a necessary part of the definition of subject clitics: there exist subject clitics which show no agreement at all (e.g., the vocalic subject clitics of Paduan, which will be discussed later) and subject clitics that only occur when a lexical subject is not present in an argumental position (though it might be present in a dislocated position). Some examples of subject clitics follow.

The examples in (24) to (28) exemplify the subject clitics from Friulian, which are obligatory both in the presence and in the absence of an overt subject in pre-verbal position, regardless of the thematic status of the subject. As we can see, they obligatorily occur without an overt subject, with a pre-verbal subject, with a post-verbal subject, and with a subject like 'nobody', which is taken to occupy an argumental position, as it cannot be left dislocated:

(24) a. *Al / E*   rive.   (Friulian)
        s.cl(m)/s.cl(f) comes
        'He/she is coming.'

      b. *Rive.

(25) a. Marie *e*   rive.
        Marie s.cl comes
        'Marie is coming.'

      b. *Marie rive.

(26) a. *E*   rive   Marie.
        s.cl comes Marie
        'Marie is coming.'

      b. *Rive Marie.

(27) a. Nisun   *al* rive.
        nobody s.cl comes
        'Nobody's coming.'

      b. *Nisun rive.

(28) a. No*l*   rive   nisun.
        neg-s.cl comes nobody
        'Nobody's coming.'

      b. *No rive nisun.

The following examples exemplify subject clitics from central Veneto (e.g., from the cities of Padua, Venice, and Treviso). They are obligatory when no overt subject is present; when an overt subject is present, they co-occur with it only if it can be left-dislocated but not if it is in an argumental position, as shown by their ungrammaticality with the post-verbal subject of unaccusative verbs or with elements that cannot be left-dislocated, such as 'nobody':

(29) a. *El* vien.   (central Veneto)
      s.cl comes.
      'He's coming.'

   b. *Vien

(30) a. Nane (*el*) vien.
      Nane s.cl comes
      'Nane is coming.'

(31) a. *El* vien   Nane.
      s.cl comes Nane
      'Nane is coming.'

   b. Vien Nane.

(32) a. *Nisun *el*   vien.
      nobody s.cl comes
      'Nobody's coming.'

   b. Nisun vien.

Finally, the examples in (33) exemplify a type of subject clitic that is attested in the majority of northern Italian dialects and appears only in the presence of auxiliary verbs. As shown in the example from Piedmontese, this subject clitic, *l*, may co-occur with another subject clitic, *a*:[25]

(33) a. Gneun *l*'ayet   inco vu   de bataille parë! (Valdotain)
      nobody s.cl'had yet   seen of battle   such
      'Nobody had yet seen a battle like that!'

   b. La barca a   *l*'a   andà a fond.   (Piedmontese)
      the boat s.cl s.cl'has gone to bottom
      'The boat sank.'

These elements are called clitic because they exhibit some of the same properties that characterize complement clitics (cf. Kayne 1975), among them the fact they cannot bear contrastive stress, cannot occur in isolation, cannot be coordinated, and cannot be modified.

Among the most widely spoken Romance languages, only French exhibits a system of (lexically realized) subject clitics, whereas among the less well-known Romance varieties subject clitics are well attested in the dialects of northern Italy.[26]

Though descriptively useful, the notion of subject clitic is spurious from the syntactic point of view, in that it does not identify a class of elements with uniform syntactic properties, as pointed out in Kayne (1975), Rizzi (1986), and Poletto (1991, 1993a), among others. As discussed in these works, the subject clitics of standard French exhibit a syntactic behavior that differs in several respects from that exhibited by subject clitics in many northern Italian dialects. In fact, even within the northern

Italian dialects, subject clitics do not constitute a syntactically uniform class, as has been convincingly argued in Poletto's work. At least two main classes need to be distinguished: "agreement clitics," which express phi-features of the subject, and "vocalic clitics," which either are invariant across all persons or else mark first and second person identically and in contrast with third person, while lacking number and gender distinctions. Here I focus on the subject clitics of the northern Italian dialects, which show an interesting distributional pattern with respect to the pre-verbal negative markers. Because they appear (in embedded clauses) between the complementizer and the verb, exactly like the pre-verbal negative markers that are the object of this study, they allow us to examine the behavior of the pre-verbal negative markers and address the questions put forth in the introduction.[27] In particular, the subject clitics of the northern Italian dialects occur either on the right or on the left of a pre-verbal negative marker (whereas the subject clitics of standard French always occur on the left of the pre-verbal negative marker). Does the observed variation follow from the fact that a negative marker may appear in more than one position? Or from the fact that subject clitics may occupy more than one position — that is, can be either higher or lower than the negative marker?

It is possible to make sense of the variation observed in the data if, on the one hand, we follow the distinction already suggested between pre-verbal negative markers that can negate the clause by themselves and those that cannot and, on the other, we keep separate the different types of subject clitics discussed in the literature. Then it is clear that what might at first sight seem like random variation is in fact reducible to the following simple pattern:

1. The pre-verbal negative markers that can negate a clause by themselves always follow "vocalic subject clitics" and typically precede "agreement subject clitics";

2. The pre-verbal negative markers that cannot negate a clause by themselves follow both vocalic and agreement subject clitics.

2.3.1. *Agreement clitics and vocalic clitics*

I will start the discussion with an overview of two main classes of subject clitics found in the northern Italian dialects, following the classification proposed in Poletto (1993a: ch. 2). This work classifies subject clitics on the basis of their function (where five different classes are identified) and on the basis of their position. Here, I focus on the latter distinction, since it allows us to shed light on the structure of the clause and to observe the structural position of negative markers with respect to the subject clitics. It is important to bear in mind, though, that the structural positions identified here do not correspond to the types of subject clitics identified on the basis of their function in the clause, in particular with respect to their case and argumental properties.

Applying the diagnostics proposed in Kayne (1975) and adopted in Rizzi (1986) for the analysis of subject clitics (namely, their behavior in coordinate structures and in relation to the pre-verbal negative markers), Poletto (1993a) distinguishes two main classes.

1. The first class of subject clitics is referred to as *agreement clitics*. The identifying property of this class of elements is that they are obligatorily repeated when the finite verb is coordinated with another finite verb. The following examples are from Basso Polesano, a variety of Veneto documented in Poletto's work, where this class of clitics is exemplified with the subject clitic for third person singular feminine, *la*. As we see, *la* must be repeated when two finite verbs are coordinated:

(34)   a. *La* magna pomi e   *la* beve   cafè.   (Basso Polesano)
          s.cl eats   apples and s.cl drinks coffee
          'She eats apples and drinks coffee.'

       b. **La* magna pomi e _ beve cafè

Note that the obligatory repetition of the clitic pronoun does not follow from a general requirement that subjects be repeated when finite verbs are coordinated; on the contrary, such a repetition would yield unacceptability with a full noun phrase or with a non-clitic subject pronoun. The fact that the subject clitics cannot be omitted is thus a property that reflects their special status and, as suggested in the works cited, their intimate relationship with the inflected verb. Rizzi (1986) takes the obligatoriness of their presence in the varieties of Trentino he examines as evidence for analyzing them as part of verbal inflection. His analysis rules out the possibility that these subject clitics could be in V° or in the canonical subject position and argues that they are best represented as being in Infl, the syntactic position where tense and agreement are expressed. The subject clitics of the northern Italian dialects, in this view, are the spell-out of agreement. As pointed out explicitly in Rizzi's article, this expresses in terms of the syntactic framework of the time the intuition encoded in traditional dialectological work, which calls them *rideterminazione dell'accordo* 'reduplication of agreement'. The structural representation of subject clitics in French and in the northern Italian dialects differs as follows, according to Rizzi (1986: 400):[28]

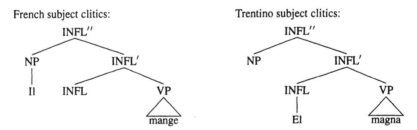

French subject clitics: Trentino subject clitics:

Poletto's work follows Rizzi's steps in distinguishing between subject clitics such as the ones in French, which do not exhibit the pattern in (34), from those of northern Italian dialects like Trentino and Basso Polesano. As we are about to see, her work assumes a more articulated phrase structure, in which the agreement clitics occupy more than two distinct structural positions.

2. The second class of clitics is referred to as *vocalic clitics* (Poletto 1993a: §2.2.2). As the label suggests, they always have the form of a vowel. The following example, from Basso Polesano, shows that vocalic subject clitics are not repeated when two finite verbs are coordinated, contrary to what happens with agreement clitics:[29]

(35) *A* magno pomi e _ bevo cafè. (Basso Polesano)
      s.cl eat   apples and _ drink coffee
      'I eat apples and drink coffee.'

If the vocalic subject clitic is repeated, the result is marginal; according to the informants, it is as strange as repeating a full noun phrase or full pronoun with the same reference (e.g., ?John$_i$ eats apples and John$_i$ drinks coffee):

(36) ?*A* magno pomi e a bevo cafè. (Basso Polesano)
      s.cl eat   apples and s.cl drink coffee
      'I eat apples and drink coffee.'

The finite verb that is the second conjunct can appear without the subject clitic, which suggests that vocalic clitics are not as closely related to the finite verb as agreement clitics. In terms of phrase structure, this can be expressed by saying that they are not part of the phrase structure that is being coordinated.

A second property that distinguishes agreement clitics and vocalic clitics concerns their position in the presence of a pre-verbal negative marker that by itself can negate a clause. The agreement clitics — those subject clitics that are obligatorily present in the coordination of two finite verbs — occur to the right of such a pre-verbal negative marker, as shown in the following examples:[30]

(37) *No la* vien. (Basso Polesano)
      neg s.cl comes
      'She's not coming.'

(38) *No te* ghe l'hai dit. (Trentino)
      neg s.cl him it'have said
      'You have not said it to him.'

(39) Maria *no la* parla. (Trentino)
      Maria neg s.cl speaks
      'Maria doesn't speak.'

In contrast, the vocalic clitics — those subject clitics that are omitted in the coordination of two finite verbs — occur to the left of a negative marker which by itself can negate the clause, as shown in (40) (from Poletto 1993a: 23):[31]

(40) a. *A* *no* vegno. (Basso Polesano)
          s.cl neg come
          'I am not coming.'
      b. **No a* vegno.

From this sort of evidence Poletto concludes that, whereas agreement clitics occur in the head of the Agr projection, vocalic clitics occupy a higher structural position. Such a difference is supported by the following properties of vocalic subject clitics:

  • They do not exhibit agreement distinctions — that is, their morphology does not change according to person,[32] number, and gender of the subject (such distinctions are expressed by the verbal ending), as shown in the following examples:[33]

(41) a. *A* magno. (Basso Polesano)
      'I eat'

　　　b. *A te* magni.
      'You eat (sg.)'

　　　c. *A*　　magnemo.
      'We eat.'

　　　d. *A*　　magnè.
      'You eat (pl.)'

- They exhibit an intricate distributional pattern with respect to complementizers and verbs that have moved to C°, which I will outline here only briefly (see Poletto 1993a for a detailed description). In some varieties, they never appear in a matrix interrogative clause, where the verb can be said to have moved to C°, but are replaced by other clitics. In other varieties, such as the variety of Friulian from Casarsa described in Benincà (1986), they appear in a matrix interrogative, but they are always on the left of the verb and a different subject clitic appears on the right of the verb:

(42) *A*　vegni*al*? (Friulian)
      s.cl come-s.cl
      'Does he come?'

Notice that neither type of behavior is analogous to that of subject clitics in French, where the subject clitic appears on the right of the verb in interrogative contexts, for example:

(43) Qui avez-*vous* vu?　(French)
      Who have-s.cl seen?
      'Who have you seen?'

When the C° position is occupied by an element with WH-features (like *do* 'where' of Friulian, analyzed in Benincà 1986), the vocalic clitic is obligatorily omitted.[34] When the C° position is occupied by a complementizer, the vocalic clitic forms a unit with it, and the linear order within the unit is always *complementizer–clitic*. The following examples from the variety of Basso Polesano spoken in Adria illustrate such a case (examples from Poletto 1993a: 28):

(44) a. Vara *ca*　　　vegno doman.　(Basso Polesano from Adria)
        look that-s.cl come tomorrow
        'Note that I'll come tomorrow.'

　　　b. *Vara *che a*　vegno doman.
        look that s.cl come tomorrow

　　　c. A no so　　*sa*　　vegnarò.
        cl neg know if-s.cl will-come
        'I don't know whether I will come.'

　　　d. *A no so *se a* vegnarò.

This contrasts with the behavior of other subject clitics in this variety, as well as that of other elements that might form a unit with the complementizer (e.g., the definite determiner of a subject), but for which this is not obligatory:

(45) a. Vara *chi*   vien. (Basso Polesano from Adria)
        look who-s.cl comes
        'Note that they're coming.'
      b. Vara *che i* vien.

These data suggest that, contrary to other subject clitics, the vocalic clitics must either occur in C° (forming a unit with the complementizer or with the verb which has moved to C°) or else be omitted.

Poletto (1993a) convincingly argues that this pattern of behavior of the vocalic clitics is best accounted for by analyzing them as base-generated in a position higher than AgrP but lower than CP. Such a position is identified as a functional projection for modal elements, labeled ModP.[35] In contrast, following Brandi and Cordin (1981, 1989) and Rizzi (1986), Poletto analyzes agreement clitics — the class of clitics that is closer to the verb — as part of the agreement morphology of the verb.[36] The agreement clitics of Basso Polesano exemplified here are taken to occur in Agr°, which is treated as a morphologically complex head.[37]

To account for the position of the vocalic clitics with respect to the pre-verbal negative markers and the agreement clitics, Poletto (1993a: §2.2.2) proposes the following structure:

(46)

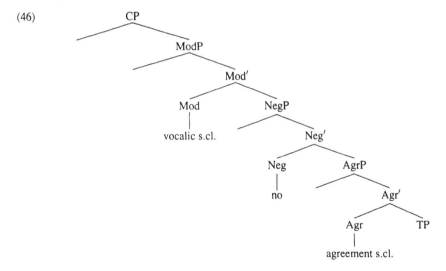

The vocalic clitics are in the head of the functional projection ModP; from this position, they cliticize onto the head of the projection CP which dominates it. The negative markers are in the head of the projection NegP; the agreement clitics "share" (cf. note 37) the head of AgrP with the finite verb.[38]

I will subscribe to this conclusion, insofar as it concerns the relative position of the negative markers that can negate a clause by themselves and these subject clitics.

In this view, then, the fact that such a negative marker follows subject clitics in certain cases and precedes them in others is not a consequence of the negative marker itself occupying more than one structural position, but of the subject clitics occupying two different structural positions. I therefore conclude that the pre-verbal negative markers that can negate a clause by themselves are in the head of NegP in all cases. Further support for this conclusion comes from the data from Friulian of San Michele al Tagliamento, discussed in Benincà (1986). The third person singular subject clitic *al* consists of a vocalic clitic *a* and an agreement clitic *l* and the pre-verbal negative marker *no* can only occur after the vocalic clitic and before the agreement clitic:[39]

(47) a. *Al* ven.   (Friulian of S. Michele)
         s.cl comes
         'He comes.'
     b. *A nol* ven
     c. **A 'l no* ven.
     d. **No al* ven.

So far we have focused our attention on the interaction of subject clitics and negative markers of varieties in which the pre-verbal negative marker can by itself negate a clause. What about pre-verbal negative markers that cannot negate a clause by themselves? They generally follow *both* vocalic subject clitics and agreement subject clitics, as we can see in the following examples (all taken from ASIS — see Benincà et al. 1990–present):[40]

(48) a. Ti te *n*'catti mai d' mèji. (Carcare)
         you s.cl neg'buy never of apples
         'You never buy apples.'

     b. A nui u *n'* interessa nent.
        to us s.cl neg interests neg
        'It doesn't interest us.'

(49) a. A*n*   so   mia csa fasa Giani. (Emiliano from Carpi)
         s.cl-neg know neg what does Giani
         'I don't know what John is doing.'

     b. La compre-t o a*n*   la compre-t mia?
        it buy-s.cl or s.cl neg it buy-s.cl neg
        'Do you buy it or don't you buy it?'

In sum, in this section I have shown that the position of pre-verbal negative markers with respect to subject clitics remains constant once we identify two major classes of clitics: vocalic versus agreement clitics. We have seen that the pre-verbal negative markers that can negate a clause by themselves follow vocalic clitics and precede agreement clitics, whereas those that cannot negate a clause by themselves follow both classes of subject clitics. For ease of reference, let us call the pre-verbal negative markers that can negate a clause by themselves "strong negative markers" and the others "weak negative markers." Then we can summarize our discussion in the following diagram:[41]

(50)

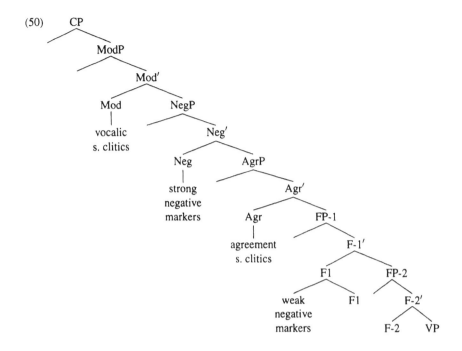

In the next section I will discuss some potential counterexamples to the proposed generalization insofar as it concerns negative markers and agreement clitics.

2.3.2. *Two structural positions for agreement clitics*

The discussion in the previous section might lead us to expect that the pre-verbal negative markers that can negate a clause by themselves always precede all the subject clitics that have been analyzed as agreement clitics, and that, in contrast, those that cannot negate a clause by themselves always follow them. In this section I will examine some counterexamples to that generalization.

Let us start with the first class of pre-verbal negative markers. Having observed their relative position with respect to agreement clitics in a variety of Veneto (i.e., Basso Polesano), Friulian, and Trentino, let us now discuss briefly some examples from other northern Italian dialects, where the distribution of these two elements is different from the cases examined so far. Since the only languages relevant to this discussion are those that have both a system of subject clitics and a pre-verbal negative marker that can negate the clause alone, when we move away from northeastern Italy our choice is limited to one other group of dialects, namely those spoken in Liguria, the northwestern Italian region immediately below Piedmont.

The dialect of Ventimiglia (Ventimigliese) does not have a system of vocalic clitics parallel to that exhibited by Basso Polesano. As for agreement clitics, while it lacks a form for the first person, it has forms for the second person singular (*ti*) and for the third person singular and plural (the singular form varies according to gender):[42]

(51) a. Tü *ti* mangi. (Ventimigliese)
          you s.cl eat
          'You eat.'

      b. Paulin *u* ven.
          Paulin s.cl comes
          'Little Paul comes.'

      c. *A* mangia.
          s.cl eats
          'She eats.'

      d. E done *i* sun sciurtie.
          the women s.cl are left
          'The women have left.'

      e. I tundi *i* sun brüti.
          the dishes s.cl are dirty
          'The dishes are dirty.'

Contrary to what one might expect in light of the discussion above, the negative marker *nu*, which by itself can negate the clause, does not precede but rather follows the subject clitics of third person singular and plural:[43]

(52) a. Se **a** *nu* gu u vò dà. (Ventimigliese)
          if s.cl neg him it wants to-give
          'If she doesn't want to give it to him.'

      b. I *nu* ven.
          s.cl neg come
          'They're not coming.'

      c. I *nu* l'han mia freidu.
          s.cl neg cl-have neg cold
          'They're not cold.'

Similar examples are also found in the dialect of Novi Ligure, where the negative marker *n* does not precede but follows the third person subject clitic:[44]

(53) a. L'a ditu ke Mario **u-***n* ñirà. (Novi Ligure)
          cl-has said that Mario s.cl-neg come(fut)
          'He said that Mario won't come.'

      b. **A-***n* mangia moi a früta, sa fía.
          s.cl-neg eats   never the fruit, that girl
          'She never eats fruit, that girl.'

      c. **I-***n* kata moi a früta, e mè surèle.
          s.cl-neg buy never the fruit, the my sisters
          'They never buy fruit, my sisters.'

These clitics cannot be considered vocalic clitics in the sense described in the previous section, since they are repeated in the coordination of two finite verbs and they exhibit agreement (they mark person, number, and gender distinctions, in the third person singular). Rather, they satisfy the diagnostics of the agreement clitics like those of

Basso Polesano. Why is it, then, that they precede the negative marker, rather than following it, thus differing from the agreement clitics of Basso Polesano?

Note that, contrary to the third person subject clitics, the second person subject clitic in Ventimigliese follows the negative marker, thus patterning like the agreement clitics of Basso Polesano:[45]

(54) a. *Nu* **ti** sai   (Ventimigliese)
        neg s.cl know
        'You don't know.'

      b. *Nu* **ti**   mangi ciü.
        neg s.cl eat   more
        'You don't eat anymore.'

These data are parallel to those mentioned by Parry for another Ligurian dialect, Savonese (data from Besio and Buzzano 1979: 15, cited in Parry in press a):[46]

(55) De cunseggi *nu* **ti** ne veu. (Savonese)
      of advice   neg s.cl cl want
      'Of advice, you don't want any.'

As for the distribution of third person agreement clitics, two possibilities come to mind at this point: either the agreement clitics of Basso Polesano on the one hand and those of the dialects of Ventimiglia and Novi Ligure on the other occupy different positions in the clause (in particular, the former are structurally lower than the latter), or else the agreement clitics occur in the same structural position in all these varieties, but the position of the negative markers differs.

It could be argued, for example, that in these Ligurian dialects the negative marker right-adjoins to the subject clitics of third person. Though logically possible, such a solution would require that the negative marker be sensitive to the person specifications of the subject clitics. Morever, it would involve lowering the negative marker and right-adjunction, two operations that we want to rule out for theoretical reasons. Alternatively, it could be argued that third person subject clitics left-adjoin to the negative marker, or that subject clitics, depending on person specifications, may occupy different structural positions. Work on subject clitics leads me to suggest that, at least in this case, the correct solution is the latter. Both synchronic and diachronic studies of the systems of subject clitics in the languages we are discussing point out that they can occupy different structural positions. Synchronically, as I already mentioned, we find subject clitics whose position differs across languages, as in the case of French on the one hand and Trentino or Basso Polesano on the other. Diachronically, we know that subject clitics can change their function and their structural position (cf. Poletto 1993a, Vanelli 1987 and Vai 1996, among others).[47] Even within the same language, as mentioned in notes (31) and (47), different forms of a clitic paradigm can diverge and end up with a different function and a different position. Thus the diagram in (46) indicates one position where agreement clitics might occur, but not the only one. Simplifying grossly, one can say that agreement clitics change, diachronically, from occupying the position of the subject NP to occupying a position closer to the inflectional head that hosts the finite verb. The agreement clitics I have been describing differ precisely along this dimension: some are closer to the canonical subject position (e.g., the third person subject clitics of Ventimigliese), while others are closer to the head hosting the finite verb (e.g., the second person subject clitics of Ventimigliese, or the subject clitics of Basso Polesano). It is often found that, in this process of change, the first form of subject clitics to appear in a different position is the subject clitic of second person singular.

I suggest that what we are witnessing in the contrast between the northwestern and the northeastern Italian dialects examined (Veneto, Friulano, and Trentino on the one hand; Ligurian varieties on the other) is a difference of this type. In the Ligurian dialects examined, subject clitics are not uniform across person specifications; the agreement clitics of third person are structurally higher than those of second person, which are closer to verbal inflection. Hence their different behavior with respect to the pre-verbal negative marker: since the agreement clitics of third person are structurally higher than the negative marker, they precede it, whereas those of second person are lower, and thus follow it. No difference in the position of the negative markers need be invoked.[48]

Let me now mention the case of Fiorentino, the dialect spoken in Florence, which is similar, though not identical, to the case of Ventimigliese. Following Antelmi's (1993: 10) description, the subject clitics of third and first person singular precede the negative marker *un*, as shown in (56):[49]

(56)   a. Lei **la** *un* mangia. (Fiorentino)
            she s.cl neg eats
            'She doesn't eat.'

        b. **E'** *un* mangio.
            s.cl neg eat
            'I don't eat.'

However, those of second person singular and plural follow it, as shown in (57):

(57)   a. Te *un* **tu** mangi. (Fiorentino)
            you neg s.cl eat
            'You don't eat.'

        b. Voi *un* **vu** mangiate.
            you neg s.cl eat
            'You don't eat.'

I suggest for this pattern an analysis similar to the preceding one proposed for Ventimigliese: the subject clitic for first person singular and third person is structurally higher than the negative marker, whereas that for second person is structurally lower. In this respect, these data do not support the conclusion in Rizzi (1986) that the pre-verbal negative marker and the subject clitics form one cluster — that is, they are adjoined to the same head and thus occupy the same structural position. Rizzi (1986: 398) reports that the negative marker *un* of Fiorentino can either precede or follow the second person subject clitic:

(58)   a. (Te) *un* **tu** parli. (Fiorentino)
            (you) neg s.cl speak
            'You don't speak.'

b. (Te) t' *un* parli.
   (you) s.cl neg speak
   'You don't speak.'

According to Antelmi (1993), though, this alternation is not possible within the same variety. The relative order of negative marker and subject clitic exhibited by the sentence in (58)b is only found in varieties spoken in isolated areas and reflects an older stage of the language. This confirms the hypothesis I have been pursuing in this section: the different positions in which the subject clitics occur with respect to the pre-verbal negative marker reflect the different diachronic stages of their development, which takes them from a structural position as high as the subject position to one closer to the verb — that is, from subjects to agreement markers.[50]

In addition to the pre-verbal negative markers that can negate the clause by themselves, those that cannot also exhibit some deviation from the expected pattern (recall that we have argued that they generally follow agreement subject clitics). I suggest that also in the case of negative markers that cannot negate the clause by themselves such deviations should be interpreted as differences in the position of the agreement subject clitic, rather than in the position of the negative markers.[51]

In sum, in this section we have examined some languages that have both subject clitics and a pre-verbal negative marker, and we have observed the linear ordering they exhibit with respect to one another. Following Poletto (1993a), I have concluded that, in varieties of Veneto, Trentino, and Friulian, the pre-verbal negative marker that by itself can negate a clause occupies a structural position lower than vocalic subject clitics and higher than agreement subject clitics. I have also proposed that the pre-verbal negative markers that cannot negate a clause by themselves, found in the dialects spoken in the Ligurian hinterland, occupy a position that is lower than both vocalic and agreement subject clitics. I have thus drawn the conclusion that, even though at first sight the pre-verbal negative marker appears to precede subject clitics in some cases and follow them in others, the pattern is in fact rather simple once we distinguish, on the one hand, between the pre-verbal negative markers that can and those that cannot negate a clause by themselves and, on the other, between vocalic and agreement subject clitics.

We have also examined languages in which a pre-verbal negative marker that by itself can negate a clause precedes some agreement clitics, but not all. In Ventimigliese, for example, the negative marker precedes the agreement clitic of second person but not that of third person. For these cases as well, I have suggested that the two different linear orders are not the consequence of the negative marker being in two different structural positions, but rather of the agreement clitics being structurally higher in the case of third person than in the case of second person. I have argued that support for this analysis comes from the observation that this class of subject clitics exhibits a shift in the structural position its members occupy, which goes from a position as high as that of full NP subjects to one as low as that of the inflected verb. In view of this, I dismissed as unnecessary the hypothesis that the pre-verbal negative markers that can negate a clause by themselves might occupy different structural positions in the languages under consideration. A similar conclusion was also suggested for the case of negative markers that cannot negate a clause by themselves.

2.4.   Pre-verbal negative markers and verb movement

The presence of a pre-verbal negative marker affects verb movement in interrogative clauses. Since not all the varieties we have been examining are equally transparent concerning the existence of verb movement in interrogative clauses, I limit the discussion here to the relatively small number of varieties that exhibit overt differences in the position of the verb in interrogative as opposed to non-interrogative contexts.

2.4.1.   *Negative markers in the absence of verb movement*

Let us consider a language that has a pre-verbal negative marker that by itself can negate the clause and in which the verb appears to occupy a different position in interrogative and in non-interrogative clauses. Paduan, the variety of Veneto spoken in Padua, is such a language, as discussed in Benincà and Vanelli (1982) and Poletto (1993a, 1993b). In Paduan, the negative marker is the pre-verbal element *no*, which by itself can negate a clause. The relative order of finite verb and subject clitic is different in interrogative and in non-interrogative clauses. As shown by the contrast between the *a* and *b* pairs in the following examples, in non-interrogative clauses the subject clitic precedes the finite verb; on the contrary, in interrogative clauses (both yes/no questions and WH-questions) the verb precedes the subject clitic:[52]

(59) a. *Te* magni. (Paduan)
s.cl eat
'You (sg.) eat'.

b. Cosa màgni-*to*?
what eat-s.cl
'What do you eat?'

(60) a. *El/la*   magna.
s.cl(m)/(f) eat
'He/she eats'.

b. Cosa màgne-*lo/*   màgne-*la*?
what eats-s.cl(m)/ eats-s.cl(f)
'What does he/she eat?'

(61) a. *I/le*   magna.
s.cl(m)/(f) eat
'They(m/f) eat'.

b. Cosa màgne-*li/*   màgne-*le*?
what eat-s.cl(m)/ eat-s.cl(f)
'What do they(m/f) eat?'

(62) a. *El* vien.
s.cl comes
'He comes.'

b. Vien-*lo*?
comes-s.cl?
'Is he coming?'

It is important to notice that the subject clitic that precedes the verb in non-interrogative clauses and the one that follows the verb in interrogative clauses are not the same. Poletto (1993b: 214) shows that Paduan has two distinct series of subject clitics. One series occurs in non-interrogative clauses and is limited to second person (singular only) and third person (singular and plural):

(63)

Non-interrogative subject clitics	
te	second singular
el/la	masculine and feminine third singular
i/le	masculine and feminine third plural

The other series is found in interrogative clauses only and shows a complete paradigm, that is, a subject clitic for each person:

(64)

Interrogative subject clitics	
i	first singular
to	second singular
lo/la	masculine and feminine third singular
i	first plural
o	second plural
li/le	masculine and feminine third plural

Although the two series exhibit some overlap (the third person feminine subject clitics of the non-interrogative and the interrogative series are identical), they differ in both the number of elements and their morphological shape. Notice the striking difference in the first person (singular and plural) and the second (plural): whereas an interrogative clitic for these persons is obligatorily present in questions, as shown in examples (65)a and (66)a, and (65)b and (66)b, no counterpart exists for non-interrogative clauses (examples from Poletto 1993b: 214):

(65) a. Cossa go-*i*   da fare? (Paduan)
       what   have-s.cl to do
       'What should I do?'

      b. *Cossa go da fare?

      c. Go   da fare na roba.
         have to do a   thing
         'I must do one thing.'

(66) a. Cossa gavì-*o*   da fare?
       what   have-s.cl(pl) to do
       'What should you do?'

      b. *Cossa gavì da fare?

      c. Gavì da fare na   roba.
         have to do one thing
         'You must do one thing.'

In addition to this morphological difference, the difference in obligatoriness between interrogative and non-interrogative clauses brings further support to the hypothesis that the subject clitics differ in the two contexts and are not simply the same type of element appearing on different sides of the verb.

Let us refer to the word order in which the verb precedes the subject clitic as "subject clitic inversion," following the literature on this topic. The pre-verbal negative marker of Paduan, *no*, typically does not co-occur with subject clitic inversion; that is, the sequence *no–verb–interrogative clitic* is ungrammatical, as shown in (67)a and (68)a. The pre-verbal negative marker is grammatical in interrogative contexts only in co-occurrence with the verb following a non-interrogative subject clitic — that is, with the word order *no–subject clitic–verb*, as shown in (67)b and (68)b. In other words, when the pre-verbal negative marker is present the word order is the same as the one found in non-interrogative clauses — *no–subject clitic–verb* — even in questions:[53]

(67) a. **No* ve-*to*   via? (Paduan)
          neg go-s.cl away
          'Aren't you going away?'

      b. *No te*   ve via?
          neg s.cl go away

(68) a. **No* vien-*lo*?
          neg comes-s.cl
          'Doesn't he come?'

      b. *Nol*   vien?
          neg-s.cl comes
          'Doesn't he come?'

Why is the pre-verbal negative marker of Paduan incompatible with one word order but compatible with the other?

Let us assume that the word order of subject clitic inversion — the one where the verb precedes an interrogative subject clitic — derives from movement of the verb to a position higher than the one it occupies in non-interrogative clauses. Suppose we extended an analysis along the lines of Rizzi's (1990, 1996) WH-criterion to the case of yes/no questions. The WH-criterion argues that a WH-operator must be in a configuration of Specifier-head agreement with a head that carries WH-features and that a head carrying WH-features must be in a configuration of Spec-head agreement with an operator specified for the same features. The following formulation of this principle is from Rizzi (1990: 378):

(69) WH-Criterion:
      a. Each +WH X° must be in a Spec-Head relation with a WH-phrase;
      b. Each WH-phrase must be in a Spec-Head relation with a +WH X°.

This combination has the effect that a moved WH-phrase, which counts as an operator in Rizzi's terms, must be in the specifier of a head with WH-features; for example, in English matrix clauses, a moved WH-phrase will be in the specifier of a projection whose head is the finite verb (which is said to have WH-features). Conversely, a

head with WH-features — for example, the finite verb in main clauses in English —
must move to the head of a projection whose specifier hosts a WH-operator. Such a
projection is assumed to be CP.

Transposing this proposal to the case of yes/no questions, one could argue that
the verb moves to C° in yes/no questions and that such movement takes place because
the finite verb, endowed with features that match those of the yes/no operator, must
instantiate a configuration of Spec-head agreement with an abstract yes/no operator
in [Spec,CP].[54] Similarly, along the lines of Chomsky (1993), where all syntactic
movement is motivated by the need to check morphological features, it could be
argued that the verb moves to C° to check certain morphological features that it
carries in yes/no questions. In either case, whether one extends to yes/no questions
Rizzi's WH-criterion or Chomsky's (1993) feature-checking mechanism, the same
prediction is made: namely, that the verb should obligatorily move in yes/no questions,
either to achieve the desired configuration (in Rizzi's terms) or to check its features
(in Chomsky's terms).

However, the data from Paduan are problematic for any approach that makes
verb movement obligatory in yes/no questions. If verb movement were obligatory,
how could it fail to take place in the presence of the pre-verbal negative marker and
not yield ungrammaticality? I would expect that failure of the verb to move would
indeed give rise to ungrammaticality. If, as has often been argued in the literature, the
presence of the negative marker between I° and C° prevents the verb from moving
to C° because it creates a minimality effect, the verb then cannot instantiate the
required Spec-head configuration or check its features. It is then surprising that the
result should be other than ungrammaticality. Notice that the sentences in (67)b and
(68)b, repeated here for convenience, are grammatical without exhibiting subject
clitic inversion, the diagnostics for verb movement to C°:

(70)   a. *No te*   ve via? (Paduan)
          neg s.cl go away
          'Aren't you going away?'

       b. *Nol*   vien?
          neg-s.cl comes
          'Doesn't he come?'

I thus formulate my analysis without making the assumption that verb movement
takes place obligatorily in yes/no questions. I will argue, instead, that the negative
marker itself (or, perhaps, its features) moves to C° in negative yes/no questions, thus
making verb movement unnecessary. In this respect, while incompatible with the
proposal in Chomsky (1993), this proposal provides support for the view expressed
in Chomsky (1995: ch. 4) concerning the trigger for overt movement: movement is
not motivated by properties of the element that moves, but by properties of the target.

In the spirit of these proposals, though departing from them in some respects,
I suggest that the syntactic properties of yes/no questions should be analyzed as
resulting from the interaction of two factors. On the one hand, they contain an
abstract yes/no operator, which contributes the question interpretation. I assume that
all operators, including the one involved in yes/no questions, must occur in a specifier
position.[55] On the other hand, because they contain an operator, I assume they are

subject to the general requirement that the head of the projection containing an operator match the features of its specifier. In the case of yes/no questions, this means that the head in whose specifier the operator occurs must have features matching those of the yes/no operator.[56] I suggest that this requirement can be satisfied if the head contains either the features of the finite verb, which has raised through TP and checked tense features, or those of the negative marker.

My proposal concerning yes/no questions in Paduan is then the following. The reason yes/no questions do not show evidence of verb movement in the presence of a pre-verbal negative marker is that the negative marker *no*, which heads the projection NegP, counts as a head with features matching those of the yes/no operator. Since I assume that this negative marker c-commands the position where the finite verb occurs (as discussed in the previous sections), it will be the element closest to the head whose projection hosts the operator. Hence, it will be attracted by such a head and left-adjoin to it, thus providing it with the features it needs. There is more than one way to think of this. The yes/no operator could be the specifier of the projection NegP; in this case, the head Neg°, which contains the negative marker *no*, matches its features. Alternatively, if CP is the syntactic locus where clausal type is specified, the yes/no operator could be taken to be the specifier of CP; in this case, either the negative marker raises and left-adjoins to C° in the syntax or its features raise at LF. As far as I can tell, the matter cannot be decided on empirical, but only on conceptual grounds. Considerations of economy of phrase structure, such as those espoused in Grimshaw (in press b), would argue in favor of viewing the operator in the specifier of NegP, since this would represent the minimal amount of structure. Still, constraints along the lines of the Neg-Criterion (which argue for a configuration of specifier-head agreement between a negative marker in the head and a negative operator in the specifier of the same projection) argue against the presence of the yes/no operator in the specifier of NegP, unless it can be taken to count as an element that satisfies the Neg Criterion (cf. Haegeman and Zanuttini 1991, 1995; Haegeman 1991, 1992a, 1992b, 1994, 1995).

For concreteness, I will assume that the yes/no operator is in the specifier of CP and that *no* can check the features of C° either by adjoining to it in the syntax or by LF-raising of its features. Since the negative marker can provide C° with the features it needs to match the operator in its specifier, the verb need not do so and therefore need not move. In fact, following economy considerations, it cannot move. In this view, then, the pre-verbal negative marker does not block verb movement: it simply makes it unnecessary.[57]

Let me now discuss some cross-linguistic support for the proposal that the negative marker can provide the features required by the functional head that has the yes/no operator as its specifier.

In Sardinian, as reported in Jones (1993), yes/no questions can be introduced by the interrogative particle *a*:[58]

(71) a. *A   mi vattus   cudda tassa?* (Sardinian)
         y/n me you+fetch that   glass
         'Will you fetch me that glass?'

b. *A* bi   venit Juanne?
y/n there comes John
'Is John coming?'

c. *A* ti   lavo cussos prattos?
y/n you wash those plates
'Should I wash those plates for you?'

Jones (1993: 25) proposes to analyze this element as occurring in C°. What is interesting for this discussion is that *a* cannot co-occur with the pre-verbal negative marker *non* (which appears as *no* in the following example):

(72)   *A no'est arrivatu Juanne? (Sardinian)
y/n neg'is arrived Juanne
'Has John not arrived?'

From my point of view, it is tempting to think that the absence of *a* stems from the fact that the negative marker can fulfill the same function, which we take to be that of providing C° with the features it needs to match those of the yes/no operator.[59]

Moving to a different language family, complementary distribution between an interrogative particle and a negative marker is also found in some dialects of Chinese (e.g., Mandarin, Cantonese, and Taiwanese), as discussed in Chen (1996) and Cheng, Huang, and Tang (in press). In Mandarin, non-negative yes/no questions exhibit the question particle *ma* in sentence final position:[60]

(73)   Ta la-lei   *ma*? (Mandarin)
he come-perf y/n
'Did he come?'

This element has been argued to occur in C° in Huang (1982), Tang (1989), and Aoun and Li (1993), among others. When a negative marker is present in the canonical pre-verbal position, it may co-occur with *ma*, as shown in (74):[61]

(74)   a. Lisi *bu* lai   *ma*? (Mandarin)
Lisi neg come y/n
'Won't Lisi come?'

b. Lisi *meiyou* lai   *ma*?
Lisi neg   come y/n
'Hasn't Lisi come?'

Alternatively, the negative marker *meiyou* can occur in sentence final position, as shown in (75). Crucially, though, *ma* and a negative marker cannot co-occur in sentence final position, in either order, as shown in (76):[62]

(75)   a. Hufei qu-le   *meiyou*? (Mandarin)
Hufei go-perf neg
'Did Hufei go?'

(76)   a. *Zhangsan lai-le   *meiyou ma*?
Zhangsan come-perf neg   y/n

b. *Zhangsan lai-le   *ma meiyou*?
Zhangsan come-perf y/n neg

Both Chen (1996) and Cheng, Huang, and Tang (in press), working independently, come to the conclusion that these data should be accounted for by taking the negative markers, base-generated in the head of NegP, to have moved to C°.[63] Both these works suggest that the negative marker in Mandarin can fulfill the same function as the question particle *ma* — that of licensing an abstract yes/no operator in the specifier of CP.[64]

Having seen some cross-linguistic evidence in support of the proposal that the negative marker can provide features matching those of the operator of yes/no questions, let us now turn our attention back to Paduan. Two main questions arise from this proposal. The first concerns embedded yes/no questions: If the negative marker *no* can make verb movement unnecessary in matrix yes/no questions, can it also take over the function of the complementizer in embedded yes/no questions?[65] That is, does one find embedded yes/no questions where the negative marker has moved to C° in the syntax, or its features move to C° at LF, thus making the complementizer unnecessary? The answer is negative. I believe this is not necessarily to be taken as evidence that my analysis is on the wrong track, but rather is to be related to the parallel impossibility of verb movement to C° in embedded questions. That is, similarly to movement of the verb, raising of the negative marker also is a root phenomenon. In selected contexts, insertion of a complementizer is preferred to both movement of the verb and movement of the negative marker. This might stem from the fact that the embedded CP, which is selected by the matrix verb, has features that can only be checked by a subordinating complementizer, such as 'if' or 'whether'.[66]

The second issue concerns WH-questions: If Paduan *no* is the closest head with features matching those of the operator of yes/no questions, is it also the closest head with features matching those of other question operators? In particular, can *no* provide the features for the head whose specifier is a WH-constituent, thus making movement of the verb unnecessary? The answer to this question can be found in the data, to which I now turn. WH-questions in Paduan exhibit subject clitic inversion — that is, the word order where the finite verb precedes the interrogative subject clitics. As mentioned, this word order is standardly taken to mark contexts where the verb has moved further than in declarative clauses (cf. Poletto 1993b: 245):

(77) a. Cossa fa-*lo*?   (Paduan)
        what does-s.cl
        'What is he doing?'

      b. Cossa magne-*lo*?
        what eats-s.cl
        'What is he eating?'

      c. Cossa ga-*lo*   fato?
        what has-s.cl done
        'What has he done?'

      d. Cossa ga-*lo*   magnà?
        what has-s.cl eaten
        'What has he eaten?'

In the presence of a negative marker, the same type of structure is ungrammatical. Interestingly, it is ruled out regardless of the position of the verb with respect to the subject clitics, as we can see in the following examples:[67]

(78)　a.　*Cossa *no* ga-*lo*　fato? (Paduan)
　　　　　what　neg has-s.cl done
　　　　　'What hasn't he done?'

　　　b.　*Cossa *nol*　　ga fato?
　　　　　what　neg-s.cl has done
　　　　　'What hasn't he done?'

(79)　a.　*Cossa *no* ga-*lo*　　magnà?
　　　　　what　neg have-s.cl eaten
　　　　　'What hasn't he eaten?'

　　　b.　*Cossa *nol*　　ga　magnà?
　　　　　what　neg-s.cl have eaten
　　　　　'What hasn't he eaten?'

WH-questions negated by pre-verbal *no* are grammatical only in a cleft-construction:[68]

(80)　a.　Cossa *ze* che *nol*　　ga　fato? (Paduan)
　　　　　what　is　that neg-s.cl has done
　　　　　'What is it that he hasn't done?'

　　　b.　Cossa *ze* che *nol*　　ga　magnà?
　　　　　what　is　that neg-s.cl has eaten
　　　　　'What is it that he hasn't eaten?'

These examples suggest that the answer to the question concerning the ability of the negative marker to match WH-features is negative: the negative marker *no* in Paduan cannot provide features to match those of the WH-operator. Since it is the closest head to $C°$, it (or its features) will be attracted and left-adjoin to $C°$; but then, because of feature mismatch, the derivation will either converge as gibberish or will terminate. Thus, in the presence of a WH-operator, the finite verb is the only head that can endow $C°$ with features matching those of the operator in the specifier position, whereas the negative marker *no* cannot do so.

At this point, one could object that the relevant difference might not be that between yes/no operators on the one hand and WH-operators on the other, but rather that between overt and abstract operators. In this respect, it is interesting to observe the pattern exhibited by the variety of Veneto spoken in Belluno (Bellunese), brought to our attention by N. Munaro (personal communication).[69] In this language, the WH-phrase *che* 'what' remains in situ in non-negative interrogative clauses (differing from the other WH-word corresponding to 'what', namely *cossa*):

(81)　A-lo　fat　*che*? (Bellunese)
　　　has-s.cl done what
　　　'What has he done?'

The analysis of this construction suggested both in Poletto (1993b) and in Munaro (1995) is that the WH-word in situ is interpreted in construction with an abstract

WH-operator in [Spec,CP].[70] Following them in assuming that WH-questions with the WH-phrase in situ have an abstract WH-operator in clause-initial position, we can then ask whether such an abstract WH-operator can be in the specifier of a head whose features are those of the negative marker. The answer is negative: in the presence of the pre-verbal negative marker, the structure with the WH-phrase in situ (and, by assumption, an abstract WH-operator in clause-initial position) is ungrammatical:

(82)　*No a-lo　　fat　che? (Bellunese)
　　　neg has-s.cl done what?
　　　'What hasn't he done?'

As in Paduan, a cleft must be used:

(83)　É-lo　che　che no l'a　　fat? (Bellunese)
　　　is-s.cl what that neg s.cl-has done
　　　'What is it that he hasn't done?'

This leads me to the following conclusion: whereas a finite verb can provide C° with the features it needs to match those of the WH-operator in its specifier, the negative marker cannot. Thus the constraints on which head can provide matching features are independent of whether the operator is overt or abstract; instead, they depend solely on whether it is a WH- or a yes/no operator.

I therefore conclude that, in Paduan as in Bellunese, yes/no question operators and WH-constituents have different requirements concerning the features of the heads of which they are the specifiers. Whereas both are satisfied by the features provided by the finite verb, only yes/no operators can occur in the specifier of a head whose features are provided by the negative marker.

Let me recapitulate briefly where this discussion has led us. I have discussed cases of yes/no questions in which the pre-verbal negative marker is incompatible with movement of the verb to the left of interrogative clitics. I have argued that, instead of viewing the negative marker as blocking verb movement, we should view it as making verb movement unnecessary. In particular, I have suggested that the negative marker itself can fulfill the function normally fulfilled by the finite verb. I have characterized this function as that of providing the head that hosts the operator in its specifier with features that match those of the operator. As mentioned, on empirical grounds it is impossible to determine whether a yes/no operator is in the specifier of NegP or of CP and, if the latter, whether the negative marker itself moves to C° in the syntax or whether its features move to C° at LF.

A choice among those options is forced if we adopt once again a theoretical assumption already discussed in section 2.2 — namely, that pronominal clitics are never adjoined to the verb, following Kayne (1994). Let us see why. Take a WH-question where the WH-phrase is immediately followed by the finite verb, such as the following:

(84)　Cossa ga-lo　dito? (Paduan)
　　　what has-s.cl said
　　　'What did he say?'

We could view this construction, as in standard analyses, as having the unit formed by the auxiliary and the interrogative clitic (*ga-lo*) in C°. Now take a similar sentence that contains a complement clitic:

(85)   Cossa ghe ga-lo   dito? (Paduan)
       what him has-s.cl said
       'What did he tell him?'

Recall from section 2.2 that, if we follow the assumptions in Kayne (1994), we cannot take the pronominal clitic *ghe* to be adjoined to the verb; rather, it must be left-adjoined to an empty functional head. In this case, then, we cannot take the verb and the interrogative subject clitic to be in the highest functional head of the clause, C°. Since it is reasonable to assume that the dative clitic *ghe* is adjoined to a functional head lower than C°, and since it precedes the unit formed by the verb and the interrogative subject clitic, we conclude that it is in a position structurally higher than the one occupied by the verb and the interrogative subject clitic. Assuming that the verb has raised and left-adjoined to the head hosting the interrogative subject clitic, we then obtain the following configuration:

(86)

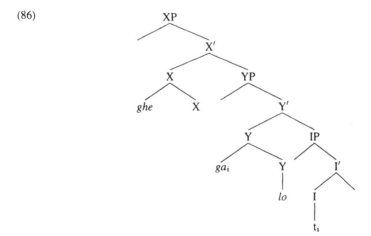

Let me now point out two consequences of the proposal just outlined.

First, in this configuration, interrogative subject clitics, which follow complement clitics in linear order, are structurally lower than complement clitics. This conclusion contrasts with the one reached for subject clitics of the non-interrogative series: they always precede complement clitics in linear order and, as discussed in section 2.2, they are structurally higher than complement clitics. I am then led to conclude that the two series of subject clitics occupy different structural positions: the non-interrogative subject clitics are structurally higher than the complement clitics, which in turn are structurally higher than the interrogative subject clitics.[71]

Second, given a configuration like the one sketched in (86), it is impossible to argue that the WH-operator is in the specifier of the head in which the finite verb occurs. If it were, it would follow the complement clitics in linear order; in fact, though, fronted WH-constituents always precede complement clitics. Thus, I have to argue that, in WH-questions, the finite verb raises to a head other than the one that has the WH-operator in its specifier. If this is true, then the relation between verb movement and the presence of a WH-operator must be less straightfoward than it is usually taken to be; that is, the verb does not move to the head that has the operator in its specifier, but to a lower head. This conclusion raises a number of questions, in particular concerning the precise characterization of the extent of verb movement, its landing site, and the reason why it needs to move.[72]

Though I will not explore these consequences any further here, let me conclude this section by mentioning three pieces of evidence that suggest a structure such as the one just sketched is indeed plausible.

First, it is possible to find non-interrogative subject clitics and interrogative subject clitics in co-occurrence. When this happens, the order is one an analysis along these lines would predict, that is: *non-interrogative subject clitic–finite verb–interrogative subject clitic*. This is illustrated in the following examples:[73]

(87) a. *A*   ven-*lo*   'co Toni? (Piedmontese from Torino)
         s.cl comes-s.cl also Toni
         'Is Toni coming as well?'

      b. Quant *a*   van-*u* a Pordenon? (Friulian)
         when s.cl go-s.cl to Pordenon
         'When are they going to Pordenon?'

      c. Ks   *a*   fen-*i*? (Emiliano from Bologna)
         what s.cl do-s.cl
         'What are they doing?'

      d. Parchè *a*   magna-*t* an pom? (Emiliano from Guastalla)
         why   s.cl eat-s.cl an apple
         'Why are you eating an apple?'

      e. N'èn-neuy? (Valdotain from Ayas)
         s.cl'eat-s.cl
         'Should we eat?'

      f. T'o-heu   vu ton laon? (Valdotain from St. Nicholas)
         s.cl'have-s.cl seen your uncle
         'Have you seen your uncle?'

Second, as discussed in Poletto (1992: 300, 1995), it is possible to find an overt complementizer followed by a vocalic subject clitic, in turn followed by the finite verb and an interrogative subject clitic. This is illustrated in the following examples, from Poletto (1995):[74]

(88) a. Chi *ch* *a*   fasi-*v*? (Romagnolo from Forlì)
         what that s.cl do-s.cl
         'What are you doing?'

      b. Cosa *ch'a*   l'a-*lo*   fait? (Piedmontese from Torino)
         what that-s.cl s.cl'has-s.cl done
         'What did he do?'

Poletto (1995) takes these data as evidence for the existence of more than one CP projection in the clause. In particular, she argues that the verb left-adjoins to the interrogative subject clitic in a position lower than the one where the complementizer *che* occurs, which is part of a split CP. This is consistent with the implications of structure (86), according to which the verb that has raised to the left of an interrogative subject clitic is not in a position as high as $C°$ (at least if we define $C°$ as the position where a complementizer occurs).[75]

Third, evidence that the verb that occurs on the left of a pronominal subject has not raised to the position of the complementizer comes from French, if we follow the proposal in Sportiche (in press b). Sportiche's paper argues that the finite verb in French moves to $C°$ only at LF.[76] Such a proposal allows a straightforward account of the traditionally problematic French construction that goes under the name of "complex inversion," exemplified in (89):[77]

(89) a. Depuis quand Jean est-il malade? (French)
         since   when Jean is-s.cl ill
         'Since when is Jean ill?'

      b. Jean est-il malade?
         Jean is-s.cl ill
         'Is Jean ill?'

These examples show that a pre-verbal subject (*Jean*) can be followed by the verb that occurs on the left of the subject clitic (*il*). If the finite verb were taken to be in $C°$, the position of the pre-verbal subject would be problematic: What position could it be occupying, between the specifier of CP and $C°$?[78] If, however, the verb is not taken to be in $C°$ but in a lower position, these examples can be accounted for straightforwardly.[79] The assumption that the verb does not move to $C°$ in the syntax in French also allows for a simple account of the contrast in (90), if combined with the assumption that full subjects can only occur in a specifier position below CP in French:

(90) a. Est-*il* à Paris? (French)
         is-s.cl at Paris
         'Is he in Paris?'

      b. *Est *Jean* à Paris?

These pieces of evidence thus support a structural representation such as the one sketched in (86) for complement clitics, finite verb, and interrogative subject clitics. This in turn suggests that (the features of) the verb raise to $C°$ at LF, not in the syntax.

2.4.2. *Negative markers in the presence of verb movement*

The previous section discussed cases in which the presence of a pre-verbal negative marker that by itself can negate the clause (e.g., Paduan *no*), is incompatible with subject clitic inversion — that is, with a word order where the verb precedes an interrogative subject clitic. This section, in contrast, examines some contexts in which the presence of a pre-verbal negative marker co-occurs with subject clitic inversion. The first such case involves pre-verbal negative markers that cannot negate the clause

by themselves, such as those of French and Walloon. Then we turn our attention back
to Paduan *no*, since there are certain contexts in which it co-occurs with subject clitic
inversion.

Of the languages with pre-verbal negative markers that cannot negate the clause
by themselves, the ones that exhibit overt differences in the position of the verb in
interrogative and non-interrogative clauses are Walloon and French. Others, like the
dialects of the Ligurian hinterland studied in Parry's work, do not exhibit as clearly
a special position for the verb in interrogative clauses and therefore are not as useful
for the issue under investigation. The pre-verbal negative markers of French and
Walloon co-occur with subject clitic inversion in interrogative clauses. As shown in
the following examples, the negative marker maintains its pre-verbal position and,
along with the verb, appears on the left of the pronominal subject:[80]

(91) a. *N'*è-ç' nin come dès   cantikes ou cwè? (Walloon)
         neg-is-it neg like some odes   or what
         'Isn't it like odes or what?'

      b. *N'*èsteût-ç' nin avou d' l'angrês   ou kî   sèt?   (Walloon)
         neg-was-it neg with of the'fertilizer or who knows
         'Wasn't it with fertilizer or who knows?'

      c. N'est-il   pas heureux? (French)
         neg'is-he neg happy
         'Isn't he happy?'

In the previous sections I characterized the distinction between negative markers
that can and those that cannot negate a clause by themselves by arguing that the
former class of negative elements are the head of the projection NegP, while the latter
are base-generated in a lower position and then left-adjoined to an independently
existing head in pre-verbal position (see diagram (18)). This characterization can
help us express the difference between these two classes that we see in interrogative
clauses, as follows. The negative markers that can negate the clause by themselves are
the head of a NegP projection higher than the finite verb (NegP-1), thus they count as
the closest head to C° with features that can match those of the yes/no operator. As
discussed, the negative marker is attracted to C°, and verb movement is not necessary
(thus, not possible). In contrast, the negative markers that cannot negate the clause
by themselves originate in a lower structural position (NegP-2); though they move
to pre-verbal position, they do not constitute the head closest to C° with features
that can match those of the yes/no operator. This can be seen to stem from different
reasons, which I will mention briefly.

Following the traditional view of these data, which takes the negative marker
to be cliticized onto the verb, the behavior of French *ne* stems from the fact that
it counts as a unit with the verb. Thus, both the negative marker and the verb are
attracted to C° and raise as a unit. In this view, the negative marker is analyzed
as left-adjoined to the finite verb. A view along these lines is incompatible with
Kayne's (1994) approach to linear order in syntax and morphology. As mentioned,
Kayne's Linear Correspondence Axiom does not allow left-adjunction of more than
one element to the same position. An alternative compatible with Kayne's proposal
would consist in viewing the negative markers of French and Walloon as adjoined to

a functional head other than the one to which the verb is adjoined, but differing from that of Paduan in lacking the relevant features that would make C° attract them. For example, they could be viewed as purely scope markers, which do not share the same features as negative markers that can negate the clause by themselves. This view is plausible, as the negative markers of French and Walloon cannot negate the clause by themselves but must always co-occur with another negative element. Yet another possibility would be to assume that a negative marker in pre-verbal position counts as the closest head that can be attracted to C° only if it heads its own phrase, but not if it is left-adjoined to another functional head ($[_H$ Neg° H]) by virtue of its clitic nature. This is because, in the latter case, the features of the negative markers are not those of the head of the phrase. As a consequence, in the case of French and Walloon where the pre-verbal negative marker is left-adjoined to another head, the finite verb is the closest head that can be attracted to C°. This view would require that verb movement to C° be viewed as LF-attraction of its features, given that the verb follows the negative marker in linear order.

Let us now turn our attention back to Paduan *no* and examine three contexts where it co-occurs with subject clitic inversion, all described in Benincà and Vanelli (1982). This discussion is a condensed presentation of the more extensive analysis of these data given in Portner and Zanuttini (1996).

1. One such context is that of WH-exclamatives. Although they resemble WH-questions, since they are introduced by WH-phrases, these exclamative clauses differ from WH-questions in two respects that are relevant for our discussion. First, the WH-phrase in exclamatives can be immediately followed by the negative marker, something that is impossible in questions (as shown in (78) and (79)). Second, in the presence of the negative marker, the word order is not the same as that found in non-interrogative clauses, but rather obligatorily exhibits the verb on the left of the interrogative subject clitic, as shown here:

(92) a. Chi *no* invitarisse-*lo* par parere importante! (Paduan)
         who neg invite-s.cl   for to-seem important
         'What people he would invite in order to seem important!'
      b. *Chi *no* (e)l invitaresse par parere importante!

(93) a. Cossa *no* ghe dise-*lo*!
         what neg him say-s.cl
         'What things he is telling him!'
      b. *Cossa *no* (e)l ghe dise!

(94) a. Cossa *no* ga-*lo*   fato!
         what neg has-s.cl done
         'What things he has done!'
      b. *Cossa *no* (e)l ga fato!

Subject clitic inversion fails to occur only when an overt complementizer is present in the clause; in this case, it is impossible in negative as well as in non-negative clauses:[81]

(95) a. Cossa *che no (e)l* ga fato! (Paduan)
         what that neg s.cl has done
         'What things he has done!'

      b. *Cossa *che no* ga-*lo* fato!

Incidentally, a similar pattern holds in Bellunese with the WH-word *cossa*, the one of the two WH-words for 'what' that fronts. It is followed either by the complementizer *che* or by a clause without a complementizer that shows movement of the verb to the left of the subject clitic:[82]

(96) a. Cossa *che no* *l*'ha   fat! (Bellunese)
         what that neg s.cl'has done
         'What things he has done!'

      b. Cossa *no* ha-*lo*   fat!
         what neg has-s.cl done
         'What things he has done!'

Informally, sentences like (92)a and (93)a are used to convey that he would invite all sorts of people in order to feel important, and that he would tell him all sorts of things. Anyone who wasn't invited, or anything that wasn't said, is so unlikely or implausible that they do not deserve consideration.[83]

    2. A second context in which Paduan *no* co-occurs with movement of the verb around the interrogative subject clitic is that of questions introduced by *parcossa*, one of the two words for 'why' in Paduan. In these contexts, two word orders are possible. The first is that exemplified in (97), where a cleft is used, as in all the negative WH-questions examined till now:

(97) Parcossa ze che *no* te   ve anca ti? (Paduan)
      why   is that neg s.cl. go also you
      'Why aren't you going as well?'

A sentence of this form is used to request information; in this particular context, (97) is asking for the reason(s) why the hearer is not going. The second is the word order exhibited in (98), which, as pointed out in Benincà and Vanelli (1982: 18), must be associated with a particular intonational pattern:

(98) Parcossa *no* ve-to anca ti? (Paduan)
      why   neg go-s.cl also you
      'Why aren't you going as well?'

In contrast with (97), (98) is used not to request the hearer's reason(s) for not going, but instead to express surprise or dismay at the fact that he or she is not going (the fact that he or she is not going is presupposed in both cases).[84]

    The question one needs to answer is why the presence of *no* triggers the use of a cleft in (97), as in other WH-questions, but not in (98). Note that in both cases *no* negates the proposition. The difference in syntactic behavior appears to correlate with the fact that the interpretation of (98) is different from that of (97): in the latter, the proposition carries the implicature that the reasons for the hearer's not going were bad or not worthy of consideration.

3. A third context in which Paduan *no* co-occurs with subject clitic inversion is the one in which pre-verbal *no* co-occurs with the post-verbal negative marker *miga*. As we see in the following examples, the word order that is impossible in ordinary yes/no questions is possible when *no* co-occurs with *miga*:

(99)   a. *No* ve-*to*   *miga* via? (Paduan)
          neg go-s.cl neg   away
          'Aren't you going away?'

       b. *No* vien-*lo*   *miga*?
          neg comes-s.cl neg
          'Isn't he coming?'

       c. *No* lezi-*to*   *miga*?
          neg read-s.cl neg
          'Aren't you reading?'

The interpretation of these sentences is different from that of yes/no questions without *miga*. Sentence (99)a, for example, is used when the speaker expected that the hearer would leave, but realizes that the hearer is not leaving, and thus expresses surprise/dismay at that realization. Similarly, (99)b is used when the speaker expected that he would come, and (99)c when the speaker expected that the hearer would be reading. That is, these sentences differ from other negative yes/no questions insofar as they convey that, of the two possible answers to the question ('he's coming, he isn't coming'), the positive one was expected and the true one — the negative answer — is contrary to expectation.[85]

A very similar reading characterizes yet another type of yes/no question that differs from ordinary yes/no questions with respect to the effect of the presence of the negative marker *no*. This is the case in which a negative and a non-negative yes/no question are conjoined by the disjunctive particle, as exemplified here:

(100) a. Vien-lo   o *no* vien-*lo*?   (Paduan)
          comes-s.cl or neg comes-s.cl
          'Is he coming or is he not coming?'

       b. Parti-to   o *no* parti-*to*?
          leave-s.cl or neg leave-s.cl
          'Are you leaving or are you not leaving?'

The interpretation of these examples is perhaps best described as a yes/no question expressing surprise and/or impatience: the speaker realizes that the person talked about is not coming and conveys that this is contrary to expectation.[86]

The question we need to answer now is why in these contexts Paduan *no* co-occurs with subject clitic inversion, whereas in the ones we examined in the previous section it does not. As in Portner and Zanuttini (1996), my answer relates the syntactc behavior of the negative marker in these contexts to its interpretation, which is different from the one of the contexts examined in the previous section. While in those contexts *no* contributes the ordinary meaning of negation to the interpretation of the clause, in the one just discussed it also behaves as a focus sensitive particle that generates a scalar implicature. Such an implicature depends on a pragmatically provided scale, much like that familiar from the interpretation of *even* (cf. Jackendoff 1972, Karttunen and Peters 1979, Rooth 1985). For a precise semantic characterization of how the implicature is generated, I refer the reader to Portner and Zanuttini (1996).

What is relevant for my discussion here is that these examples, in which the pre-verbal negative marker *no* of Paduan co-occurs with subject clitic inversion, lead me to conclude that pre-verbal negative markers can have different syntactic properties, not only cross-linguistically (as in the case of Italian on the one hand and French on the other) but also within the same language. That is, Paduan *no* counts as an independent head that can be attracted to $C°$ when it contributes only the ordinary meaning of negation to the clause, but does not when it is a focus sensitive particle that also generates a scalar implicature. Thus its semantic ambiguity goes hand in hand with what we can call its syntactic ambiguity.

Let us focus our attention on how we can express the fact that Paduan *no* exhibits a different syntactic behavior in the two cases. There are two ways to express this. One is to say that, when the negative marker contributes the ordinary interpretation of negation, it is the head of its own functional projection, NegP-1, whereas in the other case it is left-adjoined to the same head that hosts the finite verb. This is the view adopted in Portner and Zanuttini (1996). It is then possible to say that, in the former case, the features of *no* are attracted to $C°$, making verb movement unnecessary, whereas in the latter case the negative marker and the verb, as a unit, are attracted to $C°$ and provide features that match those of the operator in the specifier.

As mentioned in the discussion of French and Walloon, this view is incompatible with Kayne's (1994) extension of his anti-symmetry requirement to the word level: assuming that extension, the negative marker cannot be left-adjoined to the verb. Thus an alternative way to express these facts compatible with Kayne's assumptions requires that we do not assume that the negative marker is left-adjoined to the verb. Note also that assuming that Paduan *no* is left-adjoined to some functional head and is not the head of NegP-1 assimilates *no* to those negative markers that cannot negate the clause by themselves, such as French *ne* or Walloon *nu*. Such an extension is not obviously desirable, since the negative marker of Paduan can indeed negate the clause by itself, even in these contexts.[87] We therefore need to explore an alternative that does not imply that the negative marker forms a unit with the verb.

What is crucial for me, given the account of cases in which the negative marker does not co-occur with verb movement provided in the preceding section, is that the negative marker should not count as the closest head with appropriate features that can be attracted to $C°$. If it does not, then the verb will be attracted to $C°$. I speculate that, in these contexts, the reason why the negative marker might not count as the head with appropriate features that is closest to $C°$ is related to the fact that it is a focus-sensitive element. Assuming that the presence of focus in the clause corresponds to the presence of a particular functional projection (call it FocusP, as in Brody 1990, Tsimpli 1990, Rouveret 1992, Agouraki 1993, Ouhalla 1993, and Puskás 1994, among others), I can further speculate that the negative marker raises to the head of this projection and cannot at the same time provide the features needed to match those of the interrogative operator. I will leave the exact characterization of this issue open for now; further research will have to provide a precise answer as to why the negative marker behaves differently in these contexts.

Before I conclude this section, let me mention two pieces of evidence in support of the view that a pre-verbal negative marker may have two distinct syntactic characterizations within a given language, which correspond to different contributions it makes to the interpretation of the clause.

One comes from the variety of Veneto I have referred to earlier as Basso Polesano. As we saw in our earlier discussion of this language, it has a pre-verbal negative marker that by itself can negate the clause, *no*; example (40)a (from Poletto 1993a: 23) is repeated here for convenience:

(101)   A   *no*   vegno. (Basso Polesano)
         s.cl neg come
         'I am not coming.'

In addition to *no*, Basso Polesano exhibits a second pre-verbal negative marker, *ne*. This negative marker is used in co-occurrence with the post-verbal negative marker *mina* and with other negative constituents in post-verbal position. The following example (from Poletto 1993b: 242) has an interpretation parallel to that of the sentences in (99):

(102)   *Ne* vien-lo   *mina*? (Basso Polesano from Loreo)
         neg comes-s.cl neg
         'Isn't he coming?'

In my view, Basso Polesano expresses with a morphological distinction the syntactic ambiguity of Paduan *no*.

Another piece of evidence in support of the distinction I have drawn in the behavior of Paduan *no* comes from the fact that the same pairing of syntactic properties and semantic interpretation is found in other languages. One is the variety of Friulian spoken in San Michele al Tagliamento.[88] Like Paduan, this variety has a pre-verbal negative marker that by itself can negate the clause, *no*; it also exhibits obligatory subject clitic inversion in yes/no questions with the ordinary reading of negation. As in Paduan, the pre-verbal negative marker does not co-occur with subject clitic inversion in the contexts in which it contributes only the ordinary interpretation of negation, as exemplified in (103):

(103)   *No* tu   mangis? (Friulian of S. Michele)
         neg s.cl eat
         'Don't you eat?'

I suggest that this case should be analyzed like the case of Paduan discussed in the previous section: the verb need not, and therefore cannot, move because the negative marker is the closest head with the features needed by C°. As in Paduan, in this variety as well there is also another type of yes/no question, which is said to be used only with appropriate contextual restrictions — that is, when an expected event is not taking place. In such a context, a negated yes/no question can be used, with a reading of surprise/dismay. As we see in example (104), in this case subject clitic inversion occurs despite the presence of *no*:

(104)   *No* mangis-tu? (Friulian of S. Michele)
        neg eat-s.cl
        'Aren't you eating?'

This example is interpreted with the same kind of implicature found in the preceding examples from Paduan. I take the existence of such cases, in this and other varieties, to confirm that the ambiguous behavior of the pre-verbal negative marker in Paduan is not a peculiarity of this language, but a more general phenomenon that must be accounted for.

2.5.   Summary and conclusion

My object of investigation in this chapter has been the class of negative markers that precede the finite verb. I have shown that those that can negate the clause by themselves exhibit different syntactic properties from those that cannot. The different syntactic properties of the two types of negative markers I have identified and discussed in this chapter have to do with their position with respect to both complement and subject clitics, and with their effect on verb movement.

I have argued that these differences can best be captured by viewing the former type of negative markers (those that can negate a clause by themselves), as heading the syntactic projection NegP in which they occur (NegP-1). Assuming that such a projection is structurally higher than the projections hosting the complement clitics and the verb, as well as the subject clitics that have been called "agreement clitics," I have recast in structural terms the observation that such negative markers precede these types of clitics. At the same time, I have argued that pre-verbal negative markers that cannot negate a clause by themselves are best analyzed as not heading the functional projection in which they occur but rather being left-adjoined to an independently existing syntactic head. That is, I view these negative markers as originating in the head of a projection NegP lower in the structure (NegP-2), and then raising to pre-verbal position for reasons having to do with their clitic nature. This view reconciles two seemingly opposite analyses that have been put forth in the literature for pre-verbal negative markers in Romance: one arguing that they are clitic elements that raise from a structurally lower position, and the other arguing that they are generated where they occur. I have shown that both these views are correct, if applied to the proper class of elements. This analysis of pre-verbal negative markers that cannot negate the clause by themselves provides me with a way to account for their distribution with respect to complement and subject clitics, which differs from that of the other class of pre-verbal negative markers.

Moreover, I have argued that a pre-verbal negative marker that by itself can negate a clause, in the head of NegP-1, counts as the head closest to C° with features that can be attracted to this position. When a yes/no operator is present in the specifier of CP, the features of the negative marker, raised to C°, match those of the operator and result in a grammatical clause. I have thus interpreted the fact that verb movement does not take place in yes/no questions in the presence of a negative marker of this type in terms of the negative marker carrying out the function normally reserved to the verb — namely, providing C° with features matching those of the abstract yes/no operator in its specifier. Similarly, when a WH-operator is present in the specifier of CP, the negative marker in the head of NegP-1 counts as the closest head attracted to C°; however, in this case the features of the negative marker and those of the WH-operator do not match; the sentence is therefore ungrammatical. I have also observed that pre-verbal negative markers that cannot negate a clause by themselves never make verb movement unnecessary in yes/no questions. I have proposed to relate this syntactic behavior to the fact that they do not count as the head closest to C° with features that can be attracted to such a position.

What is the conceptual advantage of arguing that negative markers that negate the clause by themselves make verb movement unnecessary versus a view that treats them as blocking verb movement to C° by creating a minimality effect? I believe the advantage stems from dropping the claim that the verb must move to C°. In fact, if verb movement to C° were required by some general principle of the grammar, we would expect it to take place in all cases in which that principle applies. In the case of yes/no questions in Paduan, then, it is surprising to see that verb movement takes place when the clause is not negative, whereas it fails to take place when it is negative *without giving rise to ungrammaticality*. We would expect that if a principle of grammar holds, it should hold across negative and non-negative sentences and not be able to be freely violated in one case. The approach presented here allows us to make sense of the observed pattern by allowing the features of both the negative marker and the verb to match those of a yes/no operator (though not those of a WH-operator). The task then becomes that of characterizing why yes/no- and WH-operators differ in the way they do, rather than that of explaining why a general principle of grammar fails to hold in certain contexts.

From a purely theoretical point of view, this approach provides support for the view that certain types of movement are motivated by properties of the target and not of the element that moves. Moreover, it shows that the phrase structural constraints imposed by Kayne's Linear Correspondence Axiom force certain choices that, though unconventional, find a fair amount of supporting evidence.

3

Post-verbal Negative Markers

3.1. Issues to be addressed

In the previous chapter I have examined the syntactic behavior of pre-verbal negative markers. I focused on the top part of the clause and examined their distribution with respect to subject clitics, complement clitics, and movement of the verb past I°. Now I turn to the distribution of post-verbal negative markers, a class that I define by the property of following the finite form of the verb — either the main verb, when the verbal form is simple, or the auxiliary, when the verbal form consists of an auxiliary and a participle. I focus in particular on their position with respect to the past participle and infinitival forms of the verbs and to certain classes of adverbs, which I will refer to as "lower adverbs." This investigation, combined with the one of pre-verbal negative markers, will allow me to formulate a hypothesis about the structure of clauses negated by negative markers, as well as on the proper syntactic characterization of these elements. The questions I am trying to answer are the following:

- Do all post-verbal negative markers occur in the same syntactic position? I will compare data across languages, as well as within a given language, when a language has more than one post-verbal negative marker.
- Do all post-verbal negative markers make the same contribution to the interpretation of a clause? In addition, when a language has two (or more) negative markers, what differences do they exhibit, if any? If some difference indeed exists, is it a consequence of the lexical meaning of the item involved or of the structural position in which it occurs?
- How can we encode in our grammatical description the differences exhibited by the Romance languages in the expression of sentential negation?

3.2.   The distribution of adverbs

How can we identify as precisely as possible the distribution of post-verbal negative markers? Clearly we cannot limit ourselves to an examination of their position with respect to the finite verb, since, by definition, they all follow the finite verb. We need to observe them in the context of a more detailed picture of the part of the clause in which they occur. What could constitute such a fine-grained picture of the part of clausal structure in which they occur? In other words, what other elements can be found between the finite verb and the complements? We can find help in answering this question in the work of Cinque (1994, 1995a, 1996a), which examines the distribution of certain adverbs that occur in precisely the same section of the clause. As defined in that work, the "syntactic space" of so-called lower adverbs in Romance is delimited on the left by the position that an active past participle can occupy in Italian, and on the right by the first complement of the past participle (or by the VP-internal subject).[1]

Two findings of Cinque's work will be essential for my own analysis.

1. *The relative ordering of adverbs in any given portion of the clause is rigidly fixed.* Focusing on the part of clausal structure between Infl and V, Cinque's work convincingly shows that the relative order of certain classes of adverbs in Italian is the same as that of the corresponding classes of adverbs in French and a number of Romance languages. The fixed order of these adverbs (called "lower adverbs" to differentiate them from others that occur in a higher portion of clausal structure) is the following:

(1)

Italian:	mica	già	più	sempre	completamente	tutto	bene	VP
French:	pas	déjà	plus	toujours	complètement	tout	bien	VP
	neg	already	no more	always	completely	all	well	VP

Here I will consider mainly the distribution of the first four adverbs, with occasional mention of the element corresponding to English 'all', since those are the ones that are the most helpful in determining the distribution of post-verbal negative markers.[2] In this section, I briefly describe the results of Cinque's investigation, drawing examples from French and Italian, before turning to a close examination of the distribution of the post-verbal negative markers with respect to these adverbs.

Though I cannot reproduce the wealth of evidence on which Cinque's work is based, let me simply report some of the data that are relevant for the discussion to come. Standard Italian has the post-verbal negative element *mica*, which, like all post-verbal negative constituents in this language, must co-occur with pre-verbal *non*, or with other negative elements in pre-verbal position (see Zanuttini 1991, among others). As was first discussed in Cinque (1976), the occurrence of *mica* is pragmatically restricted to those contexts in which the non-negative counterpart of the proposition expressed by the sentence is assumed in the discourse. For example, in order for *mica* to be uttered felicitously in example (2), it is necessary that the proposition that Gianni has a car be entailed by the common ground. If such a proposition is not part of the common ground, the presence of *mica* renders the sentence infelicitous and its counterpart without *mica* must be used (i.e., *Gianni non ha la macchina.*). In this work, I will informally refer to *mica*, and to other negative markers with the same pragmatic restrictions, as "presuppositional negative markers." I will signal their presence with the use of the diacritic @ in front of the English translation.

(2) Gianni non ha *mica* la macchina. (Italian)
     Gianni neg has neg the car
     '@Gianni hasn't got a car.'

Cinque (1994, 1996a) shows that Italian *mica* and French *pas* exhibit the same linear order with respect to the other adverbs mentioned before. They both precede *già/déjà* 'already':[3]

(3) a. Non hanno *mica già*   chiamato, che io sappia.   (Italian)
        neg have neg already called,   that I know (subj.)
        '@They haven't already called, as far as I know.'

     b. Si tu n'as   *pas déjà*   mangé, tu peux le prendre. (French)
        if you neg'have neg already eaten, you can it to-take
        'If you haven't already eaten, you can take it.'

In both languages, 'already' in turn precedes 'no more':[4]

(4) a. Non hanno ricevuto *già*   *più*   nulla. (Italian)
        neg have   received already more nothing
        'Already they weren't receiving anything anymore.'

     b. Ils n'ont   *déjà*   *plus* rien   reçu.   (French)
        they neg'have already more nothing received
        'Already they weren't receiving anything anymore.'

As expected, since *mica* precedes *già* and *già* precedes *più*, *mica* also precedes *più*:

(5) Non hanno chiamato *mica più*, da   allora. (Italian)
     neg have   called   neg more, from then
     '@They haven't called anymore, since then.'

The respective order of *pas* and *plus* in French cannot be tested, since the two do not co-occur.[5]

Finally, *mica* and *pas* precede the class of adverbs of 'always'. This can be readily observed in the case of both Italian *mica*, which can co-occur with both *più* and *sempre*, (6)a, and of French *pas*, (6)b:

(6) a. Da allora, non ha   accettato *mica più* *sempre* i   nostri inviti.   (Italian)
        from then, neg have accepted neg more always the our   invitations
        '@Since then, he hasn't any longer always accepted our invitations.'

     b. À partir de ce   moment là, il n'a   *pas toujours* vaincu. (French)
        at to-start from that moment there, he neg'has neg always won
        'Since that moment, he hasn't always won.'

2. *There exist one head position to the immediate right and one head position to the immediate left of each such adverb.* Evidence for the existence of such a head

is provided by the fact that, across the Romance languages, the past participle can occur to the immediate right and to the immediate left of each of the lower adverbs.

For example, in Italian the past participle can occur in a range of positions which go from the one immediately to the right of 'completely' to the one immediately to the left of *mica*, including all the intermediate ones. Some of these positions are illustrated in (7). The examples in (8) show that the past participle can also occur on the immediate right and on the immediate left of 'already':

(7) a. Da allora, non hanno di solito mica più sempre completamente *rimesso* tutto bene in ordine. (Italian)

  b. Da allora, non hanno di solito mica più sempre *rimesso* completamente tutto bene in ordine.

  c. Da allora, non hanno di solito mica più *rimesso* sempre completamente tutto bene in ordine.

  d. Da allora, non hanno di solito mica *rimesso* più sempre completamente tutto bene in ordine.

  e. Da   allora, non hanno di solito *rimesso* mica più   sempre completamente tutto
      since then, neg have   usually put   neg no more always completely   all
      bene in ordine.
      well in order
      'Since then, they haven't usually any longer always put everything well in order.'

(8) a. Non ha mica già *rimesso* più niente in ordine.

  b. Non ha mica *rimesso* già   più   niente in ordine.
      neg has neg put   already no more nothing in order
      'He hasn't already put anything in order anymore.'

In contrast, the Italian past participle cannot occur to the immediate right or to the immediate left of 'well', as shown here:

(9) a. *Da allora, non hanno di solito mica più sempre completamente tutto *rimesso* bene in ordine.

  b. *Da allora, non hanno di solito mica più   sempre completamente tutto bene
      since then, neg have   usually neg no more always completely   all well
      rimesso in ordine.
      put   in order

One might conclude from these examples that 'all' and 'well' are adjoined to the VP and thus there is no head position between them, or to the immediate right of 'well', in which the participle could land. But in fact, though the past participle cannot occupy those positions in Italian, it can do so in other Romance languages. The past participle can occur in a position to the immediate right of 'well' in French, as shown in (10). The past participle can occur in a position to the immediate left of 'well' and to the immediate right of 'all' in Sardinian, in the Logudorese variety, as shown in (11):

(10) a. Il a   *bien* **compris** la   question. (French)
          he has well understood the question
          'He has understood the question well.'

  b. *Il a **compris** *bien* la question.

(11) a. *Apo *bene* **mandigadu**. (Logudorese Sardinian)

    b. Apo **mandigadu** *bene*.
       have eaten   well
       'I have eaten well.'

    c. Apo *tottu* **mandigadu**.
       have all   eaten
       'I have eaten everything.'

In light of these data, Cinque takes the ungrammaticality of the examples in (9) to be due not to the lack of a head position on the right of 'all' and 'well' but to the fact that the past participle *must* raise to the head to the left of 'all' in Italian and cannot occur in any lower position. Similar restrictions hold in other languages as well. For example in Bellunese, a variety of Veneto, the past participle cannot occur in a head position to the right of 'completely', but must occur in a position to the left of 'completely', or higher:

(12) a. *L'ha   *del tut*   **pers** la testa. (Bellunese)
       s.cl.'has completely l ost   his head
       'He has completely lost his mind.'

    b. L'ha **pers** *del tut* la testa.

On the basis of these observations, Cinque (1995a, 1996a) proposes an analysis that posits the existence of one head position immediately to the left and one head position immediately to the right of each such adverb, as follows:

(13)   X [mica X [già X [piu X [sempre X [completamente X [tutto X [bene X

Moreover, he argues that each adverb occurs in the specifier position of the head on its right, with which it shares semantic properties. For example, *più*, 'no more' occurs in the specifier of a functional projection expressing perfective aspect (whose values can be perfective or imperfective), while *sempre*, 'always', in the specifier of a projection expressing progressive aspect (whose values can be progressive or generic). Cinque provides cross-linguistic evidence that the relative order of these functional projections is fixed, from which it follows that the relative order of the adverbs will be fixed as well.[6]

An alternative analysis of the data described so far could say that the adverbs are not specifiers of functional projections, but are simply adjoined either to the left or to the right of the past participle. In addition to failing to account for the fact that the relative ordering of certain classes of adverbs is fixed and is the same across languages, an approach along these lines would also make certain wrong predictions, as argued in Cinque's work. Suppose we concluded, based on examples like (14)a and (14)b, that the adverb *più* in Italian can adjoin to the left of the past participle and that the adverb *mica* can adjoin to its right:

(14) a. Non hanno *più*   **mangiato**. (Italian)
       neg have no more eaten
       'They haven't eaten anymore.'

b. Non hanno **mangiato** *mica.*
   neg have   eaten   neg
   '@They haven't eaten.'

Then we would predict that a clause where *più* precedes the past participle and *mica* follows it should be grammatical. However, this prediction is not correct, as shown by the following example:

(15)   *Non hanno *più*   **mangiato** *mica.* (Italian)
       neg   have   no more eaten   neg
       'They haven't eaten anymore.'

In contrast, Cinque's analysis can account for the ungrammaticality of (15), as it derives it from the fact that *più* precedes *mica*, thus violating the fixed linear order described in (1). Moreover, this analysis correctly predicts that the only word orders that are possible are the three given here:

(16)   a. Non hanno *mica più* **mangiato.** (Italian)
       b. Non hanno *mica* **mangiato** *più.*
       c. Non hanno **mangiato** *mica più.*

In these examples, *mica* consistently precedes *più*, in accordance with (1). The variation stems from the fact that the past participle can occur in the head position immediately to the right of *più*, or in the one immediately to the left of *più* and to the right of *mica*, or in the one immediately to the left of *mica*.

One could then argue that the adverbs are adjoined (and not in a specifier position), but they occur in a fixed order because of certain constraints related to their scope properties (for example, constraints to the effect that an element expressing perfective aspect can take scope over one expressing progressive aspect, but not vice versa). Following such a view, it might be possible to derive their fixed order without arguing that they occur in the specifier position of a given functional projection. It could be argued instead that one or more such (classes of) adverbs adjoin to the head hosting the past participle, in an order determined by their scopal properties. Such an analysis, however, would not be able to exclude certain patterns that need to be excluded, which I will describe here briefly by means of some examples. There exists no language in which the counterpart of 'well' obligatorily precedes the past participle (as illustrated in (17)) and in which the counterpart of 'all' in pre-participial position gives rise to ungrammaticality (as indicated in (18)). In other words, if a language exhibits the grammaticality pattern of (17), it does *not* also exhibit that of (18):

(17)   a. Apo *bene* **mandigadu.** (Sardinian)
          have well eaten
          'I have eaten well.'
       b. *Apo **mandigadu** *bene.*

(18)   *Apo *tottu* **mandigadu.**
       have all   eaten
       'I have eaten everything.'

Cinque's analysis correctly excludes that such a word order pattern may occur in any given language. In general, it correctly predicts that, if the past participle obligatorily follows an adverb which occupies position x in the sequence (for example, *bene* in example (17)), it will also obligatorily follow any adverb in higher positions in the sequence (such as *tottu* in example (18)). Conversely, it predicts that, if the past participle can precede an adverb in position x in the sequence, it can also precede any adverb in lower positions in the sequence. To give an example, it correctly predicts that, if a language allows the participle to precede *tottu*, it will also allow it to precede *bene*. In other words, it correctly excludes patterns like the one in example (19):

(19) a. Apo **mandigadu** *tottu.*
     b. *Apo **mandigadu** *bene.*

An analysis that views such word order facts as stemming exclusively from the adjunction possibilities of the adverbs disposes of no principled means to express that neither (17) and (18) nor (19)a and (19)b can be part of the same language. If the order of adverbs derives from constraints related to their scopal properties, there is no way to predict the position of the adverb with respect to the past participle (unless a language allows variation that reflects different scopal relations). Thus a statement is needed to stipulate that, in a given language, an adverb class must adjoin to the left (or to the right) of the past participle. In general, for each language, this approach needs to state that, given adverb classes a, b, c, and d, the past participle occurs in a certain position (let's say, between b and c) but not in others. Moreover it must state that the relative order of a and b is fixed in order to express the fact that, if the past participle follows adverbs of class b, it also follows adverbs of class a, even when the relative scope of a and b is not at issue. Both such statements, though, constitute a departure from a purely semantic approach to the ordering of adverbs.

Moreover, an analysis that derives the order of adverbs from their scopal properties would provide no account of the parallelism between verb movement of finite forms, infinitivals, and participles exhibited within the Romance family and beyond. Pollock (1989) shows that in both French and English the relative order of verbs and adverbs is sensitive to whether the verbal form is finite or infinitival, and whether it is an auxiliary or a main verb. For example, in both languages auxiliaries occur in higher structural positions than main verbs.[7] Similarly, here I show that the relative order of negative markers and verbs is sensitive to the type of verbal form (finite versus participial versus infinitival), as well as to the distinction between auxiliaries and main verbs. An analysis based on the adjunction possibilities of certain classes of adverbs, without appeal to verb movement, will have to state for each language that some adverb classes adjoin to the left of certain verbal forms (e.g., main verbs) but to the right of others (e.g., auxiliaries). It seems that such a list of statements would be more complex than a statement concerning the extent to which certain types of verbs move. Finally, an analysis in terms of adjunction of adverb classes does not immediately account for Cinque's observations about the parallelism between the ordering of adverbs and of functional morphemes.

I will therefore adopt Cinque's proposal for the purposes of this work. To the extent that an alternative analysis provides answers to these problems, I suspect that my results will translate directly.

The background given in this section provides us with some of the tools we need to examine the distribution of post-verbal negative markers in the northern Italian dialects that are the object of this investigation. We now have a fine-grained analysis of the syntactic space between the finite verb and the complements of the verb. I can thus ask the question concerning where exactly the negative markers occur in the structure by examining their position with respect to the lower adverbs discussed in Cinque's work. An answer to this question will also allow me to find out whether they all occur in the same position or whether they occupy different structural positions. In the sections that follow I will pursue an answer to this question, as well as to the second question outlined in section 3.1 — namely, whether these dialects differentiate between a negative marker that negates a proposition without any particular discourse status (a "regular" or "non-presuppositional" negative marker) and one that negates a proposition that is assumed in the discourse (a "presuppositional" negative marker).

3.3.   Presuppositional versus non-presuppositional negative markers

3.3.1.   *Two structural positions for Piedmontese* pa *and* nen

Let us begin this investigation with Piedmontese, a language with two distinct lexical items functioning as sentential negative markers — *pa* and *nen*. I will discuss mainly the variety of Piedmontese spoken in Turin and in the area immediately to the north of Turin called Canavese. Toward the end of the section I will mention briefly the variety of Piedmontese spoken in Cairo Montenotte, studied in Parry (1985, 1989, in press a).[8]

Pa is typically used with the same function of Italian *mica*, as a presuppositional negative marker; *nen*, however, is typically used as the regular negative marker, one that negates a proposition without any particular discourse status. I say that *pa* is *typically* used as a presuppositional negative marker because it is possible to find it in contexts where it is interpreted as a regular negative marker.[9] In this chapter, we will see that this situation is not unusual in the languages under investigation: if they have two negative markers, the one used as a presuppositional negative marker can sometimes serve as a regular negative marker; similarly, the one that is typically used as the regular negative marker can sometimes function as a presuppositional negative marker, with some degree of marginality. Let us see how this works in Piedmontese.

Both *pa* and *nen* follow the finite verb in a simple form and precede all complements, whether they are DPs or quantifiers like *tut* 'all', as shown in the examples here:[10]

(20) a. Maria a   mangia *pa/nen* la carn. (Piedmontese)
          Maria s.cl eats   neg   the meat
          'Maria doesn't eat meat.'

      b. Gianni a   capis   *pa/nen* tut.
          Gianni s.cl understands neg   everything
          'Gianni doesn't understand everything.'

When the verb is followed by a verbal particle, both *pa* and *nen* precede the particle:

(21) Gianni a campa *pa/nen* giu la pasta da sul. (Piedmontese)
      Gianni s.cl throws neg   down the pasta by alone
      'Gianni doesn't put in the pasta by himself.'

When the verbal form consists of an auxiliary and a past participle, *pa* and *nen* follow
the auxiliary and systematically precede the past participle (the opposite order yields
ungrammaticality). The past participle, in turn, precedes all complements:

(22) a. Maria a l'ha   *pa/nen* **mangià** la carn. (Piedmontese)
          Maria s.cl s.cl'has neg   eaten   the meat
          'Maria hasn't eaten the meat.'

      b. Gianni a l'ha   *pa/nen* **capì**   tut.
          Gianni s.cl s.cl'has neg   understood everything
          'Gianni didn't understand everything.'

      c. Gianni a l'ha   *pa/nen* **campà** giu la pasta da sul.
          Gianni s.cl s.cl'has neg   thrown down the pasta by alone
          'Gianni didn't put in the pasta by himself.'

Thus we can preliminarily conclude that the past participle in Piedmontese raises to
a position higher than *tut* 'all' but cannot raise to a position higher than either of the
negative markers. In these examples, the difference between the use of *pa* and the use
of *nen* is not at all readily apparent. My informants say that the difference parallels
the one exhibited by *mica* and *non* in Italian. That is, *pa* corresponds to the negative
marker that negates a proposition assumed in the discourse (Italian *mica*), whereas
nen to the one that does not (Italian *non*).

    In Piedmontese interrogative clauses, inversion of the verb around the subject is
rather rare and has an archaic feeling. However, when it occurs, neither *pa* nor *nen*
interferes with it in any way (examples from Brero 1988: 119):

(23) a. It veddes-to *nen*? (Piedmontese)
          s.cl see-s.cl   neg
          'Don't you see?'

      b. It ses-to *nen* andàit?
          s.cl are-s.cl neg gone
          'Didn't you go?'

This is not surprising if we assume that the post-verbal negative marker is structurally
lower than the finite verb even in non-interrogative clauses, once the finite verb has
raised from V to I. Then in interrogative clauses, where the verb moves further,
no interference on the part of the negative marker is expected. Note that the fact
that the verb can raise past the negative marker in finite declaratives suggests that
the negative marker is not a syntactic head; if it were, we would expect it to block
head-to-head movement of the verb. In the terms of standard X-bar theory, this would
lead us to conclude that the negative marker is either an XP in the specifier of a
projection whose head is empty or an XP adjoined to another maximal projection. In
the more restricted system developed in Kayne (1994), only one option is permitted:
the negative markers of Piedmontese must be XPs adjoined to the combination of an
empty head and its complement, what in Kayne's system corresponds to a specifier:

(24)

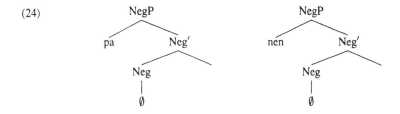

I will subscribe to this view and suggest that post-verbal negative markers be characterized, syntactically, as being in the configuration diagrammed here with an empty head. As for the label of this syntactic phrase, either NegP or PolP would be appropriate. NegP denotes a syntactic constituent hosting a negative marker; because I focus on negative markers, such a label is appropriate for this discussion in most cases. The choice of the label PolP, denoting a Polarity Phrase (cf. Belletti 1990 and Culicover 1992, among others), expresses the fact that the distribution of these negative markers often coincides with that of other elements whose meaning is not negative but rather that of emphatic affirmation. Such cases are discussed, inter alia, in Belletti (1990), which points out that the distribution of Italian *mica* coincides with that of *ben*, an affirmative element; in Laka (1990), where Spanish *no* is shown to have a positive counterpart, *sí*, which expresses emphatic affirmation; and in Kayne (1989), where the English negative marker *n't* is analyzed as occupying the same structural position as the particles for emphatic affirmation *so* and *too*. I will use NegP in this book, since I will not be discussing elements that express emphatic affirmation.

Let us now examine the position of *pa* and *nen* with respect to the adverbs studied in Cinque (1994, 1995a, 1996a). The data from Piedmontese replicate the relative order among the lower adverbs described in the previous section. Limiting our investigation to 'already', 'no more', and 'always', we find that their relative order is the same as that described by Cinque for Italian and French, with 'already' preceding 'no more', which in turn precedes 'always'. As for the relative order of the negative marker with respect to these adverbs, what we find is the following. Piedmontese *pa* parallels the distribution of Italian *mica*. In all the cases I am about to present, it functions as a presuppositional negative marker — one that negates a proposition which is assumed in the discourse. (Recall that I mark this particular reading by placing the diacritic @ before the English translation.) Like *mica*, *pa* precedes the adverb *gia* 'already', as shown in (25):

(25) a. A l'ha   *pa gia*   ciamà, che mi i   sapia. (Piedmontese)
          s.cl. s.cl'has neg already called, that I   s.cl know
          '@He hasn't already called, that I know.'

      b. A l'è   *pa gia*   partì.
          s.cl. s.cl'is neg already left
          '@He hasn't already left.'

Pa also precedes the adverb corresponding to 'no more', *pi*:

(26) a. A l'han   *pa pi*   telefuna,   da   'ntlura. (Piedmontese)
          s.cl. s.cl'have neg more telephoned, since then
          '@They haven't called anymore, since then.'

    b. Da 'ntlura, a   l'ha   *pa pi*   sempre acetà   i   nost invit.
       since then,   s.cl s.cl'has neg more always accepted the our invitations
       '@Since then, he hasn't any longer always accepted our invitations.'

Note that *gia* in turn precedes *pi*:

(27) a. A   mangia 'n bucun e   a   veul *gia*   *pi* gnente. (Piedmontese)
       s.cl. eats   a bite   and s.cl wants already no more   nothing
       'He eats a bite and already doesn't want anything anymore.'

    b. Purtrop,   subit dopu l'uperasiun, a   conusia   *gia*   *pi*   gnun.
       Unfortunately, right after the'surgery, s.cl recognized already no more anyone
       'Unfortunately, right after the operation, already he didn't recognize anyone.'

From the observation that *pa* precedes both *gia* and *pi*, combined with the observation that *gia* precedes *pi*, I conclude that the respective ordering among these adverbs is the following: *pa–gia–pi*.

    The distribution of *nen* contrasts with that of *pa* notably with respect to *gia* 'already' and *pi* 'no more'. My informants resist having *nen* in a position preceding *gia* 'already'. Thus (28)a is judged marginal and contrasts with the perfectly acceptable (28)b and with the sentences in (25):

(28) a. *?A l'e   *nen gia*   andait a ca'.   (Piedmontese)
       s.cl. s.cl'is neg already gone   to home
       'He hasn't already gone home.'

    b. A l'e *pa gia* andait a ca'.

Interestingly, sentence (28)a is judged somewhat acceptable by my informants if they stress *nen* and assign the sentence the same reading it has in the presence of *pa*: that of negating a proposition assumed in the discourse (in this case, that he has already left). In other words, *nen* is marginally possible in a position preceding *gia* (where the presence of *pa* is perfectly acceptable) only if it is interpreted as a presuppositional negative marker. This pattern suggests that *pa* and *nen* typically do not occur in the same structural position; rather, *pa* is structurally higher than *gia*, whereas *nen* typically is not.

    In contrast with (28)a, the opposite linear order for the two adverbs (i.e., *gia nen*) is readily available (cf. (29)). In this case, *gia* does not fall within the scope of negation (unlike all the cases we have seen so far):

(29) a. A   l'avia   *gia*   *nen* vulu   'ntlura. (Piedmontese)
       s.cl. s.cl'had already neg wanted then
       'Already at that time he had not wanted to.'

    b. A   l'avia   *gia*   *nen* salutami   cul di la.
       s.cl s.cl'had already neg greeted-me that day there
       'Already on that day he had not greeted me.'

This linear order is not available for *pa*, according to my informants:

(30) a. *?A l'avia   *gia*   *pa* vulu   'ntlura. (Piedmontese)
       s.cl s.cl'had already neg wanted then
       'Already at that time he had not wanted to.'

b. *?A l'avia *gia*   *pa* salutami   cul di la.
s.cl s.cl'had already neg greeted-me that day there
'Already on that day he had not greeted me.'

To the extent that these sentences are acceptable, *gia* is outside the scope of negation, as was the case in (29). The negative marker *pa* in this case does not negate a proposition assumed in the discourse (thus contrasting with the examples in (25)); rather, it is indistinguishable from the reading of the corresponding sentence with *nen*. I take this to suggest that *pa* can (very marginally) occur in the same position in which *nen* occurs; when it does, it does not contribute to the interpretation of the clause a presuppositional reading, but rather the reading of negating a proposition with no particular discourse status — that is, the same reading as *nen*.

I take these data to suggest that the presuppositional reading associated with *pa* does not stem entirely from the lexical meaning of this element, but at least partly from its structural position: when it is higher than *gia*, it negates a proposition assumed in the discourse; when it is lower than *gia*, it does not. Note that it would not suffice to say that *pa* yields a presuppositional reading because it takes scope over *gia*, which itself introduces a presupposition. First, *pa* has a presuppositional reading even in the absence of *gia*. Second, what *gia* requires to be in the common ground is different from what *pa* requires. Informally, given a sentence with both elements, *gia* presupposes the event and says that it has taken place before a certain moment in time; *pa*, however, negates the proposition, assumed in the discourse, that such an event has already taken place.

The distribution of *nen* differs from that of *pa* also with respect to the adverb *pi* 'no more'. Whereas *pa* precedes *pi*, as we saw in (26), *nen* follows *pi* in linear order:

(31) a. Da 'ntlura, a   l'ha   *pi*   *nen* sempre vinciu. (Piedmontese)
from then,   s.cl s.cl'has more neg always won
'Since then, he has no longer always won.'

b. A   l'han   *pi*   *nen* ricevu gnente.
s.cl. s.cl'have more neg received nothing
'They have no longer received anything.'

Nen also precedes *sempre*, which in turn can either be preceded or followed by the past participle, as shown in the following examples:[11]

(32) a. A   l'ha   *nen* **dine**   *sempre* tut.   (Piedmontese)
s.cl. s.cl'has neg told-us alwa   ys everything
'He hasn't always told us everything.'

b. A l'ha *nen sempre* **dine** tut.

c. *A l'ha *sempre nen* dine tut.

As a side note on these data, let me point out what we can conclude about the position of the past participle in Piedmontese: it must raise to a position higher than *tut* 'all', as confirmed by the fact that the order *tut*-participle is ungrammatical. It may raise to a position higher than *sempre*, but need not. It cannot, however, raise to a position higher than *pi* or *nen*: that word order gives rise to ungrammaticality. We will see in the course of this chapter that the position of the past participle shows a great deal of variation in the different languages under examination. Moreover, we will also see that past participles uniformly raise less than infinitival verbs.

We could conclude from these data that, whereas *pa* typically precedes both *gia* and *pi*, *nen* typically follows them both. If the position of *nen* is lower than that of *gia* and *pi*, but higher than that of *sempre*, then the linear order of these elements in Piedmontese, as compared to that of the corresponding elements in French and Italian, could be taken to be the following:

(33)

Italian:	*mica*	*già*	*più*		*sempre*
French:	*pas*	*déjà*	*plus*		*toujours*
Piedmontese:	*pa*	*gia*	*pi*	*nen*	*sempre*
	neg	already	no more	neg	always

Other ways of resolving these data are also possible, though. In particular, there is evidence that *pi nen* 'no more' is best analyzed as a syntactic unit, rather than as a sequence of two distinct elements (see discussion following diagram (45) and the examples in (46)).[12] If we analyze *pi nen* 'no more' as a unit, how can we determine the structural position of the negative marker *nen* with respect to it? That is, we know that *nen* is lower than *gia* 'already' and higher than *sempre* 'always'. We would also like to know whether it is higher or lower than *pi nen* 'no more'. Observing the position of the past participle does not help us decide the matter. Recall that the past participle can occur to the left of *sempre* 'always' but cannot occur to the left of any of the elements that precede *sempre* in linear order — *gia* 'already', *pi nen* 'no more', and the negative marker *nen*. Thus, its position simply confirms what the linear order already indicated: both *nen* and *pi nen* are structurally higher than *sempre*; but this does not reveal anything about the relative position of *nen* and *pi nen*. Observing the position of the infinitival verb, however, sheds light on the issue. Let us then turn to an examination of the relative position of infinitival verbs and the elements under discussion, 'not' and 'no more'.

A lexical verb in the infinitival form occurs on the right of the negative marker *nen*, as shown in the following examples. The opposite word order, in which the infinitival precedes *nen*, is ungrammatical:[13]

(34) a. Luigi a   s'astopa le urije per *nen* **senti**. (Piedmontese)
          Luigi s.cl self-close the ears for neg to-hear
          'Luigi is covering his ears so as not to hear.'

      b. *Luigi a s'astopa le urije per **senti** *nen*.

(35) a. L'ei   decidu da *nen* **parlete**.
          s.cl.'have decided of not to-talk-you
          'I have decided not to talk to you.'

      b. *L'hai decidu da **parlete** *nen*.

(36) a. A   l'è   mej   *nen* **parlé**.
          s.cl. s.cl'is better neg to-talk
          'It is better not to talk.'

      b. *A l'è mej **parlé** *nen*.

I take these data to result from the extent of verb movement and thus conclude that lexical verbs in the infinitival form cannot raise to a position higher than the head immediately to the right of *nen*:[14]

(37)

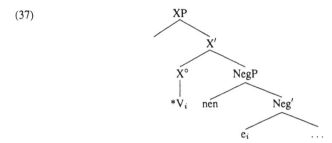

Only the infinitival form of an auxiliary verb can optionally raise to the head immediately to the left of *nen*, as shown here:

(38) a. Sun contenta da *nen* **avej**   sentu. (Piedmontese)
          am pleased of neg to-have heard
          'I am glad not to have heard.'

      b. Sun contenta d'**avej** *nen* sentu.

(39) a. A'm   dispias d *nen* **avejti**   parlà.
          s.cl-me pains of neg to-have-you talked
          'I am sorry not to have talked to you.'

      b. A'm dispias d'**avejti** *nen* parlà.

These data confirm Pollock's (1989) observation that auxiliaries move further than lexical verbs.

If we now look at the relative position of infinitival verbs and *pi nen* 'no more', we see that a lexical verb in the infinitival form can occur both on the right and on the left of *pi nen*. The position to the immediate right of *pi nen* seems to be the most natural one; hence I will put a question mark in front of the sentence with the other word order, to indicate that it is slightly marked:

(40) a. Luigi a   s'astopa le urije per *pi nen* **senti**. (Piedmontese)
          Luigi s.cl self'closes the ears for no more to-hear
          'Luigi is covering his ears so as not to hear anymore.'

      b. ?Luigi a s'astopa le urije per **senti** *pi nen*.

(41) a. L'ei   decidu da *pi nen* **parlete**.
          s.cl'have decided of no more to-talk-you
          'I have decided not to talk to you anymore.'

      b. ?L'hai decidu da **parlete** *pi nen*.

(42) a. A l'è   mej *pi nen* **parlé**.
          s.cl. s.cl'is better no more to-talk
          'It is better not to talk anymore.'

      b. ?A l'è mej **parlé** *pi nen*.

That is, the verb can occur in both the head to the immediate right and the head to the immediate left of *pi nen*. Assuming that the infinitival verb moves to the same extent in sentences with *nen* and with *pi nen*, I conclude from the contrast between (34)b, (35)b, and (36)b on the one hand and (40)b, (41)b, and (42)b on the other, that *pi nen* is structurally lower than *nen* alone, as represented in the following diagram:

(43)

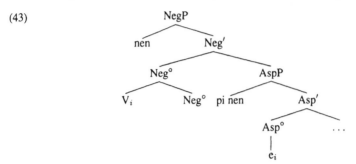

I thus conclude that the linear order of the lower adverbs and the negative marker *nen* in Piedmontese is the one shown in the following table:

(44)

Italian:	*mica*	*già*		*più*	*sempre*
French:	*pas*	*déjà*		*plus*	*toujours*
Piedmontese:	*pa*	*gia*	*nen*	*pi nen*	*sempre*
	neg	already	neg	no more	always

Turning from linear order to structural relations, following Cinque's line of reasoning, I conclude that Piedmontese exhibits the presuppositional negative marker *pa* in a position structurally higher than the adverb 'already' and the non-presuppositional negative marker *nen* in a position structurally lower than 'already' and higher than 'no more'. This can be represented as follows:

(45)

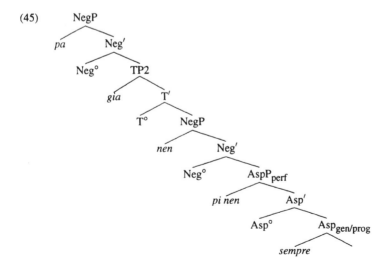

If *pa* and *nen* do not occur in the same position, we might expect them to co-occur. They can indeed co-occur, as shown here:[15]

(46) a. Fa *pa nen* sulì! (Piedmontese from Lanzo)
          do neg neg that
          '@Don't do that!'
      b. *Fa *nen pa* sulì!

Note that, in this example, the two negative markers do not cancel each other out but rather together contribute one instance of negation. The interpretation of this sentence is that of a negation of a proposition that is assumed in the discourse (namely, that the hearer is going to do that). In such examples, only the order in which *pa* precedes *nen* is possible; this is expected, given the analysis just presented, according to which *pa* occurs in a structural position higher than *nen*.[16]

Let us now examine the evidence in support of treating *pi nen* as a syntactic unit in Piedmontese. The hypothesis that *pi nen* is a syntactic unit is supported by several pieces of evidence. First, we never find lexical material intervening between *pi* and *nen*; they always occur adjacent to one other. For example, when *nen* follows *pi*, it cannot be modified by *propi* 'quite, absolutely' (e.g., (47)a), even though *nen* by itself can be so modified (e.g., (47)b):

(47) a. *Am   pias   *pi*   propi   *nen*. (Piedmontese)
          s.cl.-me pleases more absolutely not
          'I absolutely don't like it anymore.'

      b. Am   pias   *propri   nen*.
          s.cl-me pleases absolutely not
          'I absolutely don't like it.'

Second, *pi nen* can be modified as a unit, as shown in (48):

(48) Am   pias   *propri   pi nen*. (Piedmontese)
      s.cl-me pleases absolutely no more
      'I absolutely don't like it anymore.'

Third, *pi nen* can occur as a unit in isolation, in answer to a question (though with a slight degree of marginality):

(49) a. T'pensi da felu   ancura? ?No, *pi   nen*. (Piedmontese)
          s.cl'think of to-do-it again   no,   more neg
          'Do you think you'll do it again? No, not anymore.'

      b. A-y   pias   ancura? ?No, *pi   nen*.
          s.cl-him pleases still   no,   more neg
          'Does s/he still like it? No, not anymore.'

Note that these last two properties of *pi nen* are not shared by the sequence *pa pi*, which cannot be modified by *propi*, as shown in (50)a, and cannot be used in isolation, as illustrated in (50)b. Example (50)c shows that a full sentence can end with the sequence *pa pi*:[17]

(50) a. *A'm   pias   *propi*   *pa pi*.   (Piedmontese)
          s.cl-me pleases absolutely neg more
          'I absolutely don't like it anymore.'

      b. A-y   pias   ancura? *No, *pa pi*.
          s.cl-him pleases still   no,   neg more
          'Does s/he still like it? No, not anymore.'

      c. A-y   pias   ancura? No, a-y   pias   *pa pi*.
          s.cl.-him pleases still   no, s.cl-him pleases neg more
          'Does s/he still like it? No, he doesn't like it anymore.'

Further suggestive evidence that *pi nen* is a syntactic unit is provided by the variety of Piedmontese spoken in Bollengo, about 40 kilometers north of Turin. In this variety, instead of *pi nen* it is possible to find *pin*, as shown in (51). Note also that, in these examples, what in other varieties of Piedmontese is *gnun* 'no-one' appears as *piun*, and what in other varieties is *gnente* 'nothing' appears as *piente*:

(51) a. I'u   *pin*   vist *piun*.   (Piedmontese from Bollengo)
          s.cl'have no more seen no one
          'I haven't seen anyone anymore.'

      b. L'ha   *pin*   dit *piente*.
          s.cl'has no more said nothing
          'He hasn't said anything anymore.'

The three elements *pin*, *piun*, and *piente* appear to have the element *pi* in their morphological makeup, which suggests that *pi* merges with negative constituents to form a syntactic unit.[18]

Let me now summarize what we have discovered so far. Distributional evidence has led me to conclude that *pa* and *nen*, the two post-verbal negative markers of Piedmontese, do not occur in the same structural position. The relevant evidence comes from the fact that *pa* typically precedes *gia*, while *nen* typically follows it. The data concerning the interpretation of these negative markers have led me to conclude that their structural position plays a role in their interpretation. When they occur in a position structurally higher than the one occupied by *gia* 'already', they negate a proposition assumed in the discourse. When they occur in a lower structural position, they are interpreted as negative markers that negate a proposition without any particular discourse status. *Pa* typically occurs in the higher of the two positions and therefore functions as a presuppositional negative marker, whereas *nen* typically occurs in the lower of the two positions and thus typically functions as a non-presuppositional (or "regular") negative marker. But it is also marginally possible to find instances of *pa* that function as a regular negative marker, and, conversely, instances of *nen* that have the interpretation of a presuppositional negative marker. When this happens, the negative markers are in the position lower than *gia* and in the position higher than *gia*, respectively.

Another difference between the two negative elements of Piedmontese deserves some discussion, though it might or might not be related to their structural position. When the verb in the clause is in a simple form (i.e., it does not consist of an auxiliary and a past participle), *pa* can co-occur with a negative indefinite in object position, whereas *nen* cannot. Note that *pa* works as the presuppositional negative marker in these examples:[19]

(52) a. A'm   dis *pa gnente.* (Piedmontese)
         s.cl'me tells neg nothing
         '@She doesn't tell me anything.'

      b. *A'm   dis *nen gnente.*
         s.cl-me tells neg nothing
         'She doesn't tell me anything.'

(53) a. A veddu *pa gnun.*
         s.cl see   neg nobody
         '@I don't see anyone.'

      b. *A veddu *nen gnun.*
         s.cl see   neg nobody
         'I don't see anyone.'

Should we conclude from this fact that *gnente* and *gnun* occur in the same position as *nen*? Note that the contrast between *pa* and *nen* disappears when the verbal form consists of an auxiliary and a past participle. In the following examples, either *pa* or *nen* may co-occur with the negative indefinite, though neither one of them is required (*pa* has the presuppositional reading):

(54) a. I l'hai   (*pa/nen*) vist *gnun.* (Piedmontese)
         s.cl s.cl'have (neg)   seen no one
         'I haven't seem anyone.'

      b. A l'ha   (*pa/nen*) fait *gnente* ad mal!
         s.cl s.cl'has (neg)   done nothing of bad
         'He hasn't done anything bad.'

It might be the case that the negative indefinite raises to the position of *nen* when the verb is simple, but cannot raise as far when a past participle is present in the structure. If that were true, and if *nen* and *pa* occur in different structural positions, then it would be expected that the incompatibity of *nen* and a negative indefinite does not necessarily correspond to an incompatibility between *pa* and a negative indefinite.

The pattern is more complex, though, and more needs to be explained. Note that the ungrammaticality created by the adjacency of *nen* and a negative indefinite disappears when the latter occurs within a PP:

(55) A parla *nen* cun *gnun.* (Piedmontese)
     s.cl talks neg with no one
     'He doesn't talk with anyone.'

Moreover, while *nen* is ungrammatical and *pa* perfectly grammatical when adjacent to a negative object, *pi nen* yields an intermediate result:

(56) a. ??A'm cunta *pi nen gnente.* (Piedmontese)
         s.cl.'me tells no more nothing
         'He doesn't tell me anything anymore.'

  b. ??A veddu *pi nen   gnun.*
     s.cl see   no more no one
     'I don't see anyone anymore.'

Speakers clearly prefer *pi* without *nen*:

(57) a. A'm   cunta *pi   gnente.* (Piedmontese)
         s.cl'me tells no more nothing
         'He doesn't tell me anything anymore.'

      b. A veddu *pi   gnun.*
         s.cl see no more no one
         'I don't see anyone anymore.'

Similarly to *nen*, the grammatical status of *pi nen* improves when the negative indefinite is within a prepositional phrase; the sentence is found to be perfectly grammatical with or without *nen*:

(58) a. A parla *pi nen* cun *gnun.* (Piedmontese)
         s.cl talks no more with no one
         'He doesn't talk to anyone anymore.'

      b. A parla *pi* cun *gnun.*

I leave an analysis of these data for further research.

    Before I conclude this section, let me point out the existence of a third post-verbal negative marker in (certain varieties of) Piedmontese. Parry (in press b) mentions an unstressed enclitic negative *-nu* that is used in some dialects in the southern part of Piedmont (Monferrato) and in the Ligurian hinterland, for example in Cairo Montenotte. This negative marker must co-occur with the pre-verbal negative marker *n* and may also co-occur with *pa*:[20]

(59) a. Mi a   *(*n*)i   vag*nu* (Cairese)
         I s.cl neg-there go-neg
         'I'm not going there.'

      b. Dy'menika u   *(*n*)e (*pa*) 'vny*nu.*
         sunday   s.cl neg-is neg come-neg
         'He didn't come on Sunday.'

Parry (personal communication) reports the function of *nu* to be that of reinforcing negation (similar to English 'at all') or, possibly, contradicting a proposition salient in the discourse (similar to Italian *mica* and what we have ascribed to Piedmontese *pa*). In this section, I have not discussed this element, given the paucity of data at my disposal, focusing instead on *pa* and *nen*. Let me simply point out that it must be in a lower structural position than both *pa* and *nen*, since the participle necessarily precedes it, while it follows both *pa* and *nen*. Given that the past participle can occur to the right of the adverb *sempre* 'always' in Piedmontese, but cannot occur to the right of *nu*, I conclude that *nu* must be lower than *sempre*: *pa–nen–sempre–*participle–*nu*. Unfortunately, though, I do not have any example with both *sempre* and *-nu*.

    To summarize this section, we have seen that Piedmontese has more than one post-verbal negative marker and more than one position in which a post-verbal negative marker can occur. One of these positions, the one preceding the adverb 'already', is associated with the negation of a proposition assumed in the discourse. This position is typically occupied by the negative marker *pa*, though *nen* can be found there as well, with a certain degree of marginality. A second position, lower than the one occupied by the adverb 'already', is used to negate a proposition that has no particular discourse status. This position is occupied by the negative marker *nen* and marginally by the negative marker *pa*. A third position, lower than the two described so far, where the enclitic negative marker *nu* can occur is also possible, but for lack of data, I cannot state what exactly the position or the interpretation of this negative marker is. I can only speculate that its position is structurally lower than that of *sempre* 'always'.

3.3.2.   *Two structural positions for Valdotain* pa

The variety of Valdotain described here is the one spoken in the Valley of Cogne; I will refer to it as Cognen. Whereas Piedmontese has two morphologically distinct negative markers, Valdotain has only one, *pa*. *Pa* can be used as both a presuppositional negative marker and a regular negative marker. Because the language has only one morphological form for the negative marker, the question arises of whether or not these two functions correspond to two distinct syntactic representations. My data suggest that, when *pa* is used with the pragmatic restrictions of *mica* — that is, as a presuppositional negative marker — it occurs in a higher structural position than when it is used as the regular negative marker. Let us see the data that lead me to this conclusion.

Pa always follows the simple form of a finite verb, with either interpretation:

(60)   a.   Maréia mёndzə *pa*   la   tséar. (Cognen)
            Maréia eats   neg the meat
            'Maréia doesn't eat meat.'

      b.   Gianni compren   *pa* tot.
            Gianni understands neg all
            'Gianni doesn't understand everything.'

When the verbal form consists of an auxiliary and a past participle, *pa* always follows the auxiliary and precedes the past participle:

(61)   Maréia l'a   *pa* mёndzà la tsear. (Cognen)
        Maréia s.cl'has neg eaten   the meat
        'Maréia hasn't eaten meat.'

The past participle in Valdotain moves to a lesser degree than in Piedmontese. Recall that in Piedmontese it must raise to a position higher than *tut* 'all' and may, but need not, raise to a position higher than *sempre* 'always'. In the variety of Valdotain we are examining, on the other hand, the past participle occurs in a position lower than *tot* 'all' and cannot raise to a position higher than *toujou* 'always'. The examples in (62) show that the past participle occurs in the head position immediately to the right of *tot* and may raise to the head position immediately to the left of *tot* only with some degree of marginality:[21]

(62) a. Giani l'a   pa *tot* **compré**. (Cognen)
         Giani s.cl'has neg all understood
         'Giani didn't understand everything.'

      b. ?Giani l'a pa **compré** *tot*.

The examples in (63)b and (64)c show that the past participle cannot raise to the head position immediately to the left of *toujou* 'always'. This is not surprising in my view: since 'all' is lower than 'always' in the fixed order described by Cinque, a past participle that only marginally raises past 'all' (see (64)b) might not raise as far as the head position to the left of 'always'.

(63) a. De   adon, l'a   pa *toujou* **gaagnà**. (Cognen)
         from then, s.cl'has neg always won
         'Since then, he hasn't always won.'

      b. *De adon, l'a pa **gaagnà** *toujou*.

(64) a. L'ha   *toujou tot* **deut**.
         s.cl'has always all said
         'He's always said everything.'

      b. ?L'ha *toujou* **deut** *tot*.

      c. *L'ha **deut** *toujou tot*.

We can see the difference in the two uses of *pa* in their distribution with respect to the adverb *dza* 'already'. On the one hand, when *pa* is used as a negative marker that negates a proposition with no particular discourse status, it follows the adverb that corresponds to 'already' (thus paralleling Piedmontese *nen*):

(65) a. L'a   *dza*   *pa* volu-lu adon. (Cognen)
         s.cl'has already neg wanted-it then
         'Already then he didn't want it.'

      b. I   m'a   *dza*   *pa* saluià ce dzor lai.
         s.cl me'has already neg greeted that day there
         'Already that day he didn't greet me.'

On the other hand, when *pa* is used as a negative marker that negates a proposition that is assumed in the discourse, it precedes the adverb *dza* 'already' (thus paralleling the default uses of Piedmontese *pa*):

(66) a. L'è   *pa dza*   parti? (Cognen)
         s.cl'is neg already left
         '@He hasn't already left, has he?'

      b. L'en   *pa* 'd cò   *dza*   crià.
         s.cl'have neg at times already called
         '@They haven't already called.'

      c. L'hahé *pa* ('d cò)   *dza*   fai-lou?
         s.cl'has neg (at times) already done-it
         '@He hasn't already done it, has he?'

These data lead me to conclude that Cognen, which only has one negative marker, *pa*, distinguishes its two different functions by placing it in two different structural positions. That is, when *pa* is used as a non-presuppositional negative marker, it occurs in a position lower than *dza* 'already'. However, when it is used to negate a proposition believed to be true, it occurs in the same position as Italian *mica* and Piedmontese *pa* with the presuppositional reading — namely, in a position structurally higher than *dza* 'already'.

Pa precedes the adverb *mai* 'anymore', as illustrated in the following examples:

(67) a. L'a   *pa mai* predzà. (Cognen)
         s.cl.'has neg more talked
         'He hasn't talked anymore.'

      b. L'e   *pa mai* venu.
         s.cl'is neg more come
         'He hasn't come anymore.'

      c. L'en   *pa mai* reçu   ren.
         s.cl'have neg more received nothing
         'They haven't received anything anymore.'

Given that *pa* and *mai* co-occur in all of these examples, the question arises whether it is possible to talk about an adverbial form *mai* independent of *pa* or whether the sequence *pa mai* forms a single constituent, similarly to Piedmontese *pi nen* discussed in the previous section. The only lexical item that I have found to be able to intervene between *pa* and *mai* is *pouéi* 'then', as shown in example (68). Notice that *pa* in this case has a presuppositional reading; hence, if my proposal is on the right track, it occurs in the higher of the two positions I am postulating for this negative marker:

(68) De adon, l'en   *pa* pouéi *mai* acetó   le noutre envitachon. (Cognen)
      from then, s.cl'have neg then   more accepted the our   invitations
      '@Since then, they have then no longer accepted our invitations.'

Examples of this type lead me to speculate that *mai* can occasionally occur as an independent lexical element in a position structurally lower than the one occupied by *pa*. But other examples lead me to believe that *pa mai* can also form a syntactic unit. Note that *pa mai* can be used in isolation, as an answer to a question. In this case, the only lexical item that is sometimes found between *pa* and *mai*, *pouéi*, cannot occur:

(69) A-te   torna-lou fare? Na, *pa mai*./ *Na, *pa* pouéi *mai*. (Cognen)
      have-s.cl returned-it to-do no, neg more no,   neg then   more
      'Have you done it again? No, no more.'

The unit *pa mai* can also be modified by *fran* 'indeed, absolutely':

(70) L'a   *fran*   *pa mai* voia. (Cognen)
      s.cl'has absolutely neg more desire
      'She absolutely doesn't feel like it anymore.'

Following the reasoning applied to Piedmontese *pi nen*, I conclude that *pa* and *mai* form a unit in such cases. This is consistent with the intuitions of the native speakers I have consulted and with those of Chenal (1986), who writes it as a single word.[22]

We can now compare the sequence of adverbs in Valdotain with the corresponding elements in the languages discussed so far. If we take Piedmontese *pi nen* and

Valdotain *pa mai* (with the non-presuppositional *pa*) to form a syntactic unit, two possibilities are available for the sequence of positions of these elements. One possibility is that the non-presuppositional negative marker and the sequence *pa mai* occur in the same position, as shown in this table:

(71)

Italian:	*mica*	*già*		*più*	*sempre*
French:	*pas*	*déjà*		*plus*	*toujours*
Piedmontese:	*pa*	*gia*	*nen*	*pi nen*	*sempre*
Valdotain:	*pa*	*dza*		*pa/pa mai*	*toujou*
	neg	already	neg	neg/no more	always

A second possibility is that they occur in different positions, with the negative marker either higher or lower than the adverb 'no more'. It is impossible to choose between these alternatives exclusively on the basis of the data we have discussed so far. Data on the position of the past participle do not help, since in Valdotain it does not raise past *toujou* 'always', as we saw in examples (63)b and (64)c, and thus does not raise past higher elements such as *pa* and *mai*, either. In Piedmontese, infinitival verbs helped us shed light on the relative position of the negative marker and the adverb 'no more', as we saw in the previous section. In Valdotain, though, this is not the case, since infinitival verbs show the same range of verb movement as past participles. That is, they occur in the head to the immediate right of *tot* and occur to the left of *tot* only under the same conditions under which the past participle does (see note 21). As expected in view of this, they do not raise to the left of elements that are structurally higher than *tot* — *toujou* 'always', *pa mai* 'no more', and the negative marker *pa*. The examples in (72) and (73) show that a lexical verb in the infinitival form cannot occur in the head to the immediate left of *pa*:

(72) a. Loui se tôppe le bouignon pe *pa* **sentí**. (Cognen)
    Loui self closes the ears   for neg to-hear
    'Loui is covering his ears so as not to hear.'

   b. *Loui se tôppe le bouignon pe **sentí** *pa*.

(73) a. D'ei   decedó de *pa* te   **prèdzé**.
    s.cl'have decided of not to-you to-talk
    'I have decided not to talk to you.'

   b. *D'ei decedó de te **prèdzé** *pa*.

The examples in (74)b and (75)b show that even auxiliary verbs in the infinitival form cannot raise to the head immediately to the left of *pa*:

(74) a. Séi contenta de *pa* **avé**   sentú. (Cognen)
    am pleased of neg to-have heard
    'I am glad not to have heard.'

   b. *Séi contenta de **avé** *pa* sentú.

(75) a. Me despiiéi de *pa* t'**avé**   predzá.
    me pains   of neg you'to-have talked
    'I am sorry not to have talked to you.'

   b. *Me despiiéi de t'**avé** *pa* predzá.

Infinitival verbs also do not raise to the left of *pa mai*, as shown in the following examples:

(76) a. Loui se tôppe le bouignon pe *pa mai* **sentí.** (Cognen)
       Loui self closes the ears   for neg more to-hear
       'Loui is covering his ears so as not to hear anymore.'

      b. *Loui se tôppe le bouignon pe **sentí** *pa mai.*

(77) a. D'ei   decedó de *pa mai* te   **prèdzé.**
       s.cl.'have decided of neg more you to-talk
       'I have decided not to talk to you anymore.'

      b. *D'ei decedó de te **prèdzé** *pa mai.*

Thus, the position of infinitival verbs in Valdotain does not shed light on the relative position of *pa mai* 'no more' and the negative marker *pa*, and thus it does not help us choose between the hypotheses that they might occupy the same structural position or two different ones. Taking into account cross-linguistic evidence, though, I am led to reject the hypothesis that views the negative markers in the same position as 'no more', as in table (71). Such evidence comes from French, to which I turn directly.

If the conclusions reached on the basis of data from Piedmontese and Valdotain are on the right track, then we expect that French *pas* may also occur in two distinct structural positions. In particular, we expect that it occurs in a position higher than *déjà* 'already' when it functions as a presuppositional negative marker, while in a position lower than *déjà* when it functions as a regular negative marker. The first of the two expectations is borne out, as we see from the example in (78):

(78) Il n'est *pas déjà*   parti? (French)
      he neg'is neg already left
      '@Hasn't he already left?'

Whether or not *pas* can be in a position lower than *déjà* is harder to see, since the two elements cannot co-occur in the sequence *déjà pas*, as shown in (79):

(79) *Il n'a   *déjà*   *pas* voulu ce jour-là.   (French)
      he neg'has already neg wanted that day-there
      'Already that day he didn't want to.'

It is conceivable that the impossibility of the sequence *déjà pas* could be due to independent factors, which are not understood, and that in fact the negative marker *pas* is indeed able to occupy a structural position lower than *déjà*.[23] Certainly the negative marker can occur in sentences that lack a presuppositional reading, such as (80). Unfortunately, though, such examples do not allow us to determine the exact position of *pas* with respect to the position of *déjà*:

(80) Il n'est *pas* venu. (French)
      he neg'is neg come
      'He hasn't come.'

Let us not take the impossibility of the sequence *déjà pas* as sufficient reason to conclude that *pas* cannot be structurally lower than *déjà*. As we will see later in this chapter, there are languages where a negative marker that is structurally lower than the adverb 'already' cannot co-occur with it, for reasons that remain unclear (see sections 3.4.1 and 3.4.2).[24] Let us then assume, until we find evidence to the contrary, that non-presuppositional instances of *pas* indeed occur in a position that is structurally lower than the one occupied by *déjà*. Given this assumption, what can we find out about the relative position of non-presuppositional *pas* and the adverb *plus* 'no more'? *Pas* and *plus* do not co-occur, so we cannot conclude anything about their structural position from a direct observation of their linear order. What can help us is the data concerning the position of infinitival verbs with respect to *pas* and to *plus* pointed out in Pollock (1989: §6.3) and reported here. The data in (81) show that the infinitival form of a lexical verb can follow *pas* but cannot precede it:

(81) a. Pierre dit   ne   *pas* **manger**. (French)
         Pierre says neg neg to-eat
         'Pierre says not to eat.'

      b. *Pierre dit ne **manger** *pas*.

The behavior of *pas* exemplified in (81)b crucially differs from that of *plus*, shown in (82)b: the infinitival form of a lexical verb can follow *plus* and precede it as well:

(82) a. ?Pierre dit   ne   *plus*   **manger**. (French)
         Pierre   says neg no more to-eat
         'Pierre says not to eat anymore.'

      b. ?Pierre dit ne **manger** *plus*.

The contrast between (81)b and (82)b can be accounted for if we assume that *plus* is structurally lower than *pas* and that the infinitival form can raise past *plus* but cannot raise past *pas*. On the basis of these considerations I thus conclude, in agreement with Pollock (1989) and Cinque (1994, 1996a), that lack of co-occurrence of *pas* and *plus* does not mean they occupy the same structural position. I suggest instead that the non-presuppositional negative marker is structurally higher than the adverb 'no more' in French and tentatively propose that it occurs in a structural position between 'already' and 'no more'. Using the conclusion reached for French as indirect evidence, I argue that in Valdotain as well the non-presuppositional negative marker and the adverb 'no more' need not be viewed as occupying the same structural position. I suggest that Valdotain *pa* occurs in a position higher than 'no more', given the linear order of the two elements and the strong resemblance between Valdotain and French syntax. This is summarized in the following table:

(83)

	presup.		*non-presup.*		
Italian:	*mica*	*già*		*più*	*sempre*
French:	*pas*	*déjà*	(*pas?*)	*plus*	*toujours*
Piedmontese:	*pa*	*gia*	*nen*	*pi nen*	*sempre*
Valdotain:	*pa*	*dza*	*pa*	*pa mai*	*toujou*
	neg	already	neg	no more	always

presup. = presuppositional

3.4.   Non-presuppositional negative markers

We can now examine more closely the non-presuppositional negative markers, with the goal of defining more precisely where they can occur in the structure. In the preceding discussion, we saw that the non-presuppositional instances of Piedmontese *nen*, French *pas*, and Valdotain *pa* are structurally lower than *gia, déjà*, and *dza* 'already' and higher than *pi nen, plus*, and *pa mai* 'no more', respectively. We now turn our attention to data from two other Romance varieties that exhibit non-presuppositional negative markers in yet a different structural position — a position lower than 'always'. The examination of one of these varieties, Pavese, will also allow us to shed light on how movement of the participle interacts with the word order and the discourse status of lower adverbs and negative markers.

3.4.1.   *The structural position of Milanese* no

Milanese is a northern Italian dialect (of the Gallo-Italic group) spoken in Milan, in the Lombardy region. The grammar of Milanese by Beretta (1980) identifies three negative markers in this language: pre-verbal *no*, post-verbal *minga*, and post-verbal *nò*; it characterizes post-verbal *nò* as carrying stress.[25] The grammar of Milanese by Nicoli (1983: 238) also mentions an unstressed pre-verbal negative marker *no*, pronounced [nu], but declares it virtually absent from modern spoken Milanese and takes the negative markers currently employed in Milanese to be only post-verbal *minga* and *no*.[26] This is consistent with my findings: my Milanese informants only use the two post-verbal negative markers *minga* and *no*. Nicoli does not mention whether or not post-verbal *no* carries stress and writes it simply as *no*; I will follow this convention, which is also the one chosen by my informants.[27] Nicoli further points out that the only negative marker that can be used to negate a constituent is *minga*.

The distribution and the interpretation of *minga* parallels that of Piedmontese *pa*. It precedes *gemò* 'already', as shown in (84):

(84)   a.   L'è   *minga gemò*   partì? (Milanese)
            s.cl'is neg   already left
            '@Hasn't he already left?'

       b.   Han *minga gemò*   ciamà, che mi sappia.
            have neg   already called, that I   know
            '@They haven't already called, as far as I know.'

Gemò 'already' in turn precedes *pü* 'no more':

(85)   a.   El g'a   *gemò   pü*   fam.   (Milanese)
            s.cl. cl-has already no more hunger
            'Already he isn't hungry anymore.'

       b.   Da quel dì lì,   g'an   *gemò   pü*   ricevü la posta.
            from that day there, cl-have already no more received the mail
            'From that day, already they weren't receiving their mail anymore.'

As expected, *minga* precedes *pü* (though their co-occurrence is marginal for one of my informants):

(86) El Gianni l'ha   *minga pü*   ciamà, d'alura.   (Milanese)
      the Gianni s.cl'has neg   no more called, from-then
      '@Gianni hasn't called anymore, since then.'

Both *minga* and *pü* precede *semper*:

(87) a. L'a   *minga semper* vinciü. (Milanese)
          s.cl-has neg   always won
          '@He didn't always win.'

      b. L'a   *pü*   *semper* vinciü.
          s.cl'has no more always won
          'He didn't always win anymore.'

The relative order of the lower adverbs corresponding to 'already', 'no more', and 'always' thus reflects that found in the other varieties examined so far in this work and in those discussed in Cinque (1994, 1995a, 1996a).

Minga is typically interpreted as a presuppositional negative marker. According to my informants, however, it can also be interpreted as a regular negative marker. In that case, the sentences do not seem to be as marginal as their Piedmontese counterparts with *pa* used as a regular negative marker. Following the reasoning applied earlier for Piedmontese, French, and Valdotain, I assume that this follows from the fact that *minga* can occur in two different structural positions: the one higher than 'already' when it has a presuppositional reading, and the one lower than 'already' when it does not. The fact that sentences with both readings are grammatical suggests that this ambiguity is fully accepted in this language, contrary to Piedmontese. In this respect, then, Milanese *minga* is similar to Valdotain *pa*, which can function as a presuppositional as well as a non-presuppositional negative marker, as discussed in section 3.3.2.

Note that the possibility for a presuppositional negative marker to occur in more than one position is given in Italian as well. *Mica* typically occurs in a structural position lower than the one occupied by the finite verb and higher than the one occupied by *già* 'already' (cf. (88)a). But it can also occur in a position preceding the finite verb, as shown in (88)b. I propose that in such a case *mica* has raised to the specifier of the functional projection NegP in which *non* normally occurs:[28]

(88) a. Gianni *non* sarà   *mica* già   partito. (Italian)
          Gianni neg will-be neg already left
          '@Gianni won't have left already.'

      b. Gianni *mica* sarà   già   partito.
          Gianni neg will-be already left
          '@Gianni won't have left already.'

Northern Italian speakers find the example in (88)b to have a marked word order, where *mica* receives special emphasis, similar to a case of focalization.[29] Note that, in both positions, *mica* is higher than *già* 'already'.

These patterns suggest that, when a language employs a morphologically distinct negative marker to negate a proposition assumed in the discourse, the contribution of such an element to the interpretation of the clause will be the same regardless of its structural position, as long as it is higher than the position of 'already'. This is the case with Italian *mica*. If the presuppositional negative marker is structurally lower than 'already', though, it ceases to function as such and its contribution to the interpretation of the clause is that of a regular negative marker — one that negates a proposition with no particular discourse status. This is the case with Milanese *minga* and, to a lesser extent, with Piedmontese *pa*.[30] Still, when a language does not have a morphologically distinct negative marker for the negation of a proposition assumed in the discourse, the presuppositional and the non-presuppositional readings are distinguished solely on the basis of the structural position of the negative marker. This is the case, I argue, with Valdotain *pa* and possibly French *pas*.

The past participle in Milanese shows a range of positions. It can be as low as to occupy the position to the immediate right of *semper* 'always', as in the examples in (87) and (89)a. That position represents its lower bound. As shown by the following examples, it must be on the immediate left of *tüscòs* 'all':

(89) a. L'a   *semper* **di**   *tüscòs*. (Milanese)
          s.cl'has always said all
          'He has always said everything.'

      b. *L'a semper *tüscòs* **di**.

The participle can also be higher: it can occur to the left of *pü* and even of *gemò* 'already':

(90) a. L'han   **vist** *pü*.   (Milanese)
          s.cl'have seen no more
          'They haven't seen him anymore.'

      b. D'alura,   han minga **acetà**   *pü*   semper i   noster invit.
          from'then, have neg   accepted no more always the our   invitations
          'Since then, they haven't always accepted our invitations anymore.'

      c. Han **ricevu** *gemò* *pü*   nient.
          have received already no more nothing
          'Already they haven't received anything anymore.'

Whereas the lower bound of the participle is the position on the immediate left of *tüscòs* 'all', the upper bound is defined by *minga*: the past participle can occur on the right of *minga* but cannot occur on its left:

(91) a. L'u   *minga* **truà**. (Milanese)
          it'have neg   found
          '@I haven't found it.'

      b. *L'u **truà** *minga*.

(92) a. L'è   *minga* **partì**.
          s.cl'is neg   left
          '@He hasn't left.'

      b. *L'è **partì** *minga*.

(93) a. L'a   *minga* **mis giò** la pasta.
          s.cl'has neg   put down the pasta
          '@He hasn't put in the pasta.'

      b. *L'a **mis giò** *minga* la pasta.

These data lead me to conclude that the past participle can raise to any of the following positions:

(94) *minga*–(participle)–*gemò*–(participle)–*pü*–(participle)–*semper*–(participle)

What is most relevant for the purpose of the present discussion is that the past participle cannot raise to the position immediately to the left of *minga*.[31] This contrasts with what we find when we observe the distribution of the past participle with respect to the negative marker *no*: the past participle *must* occur in a position to the left of *no*:

(95) a. El l'ha   **scrivuu** *no*. (Milanese)
          s.cl s.cl'has written neg
          'He hasn't written.'

      b. *El l'ha *no* **scrivuu**.

(96) a. U   **vist** *no* la tuza.
          have seen neg the girl
          'I haven't seen the girl.'

      b. *U *no* **vist** la tuza.

(97) a. L'a   **mis giò** *no* la pasta.
          s.cl'has put down neg the pasta
          'He hasn't put in the pasta.'

      b. *L'a *no* **mis giò** la pasta.

The distribution of the past participle with respect to *no*, combined with its distribution with respect to the other lower adverbs, leads me to conclude that *no* is lower in the structure than *semper* 'always'. Thus, *no* occupies the following position in the sequence:

(98) *minga*–(participle)–*gemò*–(participle)–*pü*–(participle)–*semper*–(participle)–*no*

This conclusion amounts to saying that the post-verbal non-presuppositional negative marker can occur in more than one structural position cross-linguistically. Earlier in this chapter I concluded that Piedmontese *nen*, French *pas*, and Valdotain *pa* are structurally higher than *pi nen*, *plus*, and *pa mai* 'no more', respectively. On the basis of evidence of the same type, now I conclude that Milanese *no* is lower than *semper*. The overall picture built so far can be summarized as follows:

(99)

	presup.			non-presup.		non-presup.
Italian:	mica	già		più	sempre	
French:	pas	déjà	(pas?)	plus	toujours	
Piedmontese:	pa	gia	nen	pi nen	sempre	
Valdotain:	pa	dza	pa	pa mai	toujou	
Milanese:	minga	gemò		pü	semper	no
	neg	already	neg	no more	always	neg

presup. = presuppositional

Thus I have identified two structural positions in which the post-verbal non-presuppositional negative markers can occur: immediately below 'already' and immediately below 'always'. If I add the pre-verbal non-presuppositional negative markers to this picture, then I conclude that there are (at least) three different structural positions in which such elements can occur in the Romance varieties here examined.

Turning our attention back to Milanese *no*, which is structurally lower than 'already', 'no more', and 'always', we can ask whether it can take scope over such adverbs even though it does not c-command them. The answer is negative: when *no* does not c-command these adverbs, it does not take scope over them. This is shown in the following examples:[32]

(100) a. El fünsiòna *gemò no*   prima de vess finì.   (Milanese)
           s.cl works   alread y neg before of to-be finished
           'Already before being finished it doesn't work.'

       b. L'a   *semper* pagà *no* i   tas.
           s.cl'has always paid neg the taxes
           'It's always been the case that he hasn't paid taxes.'

In order to take scope over such adverbs, the negative marker *no* must precede them in linear order, as can be seen in the examples in (101). In these examples, *no* is characterized by the native speakers as being stressed and, at least in the case in which it precedes *gemò*, yielding a reading of denial of a proposition that is assumed to be true:

(101) a. La Maria l'a   *no gemò*   mangià. (Milanese)
           the Maria s.cl-has neg already eaten
           '@It's not the case that Maria has already eaten.'

       b. L'a   *no semper* di   tüscos.
           s.cl'has neg always said everything
           'He hasn't always said everything.'

       c. L'a   *no semper* pagà i   tas.
           s.cl'has neg always paid the taxes
           'He hasn't always paid taxes.'

Following our previous discussion, I suggest that *no*, at least in example (101)a, occurs in the same position in which *minga* typically occurs. Because this is not the default position for *no*, speakers perceive its occurrence as bearing contrastive stress, as is often the case with focalized constituents. In the other two cases, *no* could either be in the position typically occupied by *minga* or in a position corresponding to that of Piedmontese *nen*.

That *minga* and *no* occupy structurally different positions is confirmed by their distribution in co-occurrence with infinitival verbs. As is the case with past participles, infinitival forms as well obligatorily precede *no* (cf. (102)). This is expected, given that, in general in Romance, infinitival forms seem to raise as far as or farther than past participles (see Piedmontese, for example). Example (103) shows that, in the case of an infinitival auxiliary followed by a past participle, both verbal forms must raise higher than *no*:

(102) a. Cerchem de **spurcàs**   *no*. (Milanese)
           try   of to-dirty-self neg
           'Let's try not to get ourselves dirty.'

    b. *Cerchem de *no* **spurcàs**.

(103) a. L'è   cuntent de **vegh** **parlà** *no* trop.
       s.cl'is happy of to-have spoken neg too-much
       'He's happy not to have spoken too much.'

     b. *L'è cuntent de **vegh** *no* **parlà** trop.

     c. *L'è cuntent de *no* **vegh parlà** trop.

In contrast, an infinitival form can either precede or follow *minga*. Since *minga* in these contexts does not have the presuppositional reading, the question arises of where exactly it occurs. The fact that an infinitival verb can follow it, whereas it cannot follow *no*, suggests that *minga* is not in the same position as *no*. My informants seem to choose the pre-verbal position for *minga* more readily than the post-verbal position with infinitival main verbs, though both are acceptable. They choose both positions equally easily with infinitival modal verbs; infinitival auxiliaries, however, must precede *minga*. Some examples follow:

(104) a. Cerchem de *minga* **spurcàs**.   (Milanese)
       try   of neg to-dirty-self
       'Let's try not to get ourselves dirty.'

     b. Cerchem de **spurcàs** *minga*.

(105) a. L'era   inscì straca de *minga* **podè**   stà   in pee.
       s.cl'was so tired of neg to-be-able to-stay on foot
       'She was so tired that she couldn't stand up.'

     b. L'era inscì straca de **podè** *minga* stà in pee.

(106) a. L'è   cuntent de **vegh**   *minga* **parlà** trop.
       s.cl'is happy of to-have neg   spoken too-much
       'He's happy not to have spoken too much.'

     b. *L'è cuntent de *minga* **vegh parlà** trop.

I tentatively suggest that in these contexts *minga*, which does not have the presuppositional reading, is in a position lower than 'already' but higher than the one occupied by *no*. These data also show that infinitival auxiliaries must occur to the left of *minga*, whereas infinitival main verbs and modals may but need not do so. I express this observation in terms of different positions for the verb, and not in terms of different positions for the adverbs — that is, by saying that (adverbs of the class of) *minga* must adjoin to the right of infinitival auxiliaries, whereas they can adjoin either to the right or to the left of infinitival main verbs. Because we find that, across languages, auxiliaries and main verbs show different distributions, and we know that they have different properties, I find it more promising to see such differences as deriving from their different properties (whatever the relevant ones might be) rather than from different attachment possibilities of adverb classes.

3.4.2. *A focus position for Pavese* no

Pavese is the dialect spoken in Pavia, a town about 30 kilometers south of Milan. It has two negative markers, both post-verbal: *mia* and *no*. *Mia* is typically used to negate a proposition that is presupposed, similarly to Italian *mica*; *no* is typically used as the negative marker that negates a proposition with no particular discourse status. In this respect, Pavese *mia* and *no* exhibit the same properties as Milanese *minga* and *no*. Pavese deserves special attention, though, because of the interaction between the position of the past participle and the negative markers. To anticipate the discussion to come, the choice between the pre- and the post-participial position, for both negative markers and lower adverbs, is related to their discourse status.

Both *mia* and *no* follow the finite verb and precede all complements. When the verbal form consists of an auxiliary and a past participle, they both can occur between the auxiliary and the past participle, as shown in (107) and (108). Thus Pavese *no* differs from Milanese *no*, which must follow the past participle in these contexts. My informants find *mia* more natural than *no* in a position preceding the participle; however, I will not use any special diacritic to mark this preference, which is hard to quantify. We will see later that both *mia* and *no* can also occur in a position following the participle; in that position, *no* is perceived as more natural than *mia*.

(107) a. L'ho   *mia* truvà. (Pavese)
           it'have neg found
           '@I haven't found it.'

       b. L'é   *mia* partì.
           s.cl'is neg left
           '@He hasn't left.'

(108) a. La Maria l'ha   *no* mangià la carne.
           the Maria s.cl'has neg eaten   the meat
           'Mary hasn't eaten meat.'

       b. Al Gianni l'ha   *no* capì   tut cos.
           the Gianni s.cl'has neg understood everything
           'Gianni hasn't understood everything.'

Similar to Italian *mica* and Piedmontese *pa*, Pavese *mia* precedes the lower adverbs we have been investigating. It precedes *giamò* 'already' (109); *giamò* in turn precedes *pü* 'no more' (110). *Mia* can also precede *pü*, though their co-occurrence yields a slightly marginal result (cf. (111)):

(109) a. I   han *mia giamò* ciamà. (Pavese)
           s.cl have neg already called
           '@They haven't called already.'

       b. L'è   *mia giamò* partì?
           s.cl'is neg already left
           '@He hasn't already left, has he?'

(110) Al g'ha *giamò pü*   fam.
       s.cl cl'has already no more hunger
       'He is already no longer hungry.'

(111) ?I   han *mia pü*   telefunà.
       s.cl have neg no more telephoned
       '@They didn't call him anymore.'

Since *mia* precedes *giamò* and *giamò* precedes *pü*, I conclude that *mia* is structurally higher than *pü*. This indeed corresponds to the word order observed in (111). As expected, *mia* also precedes *sempar* 'always':

(112) a. L'ha   *mia sempar* vinciu cla gara chi. (Pavese)
           s.cl'has neg always won   this race here
           'He hasn't always won this race.'

       b. *L'ha *sempar mia* vinciu cla gara chi.

The distribution of *no* is less straightforward. As mentioned, it can either precede or follow the past participle. Thus, alongside examples like (108), we also find examples like those following, which are judged as more natural by my informants:

(113) a. La Maria l'ha   **mangià** *no* la carne. (Pavese)
           the Maria s.cl'has eaten   neg the meat
           'Mary hasn't eaten the meat.'

       b. Al Gianni l'ha   **capì**   *no* tut cos.
           the Gianni s.cl'has understood neg everything
           'Gianni hasn't understood everything.'

       c. M'e dispiasu da ves **gni** *no* prima.
           me'is displeased of to-be come neg earlier
           'I was sorry not to have arrived earlier.'

My informants relate the difference to "emphasis": while *no* in pre-participial position is said to be unstressed, *no* in post-participial position is said to bear stress. The same contrast is reported for the occurrence of *mia* in pre- and post-participial position. But whereas *mia* is said to be most natural when it does not bear stress (in the pre-participial position), *no* is reported to be most natural when it does (in a position following the past participle).

No does not co-occur with *pü* 'no more'. Note however that it also fails to co-occur with any other negative constituent (e.g., the counterparts of 'nobody', 'nothing', etc.).[33] Since *pü* is inherently negative, I suggest that the constraint against the co-occurrence of *no* and *pü* is one instance of the more general constraint against the co-occurrence of *no* with other negative constituents.

No can co-occur with *giamò* 'already' and *sempar* 'always' as follows. If it precedes them, the result is marginal; when *no* precedes *giamò*, it acquires the same interpretation as *mia* — namely, that of negating a proposition that is assumed in the discourse:[34]

(114) ??L'ha *no giamò* ciamà, di volt? (Pavese)
         s.cl'has neg alread y called, of times
         '@He didn't already call, by any chance?'

(115) ??L'ha   *no*   *sempar* vinciu cla gara chi.
         s.cl'has neg always won   this   race here
         'He hasn't always won this race.'

This suggests that, as in Milanese, where we saw marginal occurrences of *no* in the structural position of *minga* and with the same interpretation of *minga*, so in Pavese we see marginal occurrences of *no* in the structural position of *mia* and with the same interpretation of *mia*.

Pavese *no* is like its Milanese counterpart in its ability to co-occur with scope bearing elements it does not c-command: such co-occurrence is possible, but they remain outside the scope of negation (cf. parallel data from Milanese in (100) before). This is illustrated by example (116)a. Note that in these cases the past participle obligatorily precedes the negative marker, as shown by the ungrammaticality of (116)b:

(116)   a. A   i   ha *sempar* **pagà** *no*. (Pavese)
            s.cl. them has always paid neg
            'It's always been the case that he hasn't paid them.'

         b. *A   i   ha *sempar no* **pagà**.
            s.cl. them has always neg paid

The obligatoriness of the order *participle–no* could not be deduced from the Milanese examples, as in this language the participle does not have the option of occurring either right or left of the negative marker; it can only occur on its left. But it is clear in Pavese, where both options are available for the past participle. I speculate that such word order is required because, when the past participle raises to the left of *no*, it leaves *no* as the last element in the phonological phrase, a position where it can receive focal stress. If this is true, then the generalization is that *no* can co-occur with scope-bearing elements it does not c-command only when it bears focal stress, but not otherwise (for reasons that are not clear).[35] We will see that, more generally in Pavese, when the past participle raises to the left of any of the lower adverbs, the adverb is left in a position where it can receive stress, similar to the case of the negative marker.

Let us examine more closely the distribution of the past participle in Pavese. As in Milanese, it cannot be lower than 'all', as shown in the following examples:

(117)   a. L'ha   giamò **fat** *tut cos*.   (Pavese)
            s.cl'has already done everything
            'He has already done everything.'

         b. *L'ha giamò *tut cos* **fat**.

The past participle can be lower or higher than *sempar* 'always':

(118)   a. (A)   l'ha   *sempar* **dit** tut cos.   (Pavese)
            (s.cl) s.cl'has always said everything
            'He has always said everythig.'

         b. (A)   l'ha   **dit** *sempar* tut cos.
            (s.cl) s.cl'has said always everything
            'He has always said everythig.'

(119)   a. (A) l' ha   *sempar* **fat**.
            (s.cl) it'has always done
            'He has always done it.'

         b. (A)   l'ha   **fat** *sempar*.
            (s.cl) it'has done always
            'He has always done it.'

Note that the negative marker *no* appears in between *sempar* and *tut cos*, when the three co-occur, as shown in (120). In this example, focal stress falls on the negative marker, and *tut cos* 'everything' is preceded by an intonational break:

(120)   ?L'ha   *sempar* dit *no tut cos.*   (Pavese)
         s.cl'has always said neg everything
         'It's always been the case that he didn't say everything.'

The participle can be lower or higher than *pü* 'no more':

(121)   a. A l 'ho   *pü*   **vist**. (Pavese)
            s.cl him'have no more seen
            'I haven't seen him anymore.'

         b. A l'ho   **vist** *pü*.
            s.cl him'have seen no more
            'I haven't seen him anymore.'

(122)   a. L'ha   *pü*   **ricevu** la so posta.
            s.cl'has no more received the his mail
            'He didn't receive his mail anymore'

         b. L'ha   **ricevu** *pü*   la so posta.
            s.cl'has received no more the his mail
            'He didn't receive his mail anymore.'

It can be lower or higher than *giamò* 'already':

(123)   a. L'è   *giamò* **parti**. (Pavese)
            s.cl'is already left
            'He has already left.'

         b. L'è   **parti** *giamò*.
            s.cl.'is left   already
            'He has already left.'

(124)   a. L'ha   *giamò* **fat**   tut cos.
            s.cl'has already done everything
            'He has already done everything.'

         b. L'ha   **fat** *giamò* tut cos.
            s.cl'has done already everything
            'He has already done everything.'

Finally, it can be lower or higher than *mia*, the presuppositional negative marker. This contrasts with the case of Milanese discussed in the previous section, where the past participle could not raise higher than the presuppositional negative marker.

(125)   a. L'ho   *mia* **truvà**. (Pavese)
            it'have neg found
            '@I haven't found it.'

         b. L'ho   **truvà** *mia*.
            it'have found neg
            '@I haven't found it.'

(126)   a.   L'é   *mia* **partì.**
          s.cl'is neg left
          '@He hasn't left.'

       b.   L'è   **partì** *mia.*
          s.cl'is left   neg
          '@He hasn't left.'

In all these cases, I suggest that the participle moves to the left of the adverb or of the negative marker so as to leave them as the last elements in the phonological phrase. In such a position, they may (though need not) carry focal stress. When other lexical items follow the adverb or the negative marker to the right of the past participle, they are often separated by an intonational break, as right dislocated elements. In this view, then, one reason for the movement of the past participle is to leave the adverbs and the negative markers in a focal position. Other reasons must play a role as well in those cases where the participle has moved past these elements, but they are not in the right-most position in the phonological phrase, because they are followed by lexical material that is not right-dislocated. I leave those for further research.

To summarize, the negative marker *no* occurs in a position lower than *sempar* and higher than *tut cos*. The past participle can occupy a position as low as the one to the left of *tut cos* and can raise as high as to the position to the left of *mia*:

(127)

PP	*mia*	PP	*giamò*	PP	*pü*	PP	*sempar*	PP	*no*	PP	*tut cos*
	neg		already		no more		always		neg		all

PP = past participle

There is some other suggestive evidence in support of the view that the observed word order variation results from movement of the past participle to the left of each of these elements, with the result that they may occur at the end of the phonological phrase and thus receive focal stress.

First, the relative order of negative markers and lower adverbs is never altered by the position of the past participle. For example, whether the participle precedes or follows *sempar* 'always', its relative order with respect to *pü* 'no more' or *tut cos* 'all' remains the same.

Second, having one of the lower adverbs occur in post-participial position is not the result of some language specific constraint that holds in Pavese, such as a prohibition against having more than one adverb precede the participle. As we can see in the following examples, two lower adverbs can indeed precede the participle, yielding sentences that are grammatical:

(128)   a.   L'è   *mia giamò*   **partì**? (Pavese)
          s.cl.'is neg already left
          '@He hasn't already left, has he?'

       b.   ?L'ha   *no* *sempar* **dit**   tut cos.
          s.cl'has neg always said everything
          'He hasn't always said everything.'

This suggests that the word order variation is not the result of some constraint against adverb clusters in pre-participial position, but must be attributed to some other factor.

Third, when the negative marker *no* is used contrastively in co-occurrence with *si*, a marker of emphatic affirmation, it must occur to the right of the participle and does not have the option of preceding it:

(129) a. T'l'e   **fat** *no* o t'l'e   **fat** *si*? (Pavese)
          s.cl.'it'have done neg or s.cl'it'have done so
          'Have you done it or not?'

       b. *T'l'e *no* **fat** o t'l'e **fat** *si*?

This supports my proposal that the participle raises past the elements that bear focal stress. It must raise past the element *si*, which is used only for emphatic affirmation; the other option is ungrammatical:

(130) *T'l'e *si* **fat**? (Pavese)

I take these data to suggest that *no* has the option of being used with or without stress, hence it can usually be either preceded or followed by the past participle (recall, though, that my informants prefer it when it is preceded by the past participle). On the other hand *si*, which expresses emphatic affirmation but cannot be used for non-emphatic affirmation, does not have this option, and thus can only be preceded by the past participle. When the two co-occur, they must both be preceded by the past participle, given that they both bear contrastive stress.[36]

Let us now briefly turn our attention to the distribution of infinitival verbs with respect to the negative elements we have examined. As for the presuppositional negative marker of Piedmontese, *pa*, or for Italian *mica*, for Pavese *mia* as well co-occurrence with infinitival forms is impossible. The non-presuppositional negative marker *no*, which can negate infinitival forms of the verb, always follows them. This is illustrated in (131) and (132):

(131) a. Che stupid ch'a   sum stat a **gni**   *no*. (Pavese)
          what fool   that's.cl am been to to-come neg
          'What a fool I was not to come.'

       b. *Che stupid ch'a sum stat a *no* **gni**.

(132) a. Luigi al sa   stopa i   ureg par **senti** *no*.
          Luigi s.cl self closes the ears for to-hear neg
          'Luigi covers his ears so as not to hear.'

       b. *Luigi al sa stopa i ureg par *no* **senti**.

In the presence of an infinitival auxiliary followed by a past participle, the auxiliary must precede *no*, whereas the past participle exhibits the alternation we have been discussing in this section: it can either precede or follow *no*, with the expected effect on its discourse status:

(133) a. M'e dispiasu da **ves** *no* **gni**. (Pavese)
          me'is displeased of to-be neg come
          'I was sorry not to have come.'

       b. M'e dispiasu da **ves gni**   *no*.
          me'is displeased of to-b e come neg
          'I was sorry not to have come.'

This suggests that infinitival forms obligatorily raise to a position higher than *no*. Once again, this confirms that infinitival verbs raise higher than past participles.

For the sake of completeness, at the end of our discussion on the structural position of lower adverbs and post-verbal negative markers, I should mention one more position where they can occur, which I have so far left out of this discussion. When lower adverbs are coordinated, modified, or heavily stressed, they can occur in a position to the right of the VP-complements, as shown in the following examples:

(134)   a. Vori pü   andà a Ruma, *propi pü.*   (Pavese)
           want no more to-go to Rome, indeed no more
           'I don't want to go to Rome anymore, absolutely no more.'

        b. Ho parlà cui   fiò *sempar e   vulentera.*
           have talked with-the kids always and happily
           'I have always been happy to talk to the kids.'

This position can be seen in other Romance varieties as well, as described in Cinque (1994, 1996a) (see also Cardinaletti and Starke in press: §8). Though I have not documented it for each of the varieties we examined, I expect to find that it is available in all of them.

What is most relevant for this discussion is that certain Romance varieties exhibit negative markers in the position just described. For example, the post-verbal negative markers of the dialects of Cembra and Lisignago, spoken in the Trentino region in northern Italy, differ from the ones so far described because they follow not only the finite verb and the past participle but also the VP arguments. The following examples are from Zörner (1989):

(135)   a. No kredo ke pödia parlar kon elo *no.* (Cembra)
           neg believe that could to-talk with him neg
           'I don't think that I could talk to him.'

        b. No lagarlo   davert *no*! (Lisignago)
           neg to-leave-it open   neg
           'Don't leave it open!'

        c. No gaj neanka pü   en par de kalse *no.* (Lisignago)
           neg have even no more a pair of socks neg
           'I don't even have a pair of socks anymore.'

These data are reminiscent of the data from some varieties of Brazilian Portuguese spoken in the northeastern part of Brazil (for example in the state of Bahía).[37] The negative marker *não* can occur both in pre-verbal and in sentence-final position, giving rise to sentences that are judged to be somewhat emphatic. Some examples are given here:

(136)   a. *Não* sei   *não*. (Brazilian Portuguese)
           neg know neg
           'I don't know.'

        b. *Não* te   dou o livro *não.*
           neg to-you give the book neg
           'I don't give you the book.'

c. Eu *não* posso dormir quando tem barulho *não*.
I   neg can   to-sleep when is   noise   neg
'I can't sleep when there is noise.'

In the northeastern varieties, the post-verbal negative marker *não* can also occur without the pre-verbal one, as shown in the examples here:

(137)   a. Sei   *não*. (Brazilian Portuguese from the northeast)
know neg
'I don't know.'

b. Te   dou o   livro *não*.
to-you give the book neg
'I won't give you the book.'

c. Eu posso dormir quando tem barulho *não*.
I can   to-sleep when is   noise   neg
'I can't sleep when there is noise.'

Diachronically, this distribution is also exhibited by the post-verbal negative marker found in Milanese of the 17th century, as documented in Vai (1995a, 1996):

(138)   No faró   da corú *nò*! (Milanese from the 17th century)
neg will-do like him neg
'I won't do like him.'

Although I mentioned these data for completeness, in this work I will not attempt to provide an analysis of these negative markers but leave their examination for future research.

3.5.   Summary and conclusion

We can now return to the questions outlined in the introduction to this chapter and see how to answer them.

The first question was the following: Do all post-verbal negative markers occur in the same syntactic position? The answer is clearly negative: in the Romance varieties we examined we must distinguish at least three different structural positions in which negative markers occur, in the syntactic space delimited on the left by the past participle in a language like Italian and on the right by the VP-complements.[38] They are the following:

1. A position higher than the adverb 'already', where we find the presuppositional negative markers (Piedmontese *pa*, Valdotain presuppositional *pa*, Milanese *minga*, and Pavese *mia*).
2. A position between 'already' and 'no more', where we find Valdotain non-presuppositional *pa* and Piedmontese non-presuppositional *nen*.
3. A position lower than 'always', where we find Milanese *no* and Pavese *no*, both non-presuppositional.

To better illustrate these positions, let us adopt the clausal structure proposed in Cinque (1994, 1995a, 1996a), in which each adverb is in the specifier of a functional projection with which it shares semantic features (see discussion in section 3.2). The lower adverbs we are concerned with are analyzed as follows: 'already' is taken to be in the specifier of a projection TP-2 (corresponding to Giorgi and Pianesi's 1991 T-2); 'no more' in the specifier of an aspectual phrase that expresses perfectivity; 'always' in the specifier of an aspectual phrase whose values can be generic or progressive aspect. I represent the negative markers examined in this chapter as occurring in the specifier of a projection labeled NegP. Reserving the label NegP-1 for the projection headed by the pre-verbal negative markers that by itself can negate a clause (see chapter 2), I label the other projections hosting post-verbal negative markers NegP-2, NegP-3, and NegP-4, increasing the number as I move lower in the structure. The relative order of post-verbal negative marker and lower adverbs can be represented as follows:

(139)

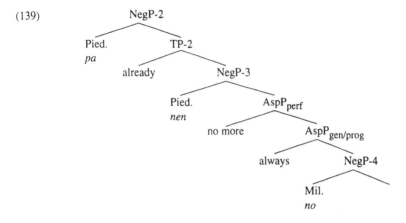

I therefore conclude that not only is it impossible to talk about one structural position for negative markers in Romance, but also it is not correct to talk about two structural positions only, one preceding and one following Infl (cf. Zanuttini 1991). Rather, the negative markers that follow the finite verb can occur in a range of structural positions, the choice among which is determined within a single language.

The second question I asked at the beginning of the chapter was the following: Do all post-verbal negative markers make the same contribution to the interpretation of a clause? If some difference indeed exists, is it a consequence of the lexical meaning of the item involved or of the structural position in which it occurs? In this chapter we have seen that we must distinguish two kinds of post-verbal negative markers, on the basis of their contribution to the interpretation of the clause:

1. Presuppositional negative markers, which negate a proposition that is assumed in the discourse
2. Non-presuppositional negative markers, which negate a proposition that does not have a special discourse status

We have seen that, when a language has two morphologically distinct negative markers, one is specialized as the presuppositional and the other as the non-presuppositional negative marker. For example, in Piedmontese, *pa* and *nen* differ along these lines. The presuppositional negative markers always occur in a structural position higher than the adverb 'already', but the non-presuppositional negative markers occur in structural positions lower than 'already'. Thus, in a language like Piedmontese, the presuppositional negative marker differs from the non-presuppositional one in both its morphological form and its structural position. There are languages, though, where the position in the structure is the only factor that distinguishes a presuppositional from a non-presuppositional negative marker. I argued that Valdotain is one such case: the negative marker *pa* can have one or the other reading, depending solely on its structural position. French might be another case of this type.

Further evidence that the structural position of the negative marker plays a role in determining its interpretation comes from the following observation. In some languages, the element that is typically used as a presuppositional negative marker can occur (perhaps with some degree of marginality) in a structural position lower than 'already' and, conversely, the element that is typically used as a non-presuppositional negative marker can occur in a position higher than 'already'. When this happens, the negative markers no longer have the reading that is typically associated with them, but they acquire the one determined by their structural position. That is, the presuppositional negative marker will contribute a non-presuppositional reading and, conversely, the non-presuppositional one will contribute a presuppositional reading. In the varieties examined in this chapter, this was seen most clearly in the case of Milanese, where *minga* can be used as a non-presuppositional negative marker and *no* can be used as a presuppositional negative marker, given the appropriate structural position.

Let us now turn to the last question asked at the beginning of the chapter: How can we encode in our grammatical description the differences exhibited by the Romance languages in the expression of sentential negation? The position where a negative marker can occur is fixed within each language, though cross-linguistically we have seen that negative markers can occupy different structural positions. Let me summarize the overall picture of where negative markers can occur in the varieties I examined, including pre-verbal negative markers that can negate a clause alone, analyzed in the previous chapter as heading NegP, here re-labeled NegP-1.

Of the four positions for negative elements discussed so far, NegP-1 stands out from all the others. As already discussed in the introductory chapter to this book, whether or not a language negates a clause with one of the elements we have described as the head of NegP-1 has wider repercussions throughout its grammar. In particular, it determines what constraints govern the distribution of negative indefinites and, as will be discussed in the next chapter, whether or not the language can have a negated "true imperative" form.

NegP-2 is the position for negative markers with a presuppositional reading — negative markers that negate a proposition assumed in the discourse. On the basis of the data examined in this chapter, those from Valdotain in particular, I concluded that it is crucial for this type of negative marker to occur above TP-2, the projection that hosts in its specifier adverbs corresponding to English 'already'. Note that these adverbs also have a presuppositional reading: 'already' presupposes the event and asserts that it has taken place before a certain moment in time. It is tempting to think that it is not a coincidence that both presuppositional negative markers and these

(140) **NegP-1**

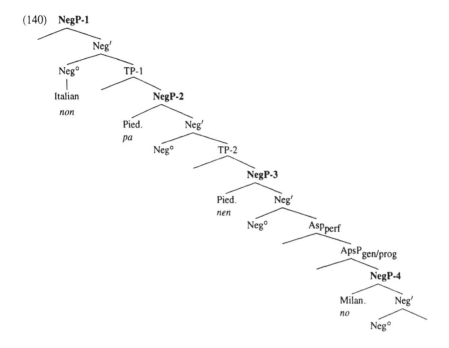

adverbs occur in the same portion of clausal structure. Though beyond the scope of this work, it would be interesting to examine these data in light of Diesing's (1992) proposals concerning the interpretation of indefinite noun phrases, where their height in the clause determines possible interpretations.

NegP-3 and NegP-4 are harder to characterize, as they do not appear to differ in their contribution to the interpretation of the clause, and the effect that they have on the grammar of the language in which they occur is less obvious than in the case of NegP-1. Based on the data collected for this work, two properties distinguish them.

The first is their ability to co-occur with other negative elements in the clause. As we saw, Piedmontese *nen*, in NegP-3, can co-occur with negative indefinites in post-verbal position in certain contexts; in contrast, this option is not available for Milanese or Pavese *no*, in NegP-4. Though I have not provided a full analysis of the case of Piedmontese, I have suggested that these data should be related to the position to which negative indefinites move. I can then speculate that such co-occurrence is never an option in languages where the negative marker occurs in NegP-4 because this position, structurally lower than NegP-3, always interferes with raising negative indefinites. Further empirical work is needed to prove this prediction.

The second property that distinguishes negative markers in NegP-3 from those in NegP-4 concerns whether or not they can take scope over an adverb like 'always', which occurs in the specifier of the projection I have labeled AspP$_{gen/prog}$.[39] Piedmontese *nen*, in NegP-3, can co-occur with *sempre* 'always' (cf. (32)) and take scope over it. This is not surprising, given that, as indicated in the structure in (140), *nen* in NegP-3 c-commands *sempre* in AspP$_{gen/prog}$. Milanese *no* and Pavese *no*, in NegP-4, behave alike in their ability to take scope over the adverb corresponding to 'always'. In both cases, the negative marker *no* can take scope over the counterpart of 'always' only if it moves to a position that c-commands it, a process tha is accompanied by a pragmatic effect similar to focalization. For convenience, I repeat here examples (101)b and (115) from Milanese and Pavese, respectively:

(141)   a. L'a   *no semper* di   tüscos.   (Milanese)
           s.cl'has neg always said everything
           'He hasn't always said everything.'

        b. ??L'ha *no sempar* vinciu cla gara chi. (Pavese)
           s.cl'has neg always won   this race here
           'He hasn't always won this race.'

When they do not c-command 'always', they cannot take scope over it but only have narrow scope. In this case, the negative marker must occur on the right of the past participle. While this requirement is not visible in Milanese, where this is the only possible position for the past participle, it becomes apparent in Pavese, where the participle has the option of either preceding or following the negative marker. I repeat the relevant data here:

(142)   a. A   i   ha *sempar* **pagà** *no.* (Pavese)
           s.cl. them has always paid neg
           'It's always been the case that he hasn't paid them.'

        b. *A   i   ha *sempar no* **pagà.**
           s.cl. them has always neg paid

In section 3.4.2, I suggested that the following generalization holds: a negative marker in NegP-4 can co-occur with a scope-bearing element it does not c-command only if it bears focal stress. In Pavese, it is possible for the past participle to raise to the left of the negative marker and leave it as the last element of a phonological phrase, where it can receive focal stress. This option must be taken for *no* to co-occur with *sempar* 'always', when it does not c-command it. Milanese *no* normally bears stress, as pointed in Beretta (1980), so it always satisfies this requirement.

If the situation observed in Milanese and Pavese is indicative of the behavior of (non-presuppositional) post-verbal negative markers, then we might try to relate the choice between a position in NegP-4 and in NegP-3 for a negative marker to the availability of a strategy for marking the negative marker as receiving focal stress (for example, movement of the past participle to the left of the negative marker). If this is true, then we predict that negative markers can occur in NegP-4 only if the language can mark them as bearing focal stress; otherwise, they will occur in a higher structural position. We also predict that, if a language looses the ability to mark the negative marker as bearing focal stress over time, the negative marker will change its position from NegP-4 to NegP-3. The negative marker might even move to a higher structural position, such as NegP-2, in particular if the language does not have another negative element that can take scope over scope bearing elements higher than NegP-3. Along this line of reasoning, it is possible that in Piedmontese *nen* occurs in NegP-3, and no higher, because of the existence of *pa*, which is structurally higher and can take scope over 'already', a scope-bearing element that *nen* fails to c-command.[40] In contrast in

Valdotain, which differs from Piemontese in that *pas* is the only negative element that can negate the clause, the negative marker occurs both in NegP-3 and in NegP-2.[41]

Besides providing an answer for the questions outlined in the introduction, which concern mainly negative clauses, in this chapter I have also shed light on certain properties of verb movement. We have seen that the relative order among the lower adverbs, as well as between the lower adverbs and the post-verbal negative markers, is not altered by the different positions of the past participle or the infinitival verb. On the contrary, as argued in Cinque's work, the order is rigidly fixed and is the same across the Romance languages; what varies is the position of the verb. The position of the past participle can vary both cross-linguistically and within a single language. To exemplify the cross-linguistic differences, in the following table I have indicated the highest and the lowest of the structural positions in which the past participle can occur in the languages discussed in this chapter.[42]

(143)

Italian:	PP	*mica*		*già*		*più*		*sempre*	PP		
Pavese:	PP	*mia*		*giamò*		*pü*		*sempar*		*no*	PP
Milanese:		*minga*	PP	*gemò*		*pü*		*semper*	PP	*no*	
Piedmontese:		*pa*		*gia*	*nen*	*pi nen*	PP	*sempre*	PP		
Valdotain:		*pa*		*dza*	*pa*	*pa mai*		*toujou*	PP		
French:		*pas*		*déjà*	(*pas?*)	*plus*		*toujours*	PP		
		neg		already	neg	no more		always		neg	

PP = past participle

In the discussion of the data from Pavese I have suggested that movement of the past participle can in some cases be motivated by discourse factors: by raising past an adverb or a negative marker the past participle leaves them as the last element in the phonological phrase. Consequently, they can bear focal stress. This cannot be the only motivation behind movement of this verbal form; further investigation is required to obtain a clearer picture of what motivates movement of non-finite verbs and of past participles in particular.

Moreover, I found that infinitival verbs can generally move higher than past participles, and, within the class of infinitival verbs, auxiliaries can move more than main verbs (thus confirming Pollock's observation for French and English). In Piedmontese, for example, although the past participle can only move to the left of *sempre* 'always' but not to the left of *pi nen* 'no more', the infinitival form of a lexical verb can raise to the left of *pi nen*, though with a slight degree of marginality.

If the word order variations I described were viewed as a consequence of the fact that adverb classes can adjoin to more than one position, we would have to express the fact that the word order is sensitive to the type of verb in the clause. Hence we would have to say that the adverb class of *pi nen* 'no more' in Piedmontese can adjoin only to the right of a past participle, but it can adjoin either to the right or to the left of an infinitival form. Similarly, the adverb class of *mia* in Milanese can adjoin only to the left of a past participle but either to the right or to the left of an infinitival verb. Moreover, we would need to say that, within the class of infinitival verbs, lower adverbs are sensitive to whether the verbal form is an auxiliary or a lexical verb: certain adverbs can adjoin to the right of infinitival auxiliaries but not of infinitival lexical verbs. Finally, for all the lower adverbs we would have to say that they can

4

Negative Imperatives

4.1. A puzzling asymmetry

In this chapter I examine the behavior of both pre-verbal and post-verbal negative markers in co-occurrence with imperative verbs. With a few exceptions, the pre-verbal negative markers that can negate a clause by themselves are incompatible with lexical verbs in the imperative form, although they are compatible with auxiliary verbs in the imperative form and with verbal forms from other verbal paradigms (indicative, subjunctive, etc.) used as imperatives. Post-verbal negative markers, however, do not show any systematic incompatibility with imperative forms. First I examine the rather complex pattern of data, and then I explore what could be the cause of such an asymmetry in their syntactic behavior.

4.2. Negative markers in imperative clauses

Two types of imperatives are found in Romance languages, depending on the morphological properties of the verb employed: (a) verbal forms that are unique to the paradigm of the imperative, in the sense that they are different from any other verbal form used for the same person in any other verbal paradigm; and (b) verbal forms that are used in the imperative but are morphologically identical to a form used for the same person in another paradigm. Following Joseph and Philippaki-Warburton (1987) and Rivero (1994a, 1994b), I refer to the former as "true" imperatives and to the latter as "surrogate" or "suppletive" imperatives.[1] The case of Italian is illustrated first, then I bring in data from other Romance languages.[2]

Among the imperative forms of the first conjugation class in Italian (verbs ending in -*are*), only the second person singular of the informal (or familiar) imperative is morphologically unique to the imperative paradigm, hence it is a true imperative (cf. (1)a). The form employed for the second person plural is formally indistinguishable from the corresponding form of the indicative, hence it is a suppletive imperative (cf. (1)b):[3]

(1) a. Telefona! (true imperative) (Italian)
         call   (imperative form; 2nd sg)
         'Call!'
     b. Telefonate! (suppletive imperative)
         call   (indicative form; 2nd pl)
         'Call!'

Imperative sentences can also employ a verb in the first person plural. As with the second person plural, in this case as well the verbal form is morphologically indistinguishable from the indicative, as shown in (2):

(2) Telefoniamo*le* subito!   (suppletive imperative) (Italian)
     call-her   immediatel y (indicative)
     'Let's call her right away!'

Besides a difference in intonation, the only other difference between the use of this verbal form in the imperative and in the indicative is the position of the verb with respect to pronominal clitics: while in clauses that do not have imperative force the verb follows the pronominal clitics, in imperative clauses it precedes them. This contrast in the position of the verb with respect to the pronominal clitics can also be observed with suppletive imperatives for the second person plural in Italian. While the verb follows the clitic in non-imperative clauses, it precedes it in imperative clauses, even though the verbal form is identical:

(3) a. *Le* telefonate tutti i   giorni? (interrogative) (Italian)
         her call   all   the days
         'Do you call her every day?'
     b. So che *le* telefonate tutti i   giorni. (declarative)
         know that her   call all the   days
         'I know that you call her every day.'
     c. Telefonate*le* tutti i   giorni! (imperative)
         call-her   all   the days
         'Call her every day!'

Italian also exhibits second singular and second plural formal (or polite) imperatives, which employ verbal forms of the present subjunctive: third person singular and third person plural respectively, as illustrated by these examples ((4)b is from Salvi and Borgato 1995):

(4) a. *Lo* dica pure! (Italian)
         it say indeed (3rd sg subjunctive)
         'Go ahead and say it!' *or* 'Feel free to say it!'

b. Corrano a casa, signori!
run   to home, gentlemen (3rd pl subjunctive)
'Rush home, gentlemen.'

These examples pattern like declarative clauses in the word order between verb and clitic: *clitic–verb*.[4]

Similar cases are reported in Rohlfs (1968: 355) from dialects spoken in southern Calabria and northeastern Sicily. In these varieties, the polite form of the second person singular imperative is expressed by means of an inflected form of the verb preceded by *mu* (or *mi* or *ma*, depending on the geographical region), a particle that the author relates to the particle *na* of the Greek substratum:[5]

(5) a. *Mu* scrivi.   (southern Calabrese)
PRT write (3rd sg)
'Write.' (2nd sg, polite form)

b. *Ma* torna subbitu.   (Catanzarese)
PRT return immediately (3rd sg)
'Come back right away.' (2nd sg, polite form)

c. *Mi* s'assètta. (eastern Sicilian)
PRT self-sits   (3rd sg)
'Sit down.' (2nd sg, polite form)

As in Italian (and in English), this construction can also be used in the presence of an overt third person subject, as shown in the following examples:

(6) a. Lu focu *mu* ti   mangia. (southern Calabrese)
the fire PRT you eats
'May the fire eat you.'

b. Num *mi*   curri nuddu. (southern Calabrese)
neg PRT run nobody
'Nobody run!'

c. *Mi*   nun nèsci. (eastern Sicilian)
PRT neg leave
'Don't go out.' (polite form)

I view these examples as parallel to the Italian cases that employ a form of the subjunctive for imperatives with third person subjects. Following Rohlfs, I suggest that the particle *mu* be analyzed as the counterpart of modern Greek *na*, which I take to be a subjunctive marker (cf. Terzi 1992, Dobrovie-Sorin 1993, and Rivero 1994a, among others).[6]

Like Italian, Catalan has true imperatives only in the second person singular of the familiar imperative, while the second person plural uses a form borrowed from the paradigm of the indicative:

(7) a. Parla! (true imperative) (Catalan)
talk   (imperative form; 2nd sg)
'Talk!'

    b. Parleu! (suppletive imperative)
       talk   (indicative form; 2nd pl)
       'Talk!'

Spanish, on the other hand, has true imperative forms in both the second person singular and the second person plural of the familiar imperative:

(8)   a. Habla! (true imperative) (Spanish)
       talk   (imperative form; 2nd sg)
       'Talk!'
     b. Hablad! (true imperative)
       talk   (imperative form; 2nd pl)
       'Talk!'

The distinction between imperative forms that are morphologically unique to this paradigm and forms that are used in sentences with imperative force but are borrowed from other verbal paradigms constitutes the basis for the description of the behavior of negative imperatives. The pattern I want to explain is the following: while some negative markers occur with all verbal forms employed in imperative clauses, others cannot occur when the verbal form employed is a true imperative. The post-verbal negative markers of Romance can negate both true and suppletive imperatives.[7] In contrast, the pre-verbal negative markers — Italian *non*, Spanish and Catalan *no* — are incompatible with true imperatives.

The Italian negative marker *non*, for example, cannot occur with a true imperative, as illustrated in the following example:

(9)   *Non telefona! (true imperative) (Italian)
     neg   call
     'Don't call!' (2nd sg)

In contrast, the occurrence of *non* with suppletive imperatives is perfectly acceptable:

(10) a. *Non* telefonate! (suppletive imperative) (Italian)
       neg call   (indicative form; 2nd pl)
       'Don't call!'
     b. *Non* telefoniamole subito!   (suppletive imperative)
       neg call-her   immediately (indicative form; 1st pl)
       'Let's not call her immediately!'

The negative counterpart of the second person singular imperative in Italian is expressed by negating an infinitive, as exemplified in (11):

(11) a. *Non* telefonarle! (suppletive imperative) (Italian)
       neg to-call-her (infinitival form)
       'Don't call her!' (2nd sg)

An analogous pattern is found in Catalan, as illustrated in (12) to (14). The form that is morphologically unique to the imperative cannot be negated by *no*:

(12)   a. Parla! (true imperative) (Catalan)
         'Talk!' (2nd sg)

       b. Parleu! (suppletive imperative)
          talk   (indicative form; 2nd pl)
          'Talk!' (2nd pl)

(13)   a. *No parla! (true imperative)
          neg talk
          'Don't talk!' (2nd sg)

       b. No parleu! (suppletive imperative)
          neg talk   (indicative form; 2nd pl)
          'Don't talk!' (2nd pl)

The negative counterpart of the second person singular imperative is expressed not by negating an infinitive, as in Italian, but by employing the second person singular form from the subjunctive paradigm:[8]

(14)   a. No parlis! (suppletive imperative) (Catalan)
          neg talk   (subjunctive form; 2nd sg)
          'Don't talk!' (2nd sg)

On the basis of the data examined so far, one could infer that the second person singular of the imperative is simply incompatible with negation, while the second plural is not. Data from Spanish provide evidence that the relevant factor is not singular versus plural, but true versus suppletive imperative. Contrary to Italian and Catalan, Spanish has true imperative forms for both the second person singular and the second person plural of the familiar imperative. Interestingly, in this language the presence of the negative marker *no* is incompatible with both forms:

(15)   a. Habla! (true imperative) (Spanish)
          talk   (2nd sg)
          'Talk!'

       b. Hablad! (true imperative)
          talk   (2nd plural)
          'Talk!'

(16)   a. *No   habla! (true imperative)
          neg talk (2nd sg)
          'Don't talk!'

       b. *No hablad! (true imperative)
          neg talk   (2nd pl)
          'Don't talk!'

The negative imperative for both the second person singular and the second person plural is expressed by means of verbal forms borrowed from the subjunctive:

(17)   a. No hables! (suppletive imperative) (Spanish)
          neg talk   (subjunctive form; 2nd sg)
          'Don't talk!' (2nd sg)

b. *No* habléis! (suppletive imperative)
   neg talk   (subjunctive form; 2nd pl)
   'Don't talk!' (2nd pl)

Let us note one visible difference between the verbal forms in true and in suppletive imperatives. While the verbal forms of true imperatives consist of the verbal root and the thematic vowel, or theme vowel (setting Spanish aside for the moment), those of suppletive imperatives consist of the verbal root, the thematic vowel and some other suffix.[9] For example, the Italian verbs in (10) show an overt agreement morpheme (-*te* and -*iamo*, respectively) and arguably an abstract tense morpheme as well, if indicative forms are taken to have one. The Italian verb in (11) exhibit the morphology of infinitival verbs (-*re*).[10] The Spanish data are interesting in this respect because they make it clear that one cannot say the peculiarity of true imperatives is that they consist merely of the verbal stem and the thematic vowel (as might be concluded from the observation of true imperatives in Italian and Catalan). While this is true for the second person singular in Spanish, the second person plural of the true imperative shows the morpheme -*d* (presumably an agreement morpheme) in addition to the thematic vowel -*a*-. This suggests that, if the difference between true and suppletive imperatives has to do with their different morphology, it is not to be related to the presence or absence of an agreement morpheme.[11]

A paradigm analogous to that of Spanish is also found in Sardinian (cf. Jones 1988: 333, 1993: 27). The true imperative forms, unique to the paradigm of the familiar imperative, are replaced by forms of the subjunctive in the presence of the pre-verbal negative marker (examples from Jones 1988):

(18)   a. Kánta! (true imperative) (Sardinian)
           sing   (2nd sg)
           'Sing!'

        b. Kantáte! (true imperative)
           sing   (2nd plural)
           'Sing!'

(19)   a. Non kántes! (suppletive imperative)
           neg sing   (subjunctive form; 2nd sg)
           'Don't talk!' (2nd sg)

        b. Non kantétas! (suppletive imperative)
           neg sing   (subjunctive form; 2nd pl)
           'Don't sing!' (2nd pl)

As in Spanish, in Sardinian, the true imperative for the second person plural consists of the verbal stem, the thematic vowel, and an agreement morpheme (-*te*); yet, the presence of this morpheme is not sufficient to license the presence of the negative marker *no*. Notice that the suffix on the second person plural imperative in Sardinian is identical to the one on the suppletive imperative in Italian: in both cases, it is the agreement marker -*te*. This confirms what was observed for Spanish — namely, that the presence or absence of the agreement morpheme does not seem to play a role in distinguishing suppletive from true imperatives, and consequently in providing an interpretation of the restrictions exhibited by the pre-verbal negative markers.

The incompatibility of the pre-verbal negative markers with true imperatives is in sharp contrast with the behavior of post-verbal negative markers. With the exception of modern central Occitan, all other post-verbal negative markers can negate true imperatives. Piedmontese, for example, is a language with a true imperative form for the second person singular; yet, the post-verbal negative marker *nen* can co-occur with this verbal form. As shown in the following examples, the true imperative form *parla* in (20)a can be negated by the negative marker *nen*, as in (20)b, with no need to employ a suppletive form:

(20)   a. Parla! (true imperative) (Piedmontese)
          talk   (2nd sg)
          'Talk!' (2nd sg)

       b. Parla *nen*!   (true imperative)
          talk   neg (2nd sg)
          'Don't talk!' (2nd sg)

Similarly, in Valdotain and in Milanese, the form for the second singular is unique to the paradigm of the imperative, and yet the presence of the negative marker does not generate ungrammaticality, as illustrated in (21) from Chenal (1986), and in (22) from Nicoli (1983) and Vai (1995a):

(21)   a. Gèina-tè   *pa.* (true imperative) (Valdotain)
          bother-you neg (2nd sg)
          'Don't worry.' (2nd sg)

       b. Feé-mè   *pa* rire.   (true imperative)
          make-me neg to-laugh (2nd sg)
          'Don't make me laugh.' (2nd sg)

(22)   a. Guarda *minga* i   tosànn! (true imperative) (Milanese)
          look   neg   the girls   (2nd sg)
          'Don't look at the girls!' (2nd sg)

       b. Vén   *minga* sénza   danee! (true imperative)
          come neg   without money (2nd sg)
          'Don't come without money!' (2nd sg)

       c. Vuza *no*! (true imperative)
          shout neg (2nd sg)
          'Don't shout!'

These data show that a true imperative is not inherently incompatible with a negative marker; incompatibility seems to exist only between true imperatives and *a particular type* of negative marker. It is tempting to think that the relevant factor is the type of negative marker employed in the clause. The relevant generalization seems to be the following:

(23)   Generalization on negative imperatives (preliminary version):
       In Romance, pre-verbal negative markers do not co-occur with true imperatives; post-verbal negative markers do.

Standard French and Walloon might appear to be a counterexample to (23), given examples like those in (24) (example (24)b is from Remacle 1952, II: 256):

(24) a. *Ne* mange pas! (French)
         neg eat   neg
         'Don't eat!' (2nd sg)
      b. *Nu* l'houke nin! (Walloon)
         neg him-call neg
         'Don't call him!' (2nd sg)

These examples show that, in these languages, the pre-verbal negative marker can occur with imperative forms that are not morphologically identical to the corresponding form in the present indicative or subjunctive (such forms would be *manges* for French and *houkes* for Walloon). Two observations are in order, though. First, the pre-verbal negative markers of French and Walloon differ from those of Italian and Spanish, both in not being able to negate a clause by themselves and in their distribution in contexts that involve subject clitic inversion, as was discussed at length in chapter 2. Second, while it is true that the indicative form for the second person singular has an -*s* ending whereas the imperative form does not, it is important to notice that the -*s* is silent. Hence, the difference between the indicative and the imperative form might be simply an orthographic one, as suggested in Kayne (1992).[12]

Even though I do not think that French and Walloon are counterexamples for my generalization, in light of these data I will revise the generalization in (23) by specifying that the negative markers that systematically exhibit incompatibility with true imperatives are those that can negate a clause by themselves:

(25) Generalization on negative imperatives (preliminary version):

      In Romance, pre-verbal negative markers that can negate a clause by themselves do not co-occur with true imperatives; post-verbal negative markers do.

I will not discuss the case of French and Walloon any further in this chapter.

One language does exhibit a post-verbal negative marker that appears to be incompatible with true imperatives: modern central Occitan, already mentioned in note 7. In this Romance variety, the negative marker *pas* follows the finite verb, like the negative markers of Piedmontese, Milanese, and Valdotain and contrary to the negative markers of Italian, Catalan, and Spanish. Yet the negative imperative in this variety employs a form of the subjunctive:

(26) a. Canta! (true imperative) (modern central Occitan)
         'Sing!' (2nd sg)
      b. Cantes *pas*! (suppletive imperative)
         sing   neg (subjunctive; 2nd sg)
         'Don't sing!' (2nd sg)

Ronjat (1980) describes the negative imperative as normally using the subjunctive (the following examples are from Ronjat 1980: 608). Interestingly, as shown in examples (27)b, (27)c, and (27)d, the subjunctive is used even when the negative marker *pas* is not present, and a different negative constituent (an argument, an adverb, or an adjunct) contributes an instance of negation to the clause:

(27) a. Vous trompés *pas*! (suppletive imperative) (modern central Occitan)
          you err   neg (subjunctive; 2nd pl)
          'Don't make mistakes!' (2nd pl)

      b. Touqués *rèn*!   (suppletive imperative)
          touch   nothing (subjunctive; 2nd pl)
          'Don't touch anything!' (2nd pl)

      c. Cantes *plus*!   (suppletive imperative)
          sing   no-more (subjunctive; 2nd sg)
          'Don't sing anymore!' (2nd sg)

      d. Anes *en-liò*! (suppletive imperative)
          go   no-place (subjunctive; 2nd sg)
          'Don't go anywhere!' (2nd sg)

These data differ from those of Italian, where the restriction on the use of a true imperative is limited to its co-occurrence with the pre-verbal negative marker and does not extend to other negative constituents, as witnessed by the grammaticality of the examples in (28). I have used capital letters to indicate that the preposed constituent is stressed:[13]

(28) a. *NIENTE* digli!   (Italian)
          nothing tell-him
          'Tell him NOTHING!'

      b. A *NESSUNO* fallo   vedere!
          to no-one   make-it to-see
          'Show it to NO ONE!'

      c. Esci senza   *niente*!
          leave without nothing
          'Go out empty handed!'

This difference between modern central Occitan and Italian suggests that the use of the subjunctive in Occitan might be due to factors other than the presence of a particular type of negative marker. Ronjat's description points out that, in the area of Nice, the infinitive is used in negative imperatives, along with the subjunctive, which is employed especially in the second person singular. Moreover, in the Perigord area, in addition to the subjunctive, forms of the true imperative are found in co-occurrence with the post-verbal negative marker *pas*, for example:

(29) Vous geinàs *pas*. (true imperative) (Occitan du Perigord)
      you worry neg
      'Don't worry!' (2nd pl)

This example, which conforms to the pattern of other post-verbal negative markers, further suggests that the use of the subjunctive in negative imperatives in this language might stem from a reason other than the impossibility of the negative marker and a true imperative verb to co-occur.

My goal in the rest of this chapter is to shed light on the distributional pattern expressed by the generalization in (25) and to identify the relevant properties that distinguish pre-verbal negative markers that can negate a clause by themselves from other negative markers in their distribution with respect to imperative forms.

In the rest of the chapter, first I take a closer look at true imperatives (section 4.3) and then at suppletive imperatives (section 4.4), with the goal of understanding how they differ in their morphological makeup. Then I propose a way of analyzing the observed incompatibility between negative markers that can negate a clause by themselves and true imperatives, building in part on the different morphological makeup of true and suppletive imperatives.

4.3. True imperatives

Let us examine in some detail some of the properties of true imperatives in Italian. The goal is to characterize what distinguishes true imperatives from other verbal forms, in particular from suppletive imperatives.

As already mentioned in section 4.2, Italian verbs of the first conjugation class are the ones that exhibit, in the second singular familiar imperative, a verbal form that is unique to the imperative and does not correspond to the second person singular in any other tense and mood. Imperative morphology in verbs of this class corresponds to the verbal root plus the vowel *-a*, the so-called thematic vowel or theme vowel (see Napoli and Vogel 1990). As we can see in the examples in (30), the thematic vowel is found immediately following the verbal stem in infinitives, past and present participles, gerunds, imperfect indicative, present indicative, and past subjunctive. The second singular familiar imperative is illustrated in (31). These examples are with the verb *parlare* 'to talk':

(30) a. Parl*a*re. (infinitive) (Italian)
       b. Parl*a*to. (past participle)
       c. Parl*a*nte. (present participle)
       d. Parl*a*ndo. (gerund)
       e. Parl*a*vo. (imperfect, 1st sg)
       f. Parl*a*te. (present indicative, 2nd pl)
       g. Parl*a*ssi. (simple past subjunctive, 2nd sg)

(31)   Parl*a*! (2nd sg familiar imperative)

The thematic vowel distinguishes the first conjugation class from the other verbal classes, whose thematic vowels are *e* and *i*, respectively. Following Napoli and Vogel (1990), I exemplify the second conjugation class with the verb *battere* 'to hit' and the third with the verb *partire* 'to leave':

(32) a. Batt*e*re. (infinitive) (Italian)
       b. Batt*u*to. (past participle)
       c. Batt*e*nte. (present participle)
       d. Batt*e*ndo. (gerund)
       e. Batt*e*vo. (imperfect, 1st sg)
       f. Batt*e*te. (present indicative, 2nd pl)
       g. Batt*e*ssi. (simple past subjunctive, 2nd sg)

(33) a. Part*i*re. (infinitive)
      b. Part*i*to. (past participle)
      c. Part*e*nte. (present participle)
      d. Part*e*ndo. (gerund)
      e. Part*i*vo. (imperfect, 1st sg)
      f. Part*i*te. (present indicative, 2nd pl)
      g. Part*i*ssi. (simple past subjunctive, 2nd sg)

As we can see in these examples, even regular verbs of the second and third class, such as the ones chosen, are less regular than verbs of the first conjugation class. The thematic vowel that appears on the past participle of the second conjugation class is *u*, instead of *e*; the thematic vowel that appears in the gerund of the third conjugation class is *e* instead of *i*.[14] As Napoli and Vogel (1990: §7.1) point out, verbs of the second class exhibit *i* instead of the expected *e* also when the verb undergoes derivation by the addition of a suffix, as shown in (34) with the verb *godere* 'to enjoy' and in (35) with the verb *fondere* 'to melt', both of the second class:

(34) a. God*i*bile. (Italian)
         'Enjoyable.' (adjective)

      b. God*i*mento.
         'Enjoyment' (noun)

(35) a. Fond*i*bile.
         'Meltable.' (adjective)

      b. Fond*i*tore.
         'The one who melts.' (noun)

The same phenomenon is observed in compounding as well: from the verb of the second class *tergere* 'to wipe',[15] we have the compound *tergicristallo* 'windshield wiper', with the thematic vowel *i* instead of *e*.[16]

In the second singular familiar imperative, verbs of the second conjugation class as well as verbs of the third exhibit the vowel *i* after the verbal stem:

(36) a. Batt*i*! (from *battere*, second class) (Italian)
         'Hit!'

      b. Part*i*! (from *partire*, third class)
         'Leave!'

Along with Napoli and Vogel, I argue that these imperative forms, just like the ones for the first conjugation class, correspond to the verbal stem plus the thematic vowel. I take the fact that the verbs of the second class exhibit an *i* instead of an *e* as simply another instance of the oscillation between the two vowels exhibited in this class. Moreover, I take the fact that these forms coincide with the second singular of the present indicative to be a mere coincidence (the second singular ending of the present indicative is -*i*, for all verb classes) and not an indication that the imperative uses a form of the indicative. Hence, I consider the second person singular familiar imperative of the second and third conjugation class to be true imperatives in the same sense in which the corresponding forms with verbs of the first class are — that is, forms consisting of the verbal stem plus the thematic vowel.

What is the function of the thematic vowel? It is not the morphological realization of person agreement, as we can see from the fact that the finite forms exhibit another morpheme for person agreement (e.g., *-o* in (30)e, *-te* in (30)f). It is not the form expressing tense or aspect, either, given the presence of tense and aspect morphemes in (30)e and in (30)f (tense marker: *-v-*, aspect marker: *-t-*, following Belletti 1990). I would like to make a proposal along the lines of Harris (1991) and suggest that the vowel is a word marker that is attached to the root by default. Harris's proposal concerns the morphology of nouns in Spanish: it suggests that, while the vowel *-a* is the morpheme that corresponds to feminine morphological gender, the vowel *-o* is simply a word marker that is attached by default to the root in order to allow syllabification according to the rules of the language. I will transpose this idea to the case of verbs and propose that the thematic vowel of verbs is also attached by default and does not correspond to tense, agreement, or aspect morphology. I will leave open the question of whether it is attached to satisfy syllabification requirements or for other reasons.[17]

The discussion up to this point has led me to the following conclusion: true imperatives in Romance differ from other verbal forms (including suppletive imperatives) in the amount of morphological specification they exhibit. True imperatives consist of the verbal root, followed by the thematic vowel and (in some cases) by an agreement morpheme; they never exhibit morphological marking for tense or aspect. Other verbal forms, on the contrary, including suppletive imperatives, can have (overt or abstract) morphological marking for tense and aspect. This is particularly clear in the cases where the suppletive imperative employs a form of the subjunctive or an infinitival verb.

Now we can ask whether and how the incompatibility of true imperatives and pre-verbal negative markers (and the compatibility of suppletive imperatives and pre-verbal negative markers) can be related to their different morphological markings. Could it stem from the presence of the thematic vowel, or from the fact that the verbal form is lacking some morphological specification? It cannot be the presence of the thematic vowel that rules out the co-occurrence of true imperatives and pre-verbal negative markers, since other verbal forms (from the indicative, subjunctive, infinitive, gerund) containing such a vowel can co-occur with the pre-verbal negative marker. It is not even some constraint on word length (e.g., a constraint requiring that a verb must have a certain number of segments following the root). We have already observed that in Spanish and in Sardinian the second person plural, a true imperative, has an agreement morpheme in addition to the root and the thematic vowel; yet these forms, like all true imperatives, are incompatible with the pre-verbal negative markers. Moreover, in Italian, certain verbs of the third conjugation class (ending in *-ire*) form the singular forms, as well as the third person plural form, by adding the morpheme *-sc-*, as shown in the following examples from the verb *finire* 'to end':

(37)   a. Fini*sc*o. (Italian)
          'I finish.'

       b. Fini*sc*i.
          'You (sg) finish.'

c. Fini*sce*.
'He finishes.'

This morpheme is present in the true imperative form as well, and yet these verbal forms are incompatible with the presence of *non*, like all true imperatives:[18]

(38) a. Fini*sc*ilo! (Italian)
       finish-it (2nd sg)
       'Finish it!'

     b. **Non* fini*sc*ilo!
        'Don't finish it!' (2nd sg)

Finally, as already mentioned (see the discussion of examples (1)b and (2)), the verbal form of the imperative might be formally identical to the one of the indicative (this is always the case with verbs of the second and third conjugation class). Yet, the indicative form can co-occur with the pre-verbal negative marker, whereas the true imperative form cannot.

If the incompatibility between true imperatives and pre-verbal negative markers is not a consequence of the presence of the thematic vowel or of the verbal form having an insufficient number of segments or syllables, a third possibility suggests itself. True imperatives lack any kind of marking for tense, aspect, or mood, whereas suppletive imperatives exhibit some; this difference could be what lies behind their different behavior with respect to pre-verbal negative markers. To explore this possibility, let us turn our attention to suppletive imperatives.

4.4.   Suppletive imperatives

Here I examine suppletive forms used in imperative clauses.[19] In the Romance languages under examination, I have found four different strategies for negating an imperative.

1. *One strategy employs a verbal form from the paradigm of the indicative.* As mentioned in section 4.2, Italian employs a form of the indicative for the second person plural imperative and forms the negative imperative for this person by negating the indicative. We have already seen examples in (1)b and (10)a, and I provide two more in (39):[20]

(39) a. Non fatelo! (Italian)
       neg do-it   (indicative form; 2nd pl)
       'Don't do it!'

     b. Non diteglielo!
        neg tell-him-it (indicative form; 2nd pl)
        'Don't tell him that!'

Other varieties also employ a form of the indicative in the second person plural and maintain the same verbal form in the negative imperatives in the presence of a pre-verbal negative marker. Among these are some varieties spoken in southern Italy, in the regions of Abruzzo, Lazio, Campania, Calabria, and Sicily:[21]

(40) a. Nən kaskétə. (Capestrano, Abruzzo)
      b. Nuŋ kadíte. (Ronciglione, Lazio)
      c. Noŋ gatéte. (Ausonia, Campania)
      d. Non kadíti. (Polistena, Calabria)
      e. Un kadíti. (Naro, Sicily)
         neg fall
         'Don't fall!' (2nd pl)

2. *A second strategy negates a verbal form from the subjunctive paradigm.*
Catalan, Spanish, and Sardinian form a negative imperative by negating a form of
the present subjunctive, as we saw above in section 4.2 and in (14), (17), and (19).
Rohlfs (1968) reports some examples of varieties spoken in Italy where the past
subjunctive is used instead of the present. Example (41)a is from the city of Bologna,
in the northern Italian region Emilia Romagna, while (41)b is from the central Italian
region Marche:

(41) a. N'ev   figurassi. (Bolognese)
         neg'you figure   (past subjunctive form, 2nd pl)
         'Don't imagine that!'

      b. 'N te   credisse. (Marche)
         neg s.cl believe   (past subjunctive form, 2nd sg)
         'Don't believe that!'

3. *A third strategy has the pre-verbal negative marker followed by the verb in
the infinitival form.* This is found in Italian for the second person singular, as well
as in Romanian and in many varieties of central and southern Italy. The following
examples are from Rohlfs (1968: 356) from the varieties spoken in Rome, Naples,
and Sicily, respectively:

(42) a. *Non* te   mòvere. (Romanesco)
         neg you(acc) to-move
         'Don't move!' (2nd sg)

      b. *Nun* də   mòvərə. (Neapoletan)
         neg you(acc) to-move
         'Don't move!' (2nd sg)

      c. *Un* ti   mòviri. (Sicilian)
         neg you(acc) to-move
         'Don't move!' (2nd sg)

Focusing on Italian, Kayne (1992) notes that two things are surprising about
employing an infinitive to express a negative imperative. First, infinitives are not
normally allowed in matrix contexts, but only in embedded contexts. Second, whereas
the order of the verb with respect to the clitics is usually $verb_{infn}–clitic(s)$, in the case
of an infinitive used as a negative imperative the order can also be $clitic(s)–verb_{infn}$.
How can these two distinguishing properties be accounted for? Kayne observes that
the infinitives characterized by these two properties only occur in the presence of
negation, and furthermore only in the presence of the negative marker *non* and not of
negation in some more general sense. That is, preposing a negative constituent such
as *a nessuno* 'to nobody' yields a marginally acceptable result only if the negative

marker *non* is present, as in (43)b. If *non* isn't present, the result is completely unacceptable, as in (43)c:

(43)   a. *Non* parlare a nessuno! (Italian)
          neg to-talk to no one
          'Don't talk to anyone!' (2nd sg)

       b. ?A nessuno *non* parlare!
          to no one neg to-talk
          'Don't talk to anyone!' (2nd sg)

       c. *A nessuno parlare!

Note that this is contrary to what is the case in ordinary finite sentences, where, for many speakers, preposing a negative constituent in Italian requires that the negative marker *non* be dropped, as indicated by the contrast in (44):

(44)   a. A nessuno parlo. (Italian)
          to no one speak (1st sg)
          'To no one I am talking.'

       b. *A nessuno *non* parlo.

Kayne's (1992) proposal is that what the negative marker licenses is not the infinitive per se, but rather an empty modal that in turn licenses the infinitive. Then the unusual *clitic–infinitive* order displayed in the case of infinitives in negative imperative contexts can be seen as an instance of clitic climbing, where the clitic is not adjoined to the infinitive but to the phonetically unrealized modal. Support for this proposal comes from the northern Italian dialects that have an overtly realized verbal form specific to the negative infinitival in the imperative construction, that is, *stá* 'stay'. In Paduan, for example, the negative imperative for the second person singular has the verb *stá* followed by the infinitive, as in (45)a. In the non-negative imperative, though, the presence of this form is impossible, as we can see in (45)b. A similar contrast holds in the case of the second person plural as well, as shown in (46):

(45)   a. *No* stá parlare! (Paduan)
          neg aux to-talk
          'Don't talk!' (2nd sg)

       b. *Stá parlare!

(46)   a. *No* sté parlare!
          neg aux to-talk
          'Don't talk!' (2nd pl)

       b. *Sté parlare!

The overt *stá* resembles the empty modal postulated for Italian in that it can only be licensed by a negative marker and cannot be licensed by a preposed negative constituent without *no*, as shown in (47)b:

(47)   a. *A nissuni no* stá parlarghe!   (Paduan)
          to no one neg aux to-talk-to-him
          'Don't talk to anyone.'

       b. *A nissuni* stá parlarghe!

As Kayne notes, the sharp ungrammaticality of (47)b is unique to the imperative construction with *stá* followed by an infinitive, and contrasts with declarative sentences, where the dropping of *no* in the presence of a preposed negative phrase gives rise to a sentence whose status is marginal, but definitely not as bad as that of (47)b.[22]

I will adopt Kayne's (1992) proposal and take the examples of negated infinitives in Italian to be cases where the negative marker licenses a phonetically unrealized verb that in turn takes the infinitive as its complement. Whereas Kayne's work proposes to view this element as an empty modal, I suggest that it is a semantically empty element, akin to an auxiliary, which can embed other verbal forms.[23] I therefore take the examples from Paduan in (45)a and (47)a to be examples of the same strategy employed by Italian for negating an imperative: the negative marker is followed by a verbal form which functions as an auxiliary, which in turn is followed by the main verb in the infinitival form.[24] The difference between these two languages is simply that such an auxiliary verb is overt in Paduan, while it is abstract in Italian.[25]

Let us examine this strategy more in depth by looking at Friulian, spoken in the northeastern Italian region of Friuli. Friulian has true imperative forms both in the second person singular and in the second plural. As shown here, these forms differ from the corresponding forms of the indicative and the subjunctive, which are identical, and of the infinitive:[26]

(48)

	Second singular	Second plural	
Imperative	ven	vignît	'come'
	fevéle	fevelàit	'talk'
	sint	sintît	'listen'
	sta	stàit	'stay'
Indicative/subjunctive	végnis	vignîs	'come'
	fevèlis	fevelàis	'talk'
	sintis/sinz	sintîs	'listen'
	stâs	stàis	'stay'
Infinitive		vignî	'to come'
		fevelâ	'to talk'
		sintî	'to listen'
		stâ	'to stay'

Consistent with what we have been observing so far, true imperatives in Friulian are incompatible with the pre-verbal negative marker. Since this language has a true imperative form for both the second person singular and plural, both are incompatible with the negative marker *no*:[27]

(49) a. *No* ven!   / *No* vignît! (true imperative) (Friulian)
       neg come (sg) / neg come (pl)
       'Don't come!'

    b. *No* fevéle! / *No* fevelàit! (true imperative)
       neg talk (sg) / neg talk (pl)
       'Don't talk!'

c. *No sint!   / *No sintît! (true imperative)
neg listen (sg) / neg listen (pl)
'Don't listen!'

d. *No sta   donge il fûc! / *No stàit   donge il fûc! (true imperative)
neg stay (sg) near the fire / neg stay (pl) near the fire
'Don't stay near the fire!'

Like Paduan, Friulian forms a negative imperative by means of a form of the verb 'stay' followed by an infinitive. As expected under this analysis, whereas a form of the verb 'stay' cannot occur in a negative imperative as a main verb (cf. (49)d), it can occur in a negative imperative when it is used as an auxiliary. The following examples are from Marchetti (1952: 153, 199) and Matalon (1977: 136); note the contrast with (49)d:

(50)   a. No sta (a) crodi!   (Friulian)
neg stay a   to-believe
'Don't believe that!' (2nd sg)

b. No stàit a crodi.
neg stay a to-believe
'Don't believe that!' (2nd pl)

(51)   No sta fidâti,   no sta crodi   masse!
neg stay to-trust-you, neg stay to-believe too-much
'Don't trust them, don't believe too much.' (2nd sg)

(52)   No stàit a vêse   par mâl.
neg stay a to-have by bad
'Don't take it badly.' (2nd pl)

The same holds true in Paduan: the pre-verbal negative marker *no* is incompatible with a true imperative form of a main verb, but compatible with a true imperative form of the auxiliary, that is, *stá*. *Stá* is a true imperative form according to our definition because it is different from the second person singular form of the present indicative (*ste*), of the present subjunctive (*staghi*), and of the infinitive (*stare*). Yet, despite being a true imperative, it is compatible with the pre-verbal negative marker *no*, as shown in (45)a.

These data clearly show that it is not the form of the verb alone that gives rise to the incompatibility with a pre-verbal negative marker; whether the verb is an auxiliary or a main verb also plays a role. Thus the way we have been thinking about the incompatibility between true imperatives and pre-verbal negative markers needs to be revised. A pre-verbal negative marker is not incompatible with all true imperative forms, but rather with true imperative forms of main verbs; on the other hand, it is compatible with true imperative forms of elements that function as auxiliaries.[28]

Let me thus reformulate the generalization as follows:

(53)   Generalization on negative imperatives (final version):

In Romance, pre-verbal negative markers that can negate a clause by themselves do not co-occur with true imperative forms of main verbs, but do co-occur with true imperative forms of auxiliaries. Post-verbal negative markers do not exhibit any such restriction.

More examples of this pattern can be found in Rohlfs (1968). Note that, while example (54)a from Trentino uses a true imperative form of the verb 'stay', example (54)b from Emiliano uses the infinitival form of the same verb:[29]

(54)   a. *No* sta móverte.   (Trentino)
           neg stay to-move-you(acc.)
           'Don't move!' (2nd sg)

       b. *En* te   star   mövər.   (Emiliano)
           neg you(acc.) to-stay to-move
           'Don't move!' (2nd sg)

The option of using an infinitival form is present in Paduan as well. As reported by Paola Benincà (personal communication), besides the form *stá*, the infinitival form *star* can also be used for the negative imperative of the second person singular. Certain aspectual differences distinguish the two forms, but I will not discuss them here. An example of a negated imperative with the infinitival form of 'stay' is shown in (55)b (example (55)a is the same as (45)a):

(55)   a. *No* stá parlare! (Paduan)
           neg stay to-talk
           'Don't talk!' (2nd sg)

       b. ?*No* star   parlare.
           neg to-stay to-talk
           'Don't talk!' (2nd sg)

The form with the infinitival verb is slightly degraded in a sentence without pronominal clitics, as indicated by the question mark in (55)b. Its grammatical status improves when pronominal clitics are present, as shown in (56)b, which at the moment I cannot explain:[30]

(56)   a. *No* stá   melo dire! (Paduan)
           neg stay me-it to-say
           'Don't tell me that!' (2nd sg)

       b. *No* starmelo   dire!
           neg to-stay-me-it to-say
           'Don't tell me that!' (2nd sg)

    4. *The fourth strategy has the pre-verbal negative marker followed by a gerund.* Though at first sight different from the strategy just described, in fact the difference is a consequence of properties of the languages under study that are not unique to imperatives.

    This structure occurs in certain varieties spoken in southern Italy, in particular in the regions of Puglia, Calabria, and Basilicata; some examples can be found in Valente (1975: 34), a study of the dialects spoken in northern Puglia:

(57)   Non facennə. (Pugliese)
       neg doing
       'Don't do that!' (2nd sg)

More examples are provided in Rohlfs (1969: 110):

(58) a. Non cadènnə. (Calabrese)
neg falling (gerund)
'Don't fall!' (2nd sg)

b. Nəm magnannə. (Pugliese)
neg eating (gerund)
'Don't eat!' (2nd sg)

c. Nan dəcènnə. (Pugliese)
neg saying (gerund)
'Don't speak!' (2nd sg)

Note that when a pronominal clitic is present it always precedes the gerund, as shown in the following examples (from Rohlfs 1969: 110). As in the case of Italian discussed in Kayne (1992), this is a striking departure from the word order normally found with gerunds, where the pronominal clitic follows, and cannot precede, the verb.

(59) a. No *mə* pəngènnə. (Pugliese from Bari)
neg me stinging
'Don't sting me!'

b. Nən *də*   muvènnə. (Lucera)
neg you(acc.) moving
'Don't move!'

c. Nun *u* dicinnə a nnisciunə. (Calabrese from Diamante)
neg it saying to nobody
'Don't tell that to anyone!'

The analogy between the order *clitic–gerund* possible only in negative imperatives in these languages and the order *clitic–infinitive* possible only in negative imperatives in Italian leads me to suggest that in these cases as well the negative marker is selecting a verbal element that has no phonetic realization and to which the pronominal clitics raise. Note that these languages share with the Balkan languages the property of making limited use of the infinitive form in favor of forms of the subjunctive or of the gerund. It is then plausible to assume that the reasoning applied by Kayne for the case of *non* followed by an infinitive in Italian should be applied here as well. These languages would then have a negative marker licensing an empty auxiliary, which, in turn, takes a gerund rather than an infinitive.

Valente (1975) suggests that the negative imperative formed with the negative marker followed by a gerund is derived from a construction where the negative marker is followed by *zi* 'to go' and a gerund, as in (60):

(60) Non zi   fačénnə. (Pugliese)
neg to-go doing
'Don't do that!'

In a similar vein, Rohlfs (1969: 111) speculates that these forms derive, diachronically, from a construction where the negative marker was followed by a form of 'go' followed by a gerund.

Cross-linguistic support for their hypotheses and for my extension of Kayne's analysis is provided by a dialect spoken in the central area of Puglia, often classified as part of Salentino (rather than Pugliese): Tarantino, spoken in Taranto.[31] In this variety, regular verbs do not show any difference between verbal forms used for imperatives and for present indicative and subjunctive. Irregular verbs, though, show that the second person singular imperative is morphologically unique to this paradigm, while the second person plural coincides with a form of the indicative/subjunctive. I exemplify this with the verb *scé* 'to go':

(61)

	Second singular	Second plural	
Imperative	va	sciatə	'go'
Indicative/subjunctive	vé	sciatə	'go'
Infinitive		scé	'to go'

In Tarantino, as in the languages examined so far, the negative imperative cannot be formed by negating the true imperative form of a main verb:

(62)   *No va! (true imperative) (Tarantino)
neg go (2nd sg)
'Don't go!'

In this language, the negative imperative is formed instead with the infinitival form of the verb 'to go', *scé*, followed by a gerund:[32]

(63)   a. No scé   mangiannə. (Tarantino)
neg to-go eating
'Don't eat!' (2nd sg)

b. No scé   scennə.
neg to-go going
'Don't go!' (2nd sg)

The second person plural of the imperative can be negated by negating the form used as a suppletive imperative, which coincides with the indicative form, as shown in (64):

(64)   a. No sciatə. (suppletive imperative) (Tarantino)
neg go   (indic./subj.; 2nd pl)
'Don't go!' (2nd pl)

b. No mangjatə. (suppletive imperative)
neg go   (indic./subj.; 2nd pl)
'Don't go!' (2nd pl)

Alternatively, the second plural can be negated by employing the second person plural indicative/subjunctive of the verb *scé*, 'to go', followed by the main verb in the gerund, as shown in (65):

(65)   a. No sciatə scennə. (Tarantino)
neg go   going
'Don't go!' (2nd pl)

b. No sciatə mangiannə.
neg go   eating
'Don't eat!' (2nd pl)

Note that, except in clitic climbing contexts, pronominal clitics usually follow the gerund in Tarantino. Negative imperatives pattern like clitic climbing contexts, as shown in (66): the pronominal clitics precede the auxiliary and cannot follow the gerund. Analogous to the cases discussed previously, we can view the clitics as obligatorily raising to left-adjoin to the auxiliary:

(66)   a.   No 'u scé   pigghjannə. (Tarantino)
            neg it to-go taking
            'Don't take it!' (2nd sg)

       b.   No 'u sciatə pigghjannə.
            neg it go   taking
            'Don't take it!' (2nd pl)

This construction in Tarantino thus differs from the parallel construction in Paduan and Friulian in the choice of the verb that functions as an auxiliary ('go' versus 'stay') and in the form of the main verb (gerund in Tarantino, infinitival in Paduan and Friulian). On the use of the gerund instead of the infinitive, it must be pointed out that Tarantino, like other varieties spoken in this area, is a language where the infinitive is used in a subset of the contexts in which it is used in Paduan or Friulian. The infinitive does not occur in a complement clause, where a tensed clause is used instead (both when the subjects of the two clauses are disjoint in reference and when they are coreferential):[33]

(67)   a.   'A vogghjə cu   fazzə. (Tarantino)
            it want   that do   (subjunctive; 1st sg)
            'I want to do it.'

       b.   M'onnə dittə cu   'a fazzə oscə.
            me-have said that it do   today
            'They told me to do it today.'

The infinitive is found in clauses where it is a sentential subject:

(68)   a.   Scé a Məlanə è bellə. (Tarantino)
            to-go to Milan is nice
            'Going to Milan is nice.'

       b.   È megghjə scé a Məlanə.
            is better to-go to Milan
            'To go to Milan is better.'

As mentioned in relation to the varieties spoken in Puglia, Calabria, and Basilicata, the choice of a gerund in imperative contexts is most likely to be related to the limited use of infinitives in these languages, and not to any syntactic property of imperatives.[34]

Let us now summarize the strategies employed to negate imperatives in the Romance varieties we have examined in this section. When a language has a preverbal negative marker that by itself can negate a clause, the negative marker does not co-occur with a main verb that is morphologically a true imperative. Instead, it occurs with one of the following verbal forms:

1. A form of the indicative
2. A form of the subjunctive
3. An overt or abstract auxiliary followed by an infinitive
4. An overt or abstract auxiliary followed by a gerund

As mentioned in the course of the discussion, the third and fourth strategies differ in ways that depend on syntactic properties of the languages in which they occur that are not related to the syntax of imperatives.

Let me now provide an account of these data, building on the difference observed in this section and in the previous one between true and suppletive imperatives.

4.5.   Pre-verbal negative markers and mood

One way to interpret the data just presented that seems particularly natural is that of relating the occurrence of the negative marker to the morphological differences that can be observed between true and suppletive imperatives. In the previous two sections we have established that, while true imperatives consist of the verbal root plus the thematic vowel and, in some cases, an agreement morpheme, suppletive imperatives are either a finite form (from the paradigm of the indicative or the subjunctive) or a non-finite form introduced by an auxiliary, which might be either overt or phonetically null. It seems natural to look into these differences to find an explanation for the incompatibility of the negative marker with true imperatives.

To do this, we need to identify what exactly differentiates the two. Let us consider verbal morphology. We have already seen that agreement does not distinguish between true and suppletive imperatives, since both of them might have agreement markings. The other pieces of verbal morphology that might be relevant to explain the contrast under investigation are morphological markings for tense, aspect, and mood.

In Zanuttini (1991, 1996),[35] on the basis of a subset of the data presented here, I explored the possibility that the incompatibility of the pre-verbal negative marker with true imperatives might be due to the absence of tense morphology on these verbal forms. The empirical observation on which that proposal was based was that the pre-verbal negative marker of Italian is incompatible with both true imperatives and past participles. Assuming that the verbal morphology of past participles marks aspect but not tense, as has been argued in the literature, I concluded that in both cases the negative marker is incompatible with these verbal forms because they lack tense marking. I expressed this idea in terms of selectional properties of functional categories: I argued that the pre-verbal negative marker is a head that selects the functional projection TP as its complement. When TP is missing, NegP cannot occur, since its selectional requirements are not met.

Some data that I was not aware of at the time of that proposal now lead me to reconsider the role of the functional projection TP in accounting for the distribution of pre-verbal negative markers that can negate a clause by themselves in imperative clauses. In particular, recall what we observed in Friulian (and then confirmed with data from other varieties): a pre-verbal negative marker that by itself can negate a clause is compatible with a true imperative form if the true imperative is not a main verb but an auxiliary. In Friulian, for example, the pre-verbal negative marker *no* cannot negate an instance of the main verb 'stay' in the true imperative form, but it can co-occur with an instance of this same element when it is used not as a main verb but as an auxiliary (see (49)d on the one hand, versus (50), (51), and (52) on the other). In other words, the lack of morphological marking does not matter when the verbal form is an auxiliary rather than a main verb.

In view of this, to maintain my original proposal and incorporate this observation, I should rephrase it in different terms. The negative marker is sensitive to the presence or absence of a certain type of morphological marking; but the absence of such morphological specification can be redeemed by the presence of an (overt or abstract) auxiliary verb. It seems to me that a reasonable move at this point consists in assuming that the auxiliary element is a verbal form corresponding to the morphological marking the negative marker requires. Let me thus hypothesize that the auxiliaries we have encountered in imperative contexts are mood markers, similar in nature to the subjunctive particles (*mi/mu/ma*) of the southern dialects.

I must now rephrase my previous proposal and argue that the negative marker is not sensitive to the presence (or absence) of an element expressing tense, but rather to that of an element expressing mood. This proposal amounts to arguing that the negative markers that occur in clauses interpreted as a command, a prohibition, an invitation, or a recommendation (the range of interpretations associated with the illocutionary force of an imperative) require the syntactic expression of mood. This requirement can be satisfied either by the presence of the corresponding morphological marking on a main verb, or by the presence of a functional element that is the realization of this grammatical category.

This reformulation of the proposal can account for the data described in the previous sections in a straightforward way, if combined with the assumption that main verbs in the true imperative form lack (overt or abstract) specification for mood. This assumption finds support in the observations made in section 4.3, which showed that true imperatives consist of the verbal root followed by the thematic vowel and, in some cases, an agreement morpheme.[36]

More generally, support for the view that the incompatibility of a pre-verbal negative marker and a true imperative verb stems from selectional properties of the negative marker comes from two considerations. First, post-verbal negative markers do not show such incompatibility, but can co-occur with true imperatives.[37] If we view the pre-verbal negative markers as heads and the post-verbal negative markers as maximal projections in a specifier position, then a natural way of expressing their differences is to build on this distinction, by saying that the negative marker that is a head selects its complement, or certain features of its complement, whereas the one that is a maximal projection does not. Second, in a given language, true imperatives are not incompatible with other negative constituents, but only with pre-verbal negative markers. At least for some speakers of Italian, for example, it is possible to have a true imperative in a sentence with a preposed negative constituent, as was illustrated in (28) and as shown in the following example:[38]

(69)   A NESSUNO dillo! (true imperative) (Italian)
        to nobody   say-it
        'Don't say it to anyone!'

An analysis in terms of selectional properties of the negative marker offers a natural way of expressing the fact that the incompatibility is indeed restricted to the negative marker itself and does not extend to other negative constituents.

Let us now consider the types of verbs that can be found in negative clauses interpreted as imperatives, discussed in section 4.4. They are forms of the indicative or the subjunctive, or else they are overt or abstract auxiliary verbs followed by an infinitive or a gerund. I have suggested that the overt or abstract auxiliaries be viewed as the realization of the syntactic category mood. This hypothesis also leads me to suggest that forms of the indicative and of the subjunctive contain some marking for mood in their syntactic representation — either in their morphological marking or as an abstract category in the head of the functional projection MoodP. In other words, according to this proposal, these verbal elements mark mood and can satisfy the selectional requirements of the negative marker that occurs in clauses with the illocutionary force of an imperative. I will provide a more detailed discussion of this point in section 4.8.

Infinitival verbs can occur in such clauses only in the presence of an auxiliary. Recall what we have already noted, following Kayne (1992): the behavior of infinitives used as suppletive imperatives is different from that of infinitives in non-imperative contexts. Two main differences appear: infinitives used as suppletive imperatives occur in main clauses; and, in the presence of the negative marker, infinitives used as suppletive imperatives allow the word order *clitic–infinitive* even in languages where such word order is not usually possible.[39] Both these properties can be accounted for by assuming that, in negative imperatives, an abstract auxiliary takes the infinitival verb as its complement. The fact that the infinitives we find in negative imperatives are always introduced by an overt or abstract auxiliary suggests that the negative marker that occurs in these clauses is not compatible with "plain" infinitives, which do not satisfy its selectional requirements. Yet we know that such "plain" infinitives can be negated in clauses that do not have the illocutionary force of imperatives. This leads me to suggest that there are two distinct negative markers in Italian, and more generally in the Romance varieties that negate a clause by means of a pre-verbal negative marker alone:

1. One negative marker requires marking for mood in the clause, either in the verbal morphology or in the presence of a functional element expressing mood; this is the negative marker found in clauses with the illocutionary force of an imperative.
2. The other negative marker does not require the presence of mood marking in the clause, and is found in clauses that lack the illocutionary force characteristic of imperatives.

In this view, Romance languages with pre-verbal negative markers are seen as maintaining a distinction that was present in Latin, which had a negative marker to be used with certain verbal forms and a different one to be used with others. In Latin, this distinction had an overt morphological reflex: *non* and *ne*; *ne* was used in so-called prohibitive sentences, a class that included negative imperatives as well as clauses in the subjunctive. Following this analysis, I am led to conclude that in contemporary

Romance languages as well, imperative clauses use a negative marker different from the one used in other contexts, one that requires the presence of functional material expressing mood.

Cross-linguistically, Sadock and Zwicky (1985) point out that when a language has two morphologically distinct negative markers, they are most often sensitive to mood distinctions of the verbal paradigm and specialize accordingly. Less frequently, they are sensitive to the aspect of the verb. Along these lines, the analysis sketched here leads me to propose that, although Romance languages with pre-verbal negative markers that can negate a clause by themselves do not exhibit two morphologically different negative markers, in fact they do have two negative markers, whose distribution is sensitive to mood distinctions. One negative marker, *non-1* in Italian, occurs in clauses with the illocutionary force of an imperative; a second negative marker, *non-2*, occurs in all other contexts, but cannot occur in imperative clauses.

In what follows, I will explore this hypothesis and make it more precise. I will discuss the difference between imperative clauses that are negated and those that are not, and suggest a way to integrate the sensitivity of the negative marker to mood specifications into my general approach to word order and clausal structure.

The remainder of the chapter is organized as follows. In section 4.6, I examine in some detail one of the most influential current proposals on the syntax of imperative clauses in Romance, that first put forth in Rivero (1994a, 1994b) and then in Rivero and Terzi (1995), which argues that true imperative verbs move to C°. In particular, I focus on how that proposal accounts for the incompatibility of true imperatives and pre-verbal negative markers in Romance. Then in section 4.7 I discuss the relative distribution of imperative verbs and certain classes of adverbs that occur in the upper part of the clause, with the goal of establishing the extent to which verbs move in imperative clauses, and whether true and suppletive imperatives differ in this respect. Finally, in section 4.8, I provide my analysis of the incompatibility of true imperatives and pre-verbal negative markers.

4.6.   A comparison of true and suppletive imperatives

Now I examine certain aspects of Rivero's (1994a, 1994b) proposal on imperative clauses, focusing in particular on two points: (a) the evidence for the claim that true imperatives move to C°, whereas suppletive imperatives move to a lower position, and (b) the claim that the negative marker creates a minimality effect that blocks verb movement to C°. As will become obvious from the discussion of my own proposal, I keep certain insights of Rivero's work, which prove very fruitful. But I do not adopt the view that true and suppletive imperatives differ radically in their syntactic representation, the former having an imperative feature in C°, the latter having this feature in I°.

Rivero (1994a, 1994b) combines the observation of the lack of co-occurrence of pre-verbal negative markers and true imperatives with two other empirical observations, and formulates a theoretical proposal intended to account for all of them. Let us review it briefly.

1. *Imperative clauses with true imperatives are root clauses*—that is, they resist embedding (cf. (70)b, (71)b)—whereas imperative clauses with suppletive imperatives can be embedded (cf. (70)c and (71)c):[40]

(70) a. Cîntă! (true imperative) (Rumanian)
         sing
         'Sing!' (2nd sg)

      b. *Ti-am   spus să   cîntă. (true imperative)
         you-have told PRT sing
         'I told you to sing.'

      c. Ti   am   spus să   cîntj. (suppletive imperative, subjunctive)
         you have told PRT sing-Pres-2s
         'I told you to sing.'

(71) a. Dad-me el libro! (true imperative) (Spanish)
         give-me the book
         'Give me the book!' (2nd pl)

      b. *Pido que dad-me el libro. (true imperative)
         ask   that give-me the book
         'I ask that you give me the book.'

      c. Ordeno que me deis el libro. (suppletive imperative, subjunctive)
         order   that me give the book
         'I order you to give me the book.'

2. *Imperative clauses with true imperatives have the verb preceding the clitic,* whereas imperative clauses with suppletive imperatives exhibit the opposite order, namely the clitic preceding the verb:[41]

(72) a. **Dă-**mi   cartea! (true imperative) (Rumanian)
         give-me book-the
         'Give me the book!' (2nd sg)

      b. Să-mi   **dai**   cartea. (suppletive imperative)
         PRT-me give book-the
         'Give me the book.'

(73) a. **Envía-**lo. (true imperative) (Spanish)
         send-it
         'Send it!' (2nd sg)

      b. Que lo **escribáis**! (suppletive imperative)
         that it write
         'Write it!' (2nd pl)

3. *True imperatives cannot be negated by a pre-verbal negative marker,* while suppletive imperatives can. I will not provide examples to illustrate this generalization, since we have discussed it and illustrated it at length in section 4.2 to introduce the topic of this chapter.

The proposal put forth in Rivero's work is that true imperatives must move to $C°$ in order to trigger the appropriate illocutionary force of the imperative clause.[42] At the same time, the true imperative verb itself is said to carry an imperative feature; such a feature must be checked and can only be checked in C°.[43] Suppletive imperative verbs, on the other hand, do not always share the syntax of imperative clauses and can acquire the appropriate illocutionary force by other means. Suppletive imperatives that employ a form of the indicative or of the infinitive are argued to have the syntax of other infinitival and indicative clauses, and not to have imperative features in their functional makeup.[44]

The proposal that true imperatives must move to C°, whereas suppletive imperatives do not, allows for the following interpretation of the empirical observations just described:

- Given that the true imperative verb moves to C°, a clause containing it cannot be embedded, because the presence of a complementizer in C° would block the required movement of the verb. A clause containing a suppletive imperative, however, can be embedded, since the suppletive imperative verb need not move to C° and therefore this position can be filled by a complementizer.
- Given that the true imperative verb moves to C°, it will precede pronominal clitics, which are taken to be in Infl. A suppletive imperative, on the other hand, will typically follow pronominal clitics, since it does not have to raise to C°.
- Given that the true imperative verb moves to C°, the presence of a pre-verbal negative marker on its path from I° to C° creates a minimality effect that yields ungrammaticality. This is because, by assumption, the verb cannot incorporate to the negative marker and then move to C° as a unit with it. A suppletive imperative, on the other hand, will not be affected by the presence of a pre-verbal negative marker, since it does not have to move to C° across it.

Conceptually, there are two parts to the proposal. The first is that there is a difference between true imperative verbs and suppletive imperative verbs in the extent to which they move; assuming such a difference provides a way of interpreting the empirical observations described previously. The second is that there is a difference in the way in which true and suppletive imperative verbs trigger the illocutionary force of the clause: true imperative verbs trigger the desired illocutionary force by moving to C° while suppletive imperatives can do so by other means. Though I see the attraction of this proposal, and I will maintain some of its insights in my own analysis, I also see some problems that I would like to discuss in the remainder of this section.

The first empirical observation whose interpretation I find problematic is the one concerning the possibility of embedding imperative clauses. Rivero suggests that imperative clauses with true imperative verbs cannot be embedded, whereas those with suppletive imperatives can. While it is true that imperative clauses with a suppletive imperative verb in the subjunctive can be embedded, it is not true that those with other types of suppletive verbal forms can. Let me illustrate this point with examples from Italian. When the suppletive imperative is a form of the indicative, it resists embedding as much as a true imperative does, as shown in the following examples:

(74) a. *Ti ordino (di/che) fallo! (true imperative) (Italian)
         you order   (of/that) do-it   (2nd sg)
         'I order you (of/that) do it!'

b. *Ti ordino (di/che) fatelo! (suppletive imperative)
   you order (of/that) do-it (2nd pl, indicat.)
   'I order you (of/that) do it!'

c. *Ti ordino (di/che) non lo fate! (suppletive imperative)
   you order (of/that) neg it do (2nd pl, indicat.)
   'I order you (of/that) do not do it!'

Embedding is indeed possible when the verb is a form of the subjunctive, as in the polite imperatives for second person singular and plural, which employ a verbal form of the subjunctive in the third person:

(75) a. Le ordino che lo faccia subito!   (suppletive imperative) (Italian)
        her order that it do   immediately (3rd sg subjunctive)
        'I order you (sg) to do it right away!'

     b. ?Ordino che corrano a casa! (suppletive imperative)
        order   that run   to home (3rd pl subjunctive)
        'I order you (pl) to run home.'

This is not surprising since verbs expressing an order or a command require subjunctive complements. But can we really consider the embedded clauses in (75) as instances of embedded imperatives? The force of a command comes from the performative nature of the matrix verb, not necessarily from a property of the embedded clause. The pattern is perhaps more revealing in the cases where the suppletive imperative is a form of the infinitive, as in negative imperatives for the familiar second person singular and plural. Infinitival clauses can normally be embedded under verbs of saying or verbs expressing a command. But, interestingly, embedding is possible only when the infinitive shows the same word order with respect to the pronominal clitics that it shows in non-imperative clauses — namely the order *verb–clitic*, as in (76)a. On the contrary, embedding is impossible when the infinitive exhibits the word order with respect to pronominal clitics that is unique to imperative clauses — namely *clitic–verb*, as in (76)b:[45]

(76) a. Gli ho   ordinato di non *prenderlo*! (Italian)
        him have ordered of not to-take-it
        (word order of non-imperative clauses)
        'I have ordered him not to take it.'

     b. *Gli ho   ordinato di non *lo prendere*!
        him have ordered of not it to-take
        (word order of imperative clauses)
        'I have ordered him not to take it.'

This shows that clauses with infinitival verbs cannot be embedded when they exhibit syntactic properties of imperatives, but only when they behave as regular infinitives. These data suggest that clauses with suppletive imperatives can be embedded only when the verbal form they employ can normally occur in subordinate clauses (as in the case of subjunctives or infinitives with the non-imperative word order). When suppletive forms have syntactic properties that are unique to the imperative, they resist embedding as much as true imperatives do. Hence, the conclusion I draw is that imperative clauses resist embedding in general in modern Romance languages;

certain verbal forms that are employed as suppletive imperatives can be embedded, but only insofar as they coincide with forms that are used in non-imperative clauses.[46] The fact that they appear embedded under verbs expressing an order or a command does not make them embedded imperatives; all they share with imperative clauses is the interpretation of a command or order, which is provided by the matrix verb. In view of this conclusion, if the impossibility of certain suppletive imperatives to occur in embedded contexts were to be taken as evidence that the verb has moved to $C°$, one would have to say that *both* true and suppletive imperatives move to $C°$.

The second empirical observation whose interpretation I find problematic is the one concerning the relative order of verb and pronominal clitics in imperative clauses. Rivero concludes from her data that imperative clauses with true imperatives exhibit the word order *verb–clitic*, whereas imperative clauses with suppletive imperatives exhibit the opposite word order, *clitic–verb*. This description of the data is not entirely accurate, in that not all suppletive imperatives exhibit the order *clitic-verb*. We have already seen in note 44 a case of suppletive imperative in Spanish in which the order is *verb–clitic*. Rivero explains this example by suggesting that suppletive imperatives can only precede pronominal clitics when $C°$ is available and when no pre-verbal negative marker is present (since it would block movement of the verb to $C°$). But in Italian, as we saw in section 4.2, suppletive imperatives that employ a form of the indicative always precede the pronominal clitics, even when the pre-verbal negative marker is present:

(77)   a. *Fatelo!* (suppletive imperative) (Italian)
            do-it   (indicative form; 2nd pl)
            'Do it!' (2nd pl)

        b. Non *fatelo!* (suppletive imperative)
            neg do-it   (indicative form; 2nd pl)
            'Don't do it!' (2nd pl)

If the order *verb–clitic* were to be taken as evidence that the verb has moved to $C°$, then we would be forced to conclude that the suppletive imperative verb in (77) has moved to $C°$ in both the absence and the presence of the pre-verbal negative marker *non* (see (77)a and (77)b, respectively). But this situation leaves us with two choices, both undesirable from the point of view of Rivero's account: either we predict that the sentence in which the pre-verbal negative marker is present will be ungrammatical, or we admit that the verb can move to $C°$ even in the presence of the negative marker. The first alternative is proven wrong by the empirical data (see (77)b). If we choose the second alternative, then we lose the possibility of accounting for the incompatibility of true imperative verbs with pre-verbal negative markers in terms of the negative marker blocking verb movement to $C°$: if the negative marker does not block verb movement to $C°$ for a suppletive imperative, like the one in (77)b, it is hard to see why it should do so for a true imperative.

This discussion leads me to the following conclusions:

• The impossibility of embedding does not necessarily distinguish true imperatives from suppletive imperatives, as in many cases it applies to both.

• The order *verb–clitic* also does not necessarily characterize true imperatives in contrast with suppletive imperatives. In both Italian and Spanish some non-negative forms of suppletive imperatives exhibit precisely that word order. If this word order results from the verb having moved to C°, then the possibility of such movement must be granted to both types of verbs; alternatively, it might not be a reflection of verb movement to C°.

• Impossibility of embeddding and *verb–clitic* word order do not necessarily go together with being incompatible with a pre-verbal negative marker: whereas true imperatives exhibit all three properties (they cannot be embedded, they precede the clitics, and they cannot be negated), certain suppletive imperatives exhibit the first two properties but not the third.

Finally, I would also like to raise the general question of why the illocutionary force should come from a feature in C° in true imperatives and from a feature in I° in suppletive imperatives. Such a difference seems arbitrary if it is not related to some other difference between the two types of verbs. An alternative analysis, which argues that the illocutionary force of imperatives always comes from the same place in syntactic structure, would be more general and thus more plausible from the point of view of the language learner.

In the next section, I will try to establish the position to which the verb moves in non-negative imperatives on the basis of its relative position with certain classes of adverbs. Then in section 4.8 I will address the issue of whether we can make the syntax of true and suppletive imperatives more uniform, while accounting for their differences.

4.7.   Imperatives and adverbs

To address the question of verb movement in imperative clauses, I now examine the position of the verb with respect to adverbs. In his study of Italian imperatives, Graffi (1996) discusses the extent of verb movement and takes the fact that imperative verbs occur to the left of *spesso* 'often' to suggest that they have moved to C°. Here I conduct a more exhaustive analysis of the relative distribution of adverbs and verbs in imperative clauses in order to see whether I can more precisely determine the extent to which the verb moves. We will see that, at least in the case of Italian, true and suppletive imperatives appear to move to the same extent in non-negative contexts.

In the tradition of Klima (1964), Emonds (1978), Pollock (1989) and most recently Cinque (1994, 1995a, 1996a), we can study the extent of verb movement by looking at its distribution with respect to adverbs. As mentioned in chapter 3, Cinque's work provides a detailed analysis of the relative position of certain classes of adverbs. In his view, each class of adverbs is associated with a particular functional projection to which it is semantically related; more precisely, adverbs are argued to occur in the specifier of a functional head with which they share semantic content. Given a sequence of adverbs belonging to different classes, exactly one head position can be found between each of them where the verb can occur.[47] Following Cinque's assumption that the order of functional projections is fixed, the relative order of the adverbs is fixed as well. Therefore, the position in which the verb occurs with respect to the adverbs reveals the extent to which it has moved. In chapter 3 we focused our attention on so-called lower adverbs and the position of the past participle or the infinitival verb with respect to them. Here I briefly summarize Cinque's proposal concerning adverbs that occur in the higher part of the clause and examine the position of true and suppletive imperative verbs with respect to both these adverbs and the lower adverbs. I will work with examples from Italian.

Both true and suppletive imperative verbs in Italian obligatorily precede all the lower adverbs discussed in the previous chapter. I exemplify this by showing that they obligatorily precede *sempre* 'always', as shown in (78) and (79):

(78) a. Ricordati *sempre* di prendere il   passaporto! (true imperative) (Italian)
         remember always of to-take   the passport
         'Always remember to bring your passport!'

      b. *Sempre* ricordati di prendere il passaporto!

(79) a. Ricordiamoci *sempre* di prendere il passaporto! (suppletive imperative)
         'Let's always remember to bring our passport!'

      b. *Sempre* ricordiamoci di prendere il passaporto!

Moreover, they obligatorily precede the highest of the lower adverbs — those that occur in the specifier of NegP-2 (see chapter 3 for discussion and in particular the diagram in (139)). Leaving aside *mica*, which occurs in NegP-2 but only in negative clauses, we can see that both true and suppletive imperatives obligatorily precede *pur* and *ben*, particles of emphatic affirmation that are argued to occur in the specifier of the same functional projection as *mica* (cf. Belletti 1990, Cinque 1994, 1995a, 1996a):

(80) a. Dagli   *ben*   una risposta! (true imperative) (Italian)
         give(sg)-him indeed an   answer
         'Do give him an answer!' (2nd sg)

      b. *Ben* dagli una risposta!

      c. Dategli   *ben*   qualche soddisfazione! (suppletive imperative)
         give(pl)-him indeed some   satisfaction!
         'Do give him some satisfaction!' (2nd pl)

      d. *Ben* dategli qualche soddisfazione!

(81) a. Fallo   *pure*! (true imperative)
         do(sg)-it indeed
         'Go ahead and do it!' (2nd sg)

      b. *Pure* fallo!

      c. Fatelo   *pure*! (suppletive imperative)
         do(pl)-it indeed
         'Go ahead and do it!' (2nd pl)

      d. *Pure* fatelo!

These examples tell us that the verb in both true and suppletive imperatives must raise at least to some functional projection higher than the one hosting these adverbs, that is, NegP-2. To determine more precisely to which functional projection the verb raises, we need to examine adverb classes that are higher in the structure.

Cinque's (1995a, 1996a) analysis of the top portion of the clause identifies three modal projections, one projection for mood, and one temporal projection. The modal projections correspond to evaluative modality, epistemic modality, and root modality. Speaker-oriented adverbs (e.g., Italian *fortunatamente, sfortunatamente, per (s)fortuna* 'fortunately, unfortunately, (un)luckily') are argued to occur in the specifier of the evaluative modal phrase. Adverbs like *probabilmente, evidentemente* 'probably, evidently' are argued to occur in the specifier of the epistemic modal phrase, which is structurally lower than the evaluative modal phrase. This is reflected in the fixed linear order of these adverbs:[48]

(82) a. Il vincitore sei *fortunatamente probabilmente* tu. (Italian)
          the winner are fortunately   probably   you
          'The winner is luckily probably you.'

      b. *Il vincitore sei *probabilmente fortunatamente* tu.
          'The winner is probably luckily you.'

Adverbs like *forse, (quasi) certamente, di sicuro* 'perhaps, (almost) certainly, for sure' are argued to occur in a lower structural position — namely, in the specifier of a functional projection where the mood of the clause is specified. They follow in linear order the previous two classes of adverbs (cf. (83)) and precede the class of subject oriented adverbs, like *intelligentemente, goffamente* 'intelligently, clumsily', as shown in (84). Subject-oriented adverbs are argued by Cinque to occur in the specifier of a functional projection that expresses root modality.

(83) a. Gianni è *probabilmente forse*   il più indicato.   (Italian)
          Gianni is probably   perhaps the most appropriate
          'Gianni is probably perhaps the best person.'

      b. *Gianni è *forse   probabilmente* il più indicato.
          Gianni is perhaps probably   the most appropriate
          'Gianni is perhaps probably the best person.'

(84) a. Gianni non ha *forse   intelligentemente* voluto restare.
          Gianni neg has perhaps intelligently   wanted to-stay
          'Gianni hasn't perhaps intelligently wanted to stay.'

      b. *Gianni non ha *intelligentemente forse*   voluto restare.
          Gianni neg has intelligently   perhaps wanted to-stay
          'Gianni hasn't intelligently perhaps wanted to stay.'

Cinque (1996a) also identifies a temporal projection, which corresponds to Giorgi and Pianesi's (1991) TP-1, in whose specifier are adverbs like *oggi, adesso, allora* 'today, now, then'. This functional projection is argued to be lower than the functional projection for epistemic modality but higher than the functional projections expressing root modality and mood.[49] Some examples of the relative position of these adverbs with respect to modal adverbs are given here:

(85) a. Gianni *fortunatamente oggi* dirà   di no. (Italian)
          Gianni fortunately   today will-say of no
          'Luckily John today will say no.'

b. Gianni *evidentemente adesso* si   comporta meglio.
   Gianni evidently   now   self behave   better
   'Evidently John now behaves better.'

c. Gianni *adesso forse*   se   ne   va.
   Gianni now   perhaps self from-there goes
   'John now perhaps will leave.'

The sequence of functional projections and adverbs occurring in their specifiers can be summarized as follows:

(86)

ModP$_{eval}$	ModP$_{epist}$	TP-1	MoodP	ModP$_{root}$
fortunately	probably	today	perhaps	intelligently

Turning now to verb movement in imperatives, we see that none of the adverbs that are argued to occur in the specifier of a modal phrase can occur in imperative clauses. Both true and suppletive imperatives in Italian fail to co-occur with all the adverbs associated with the evaluative, epistemic, and root modal projections.[50] Let me illustrate this with some examples.

(87) a. *Per fortuna* fallo! (true imperative) (Italian)
        'Fortunately do it!' (2nd sg)

      b. *Per fortuna* fatelo! (suppletive imperative)
        'Fortunately do it!' (2nd pl)

(88) a. *Probabilmente* fallo! (true imperative)
        'Probably do it!' (2nd sg)

      b. *Probabilmente* fatelo! (suppletive imperative)
        'Probably do it!' (2nd pl)

(89) a. *Intelligentemente* dì di no! (true imperative)
        'Intelligently say no!' (2nd sg)

      b. *Intelligentemente* dite di no! (suppletive imperative)
        'Intelligently say no!' (2nd pl)

Note that the ungrammaticality of these sentences is not simply a consequence of the word order *adverb–verb*; the opposite word order, in which the verb precedes the adverb, yields ungrammaticality as well.[51]

The incompatibility with the adverb classes just mentioned is also a property of infinitives and gerunds. These non-finite forms also fail to co-occur with speaker-oriented, epistemic, and subject-oriented adverbs, like true and suppletive imperatives. When a speaker-oriented adverb is present in a sentence containing an infinitival verb, it can only be interpreted with the matrix verb, as in (90), but not with the infinitival:[52]

(90) *Fortunatamente* trattare con lui è un piacere. (Italian)
       'Fortunately to deal with him is a pleasure.'

Imperative verbs, both true and suppletive, can co-occur with the temporal adverbs argued to be in the specifier of TP-1 in Cinque (1996a) (e.g., *oggi, adesso, allora* 'today, now, then') and marginally also with the adverbs argued to be in the specifier of the mood phrase. Let us start with the temporal adverbs. In non-imperative clauses, temporal adverbs in the specifier of TP-1 precede the pre-verbal negative marker:

(91) a. Gianni *oggi non* si   sente bene. (Italian)
          Gianni today neg self feels well
          'Gianni isn't feeling well today.'

      b. Gianni *adesso non* vuole andarsene da   quel posto.
          Gianni now   neg wants to-leave   from that place
          'Gianni now doesn't want to leave that place.'

But when we examine their distribution with respect to the verb, we must bear in mind two other positions for temporal adverbs; a sentence-initial and a sentence-final position. The former is a position that has been described as the one to which adverbs prepose; temporal adverbs in that position have the meaning of scene setting adverbs, for example, 'given the situation' (cf. Cinque 1990: ch. 2). Some examples are given here:

(92) a. *Adesso* Gianni lascerà   quel lavoro. (Italian)
          now   Gianni will-leave that job
          'Now Gianni will quit that job.'

      b. *Allora* il   governo   dovette raggiungere un compromesso.
          'Then the government must   to-reach   a   compromesso.'
          'Then the government had to reach a compromise.'

The latter position is used when the adverb constitutes new information or receives contrastive stress. In these cases, exemplified in (93), a (slight) pause precedes the adverb:[53]

(93) a. Non parla più   di te   *adesso*. (Italian)
          neg talks anymore of you now
          'He no longer talks about you now.'

      b. Pensava sempre a te   *allora*.
          thinked always to you then
          'He was always thinking of you then.'

Thus, when we examine the distribution of the verb with respect to these adverbs, we must always sort out which of these three possible positions the adverb is occupying.

Going back to true and suppletive imperative verbs, we see that they can follow the temporal adverbs in imperative clauses, as shown in (94) and (95).[54] Given examples of this type, though, it is difficult to say whether the temporal adverb is in the adverb preposing position (presumably, in the specifier of CP) or in the specifier of TP-1, as in the examples in (91). The most readily available interpretation is the one of the scene setting adverb, which suggests that these adverbs are not in the specifier of TP-1, but in a higher position:[55]

(94) a. *Oggi* vacci   tu! (true imperative) (Italian)
          today go-there you
          'Today you go there!' (2nd sg)

b. *Oggi* andateci voi! (suppletive imperative)
today go-there you
'Today you go there!' (2nd pl)

(95) a. *Adesso* dagli   pur   la notizia! (true imperative)
now   give-him indeed the news
'Now go ahead and tell him the news!' (2nd sg)

b. *Adesso* dategli   pur   la notizia! (suppletive imperative)
now   give-him indeed the news
'Now go ahead and tell him the news!'

In addition to following them, true and suppletive imperative verbs can also precede temporal adverbs, as shown in the following examples:

(96) a. Vacci   (tu)   *oggi*! (true imperative) (Italian)
go-there (you) today
'Today you go!' (2nd sg)

b. Andateci (voi) *oggi*! (suppletive imperative)
go-there (you) today
'Today you go!' (2nd pl)

(97) a. Dagli   pure   la notizia *adesso*! (true imperative)
tell-him indeed the news   now
'Go ahead and tell him the news now!' (2nd sg)

b. Dategli pure   la notizia *adesso*! (suppletive imperative)
tell-him indeed the news   now
'Go ahead and tell him the news now!' (2nd pl)

I argue that in such cases the temporal adverbs are in sentence final position and not in the specifier of TP-1. This is shown by the fact that they follow the object and is confirmed by their position with respect to the lower adverbs. The reasoning is as follows. I have assumed Cinque's proposal that a temporal adverb in the specifier of TP-1 is structuraly higher than the lower adverbs (i.e., *pur/mica, più, sempre*). If the verb had raised past the temporal adverb in the specifier of TP-1, it would have to have raised past the lower adverbs as well; hence it should occur on the left of both the temporal adverb and the lower adverbs. In other words, if the verb had raised past TP-1, we should obtain the linear order *verb–temporal adverb–lower adverb*. But such word order is clearly impossible, as shown by examples (98)a and (99)a, where I use the lower adverb *pur* 'indeed' for the purpose of exemplification. When the verb precedes *adesso*, the temporal adverb can only follow the lower adverb *pur* and the object, as shown in (98)b and (99)b:

(98) a. *Dagli *adesso pur*   la notizia! (true imperative)
tell-him now   indeed the news
'Go ahead and tell him the news now!' (2nd sg)

b. Dagli *pur* la notizia *adesso*!

(99) a. *Dategli *adesso pur*   la notizia! (suppletive imperative)
give-him now   indeed the news
'Go ahead and tell him now!' (2nd pl)

   b. Dategli *pur* la notizia *adesso*!

Hence I conclude that, when a true or a suppletive imperative verb precedes a temporal adverb, the adverb is in sentence final position, and not in the specifier of TP-1.

Let us now turn briefly to the other class of adverbs compatible with imperatives, the one argued to occur in the specifier of the mood projection. The occurrence of these adverbs in imperative clauses is perhaps marginally better than that of speaker-oriented or epistemic adverbs, though it yields ungrammaticality. As indicated by the asterisks and question marks, the examples with the suppletive imperative seem to be slightly better than those with the true imperatives:

(100)   a. *Certamente* fallo! (true imperative) (Italian)
           'Certainly do it!' (2nd sg)

       b. ?**Certamente* fatelo! (suppletive imperative)
           'Certainly do it!' (2nd pl)

(101)   a. **Di sicuro* vacci! (true imperative)
           'For sure go there!' (2nd sg)

       b. ?**Di sicuro* andateci! (suppletive imperative)
           'For sure go there!' (2nd pl)

The intuition is that these sentences are missing a modal element; they become perfectly grammatical if an overt modal is added, as shown here:

(102)   a. Certamente devi farlo! (Italian)
           'Certainly you must do it!' (2nd sg)

       b. Certamente dovete farlo!
           'Certainly you must do it!' (2nd pl)

(103)   a. Di sicuro puoi andarci!
           'For sure you can go there!' (2nd sg)

       b. Di sicuro potete andarci!
           'For sure you can go there!' (2nd pl)

These types of sentences improve if the verb precedes the adverb. This is shown in the examples in (104) and (105), which contrast with the ones in (100) and (101) in having the order *verb–adverb*:

(104)   a. ??Fallo *certamente*! (true imperative) (Italian)
           'Certainly do it!' (2nd sg)

       b. ??Fatelo *certamente*! (suppletive imperative)
           'Certainly do it!' (2nd pl)

(105)   a. ??Vacci *di sicuro*! (true imperative)
           'For sure go there!' (2nd sg)

       b. ??Andateci *di sicuro*! (suppletive imperative)
           'For sure go there!' (2nd pl)

I conclude from these data that, to the extent that these adverbs are possible in imperative clauses, the verb must move to a head position higher than the position they occupy when they occur in the specifier of the Mood projection. Combining this result with the one already obtained, I draw the following conclusions:

- True imperatives and suppletive imperatives do not differ in the extent to which they move when analyzed with respect to the distribution of adverbs.
- True imperatives and suppletive imperatives move to a head position higher than Mood° and higher than T°.

Let me assume that NegP-1, the functional projection headed by the pre-verbal negative markers that can negate the clause by themselves, is lower than TP-1 and higher than MoodP. This hypothesis is supported by the fact that the negative marker follows temporal adverbs and can precede adverbs in the specifier of MoodP. The structure of the clause discussed in this section, with the addition of the projection NegP-1, can then be summarized in the tree here:[56]

(106)

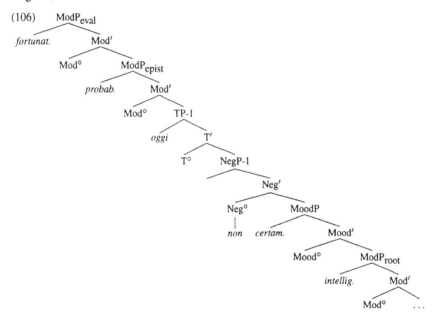

This discussion has led me to the conclusion that true imperative verbs, as well as at least some suppletive imperatives, raise to a head position higher than Mood° and higher than T°. Let me say, for the sake of simplicity, that they move to C°.[57] We can now turn our attention to what happens when a pre-verbal negative marker is present.

4.8.   The syntax of imperatives

In this section I will take as a starting point the observation that true imperatives and some suppletive imperatives move to the same extent in non-negative clauses. I then offer an account of the incompatibility of true imperatives with pre-verbal negative markers that is based on three building blocks:[58]

1. The presence of a syntactic feature that marks the illocutionary force of imperatives
2. The requirement (imposed by the pre-verbal negative marker) that mood be syntactically represented in the clause
3. The difference in the morphological makeup of true and suppletive imperatives.

We have already discussed the difference in the morphological makeup of true and suppletive imperatives in sections 4.3 and 4.4. Let me therefore comment briefly on the other two points. As for the first one, I am assuming, along with much of the existing literature, that imperative clauses are subject to the syntactic requirement that the head of a certain functional projection be filled, either in the syntax or at LF. As I mentioned at the end of the previous section, I will identify this projection with CP for simplicity. This requirement can also be expressed in terms of features, by saying that C° has a feature that needs to be checked. From this assumption it follows that some element of the right type must be in C° by LF to check this feature.[59] This requirement strongly resembles that of interrogative clauses discussed in chapter 2, where a feature in C° also needs to be checked by an element of the appropriate type. I will assume that this requirement holds of all clauses with the illocutionary force of an imperative, whether they employ a true imperative or a suppletive imperative form, whether or not they are negative. In this I depart from other analyses (like Rivero's), which take this to be the case only when the verb in the clause is a true imperative and not when it is a suppletive imperative. I assume that the elements that can satisfy the requirement that C° be filled, or that its feature be checked, are verbs, verbal features, the pre-verbal negative marker, and the complementizer. The unifying property of this class of elements is that they are all verbal elements; perhaps the easiest way to express this is that they all belong to the extended projection of V, in the sense of Grimshaw (in press a).[60]

Let me now turn to the second point, concerning the requirement that mood be syntactically represented in the clause. This stems from the discussion of the relation between negation and mood in section 4.5, where we saw that the pre-verbal negative marker that occurs in clauses with the illocutionary force of an imperative requires that marking for mood be present in the syntactic representation of the clause. I express this relation in terms of properties of the functional projection MoodP, and say that the pre-verbal negative marker of imperative clauses, in the head of NegP-1, requires that the features of its complement, MoodP, be "active." That is, whereas the Mood projection can generally be present in the structural representation of the clause with inert features, when the negative marker is present the features of MoodP must be checked by some element of the appropriate type. They can be checked either by the corresponding morphological marking on a verb or by a functional element that is the realization of this grammatical feature, such as the subjunctive marker or the (overt or abstract) auxiliaries discussed in the previous sections.

On the basis of these assumptions, I now provide an account of the contrast between positive and negative imperatives discussed so far.

4.8.1.   *Positive imperatives*

The characteristic property of the syntax of positive imperative clauses is the presence of a feature in C° that must be checked by an element of the appropriate type. The mechanism by which such a feature is checked differs depending on the verbal form employed.

I suggest that true imperative verbs, which do not have any morphological specification for tense, aspect, or mood, move to C°.[61] As should be clear from the preceding discussion, compelling evidence that shows this movement of the verb is difficult to come by; the evidence at our disposal is compatible both with the hypothesis that the verb moves to C° and with the one that its features, rather than the verb itself, move to C°. As has been argued in the literature, the hypothesis that the verb moves to C° is supported by the relative linear order of the verb with respect to clitic pronouns. Moreover, it is supported by the linear order of the verb with respect to adverbs: as we saw in section 4.7, true imperative verbs precede adverbs that are taken to be in the specifier of MoodP and TP-1; it is thus plausible to assume that the position where the verb occurs is the head of CP. An example of a true imperative is repeated here, where we can see that the verbal form precedes the adverb that corresponds to 'certainly' (which we take to occur in the specifier of MoodP) and the object clitic:

(107)   a.   *Fa*llo di sicuro! (true imperative) (Italian)
             do-it of sure
             'Definitely do it!' (2nd sg)

         b.   *Lo *fa* di sicuro!

Suppletive imperatives exhibit a more complex array of possibilities, which will be discussed in turn. Suppletive imperatives that employ a form of the indicative appear to occur in the same position as true imperative verbs, as was argued in section 4.7 for the case of Italian. They obligatorily occur to the left of complement clitics and precede the same classes of adverbs that true imperatives precede. I repeat one example here:

(108)   a.   *Fate*lo di sicuro! (suppletive imperative) (Italian)
             do-it of sure (indicative)
             'Definitely do it!' (2nd pl)

         b.   *Lo *fate* di sicuro!

The (non-visible) difference between suppletive imperatives and true imperatives might lie in the fact that suppletive forms can move through other functional projections before reaching C° since, thanks to their richer morphological marking, they can check the features of intermediate projections (MoodP and TP, for example). As pointed out for the case of true imperatives, for suppletive imperatives as well it is impossible to determine whether the verbal form itself raises to C° or whether it occurs in a lower functional projection (higher than the pronominal clitics) and only its features raise to C°. The fact that sentences with suppletive imperatives cannot be embedded, described in section 4.6, does not help distinguish between these two options, since it can be derived by assuming either that the verb has moved to C° or that its features move there.

Let us now turn to suppletive imperatives that use a form of the subjunctive. The Spanish polite imperatives for second person singular and plural use a form of the subjunctive and can exhibit the same word order found in the Italian suppletive imperatives just described, that is, the order *verb–clitic*. I repeat one example here:

(109)   a. *Den*-me el libro! (suppletive imperative) (Spanish)
            give-me the book (subjunctive)
            'Give me the book!' (2nd pl)

        b. *Me *den* el libro!

The Spanish suppletive imperatives in the subjunctive differ from the Italian counterparts in the indicative in the following respect: the word order that gives rise to ungrammaticality in (109)b becomes possible in the presence of an overt complementizer (while it is always impossible in the case of Italian suppletive imperatives with a form of the indicative). One relevant example is repeated here, from Rivero (1994b):

(110)   *Que* me den el libro! (suppletive imperative) (Spanish)
          that me give the book (subjunctive)
          'Give me the book!' (2nd pl)

Rivero's work suggests that these sentences do not have an imperative feature in C°, but rather acquire the illocutionary force of an imperative by other means. In contrast, I would like to argue that all clauses with imperative illocutionary force are characterized by the presence of a feature in C° that needs to be checked. For the Spanish case in (110) I suggest that the complementizer itself can check the imperative feature in CP. When the complementizer is missing, as in (109)a, the verb moves to a position from which it can do so. An approach along these lines has the advantage of providing a uniform analysis for all cases that have the illocutionary force of an imperative, regardless of the verbal form that expresses them.[62]

Other Romance varieties seem to always exhibit an overt complementizer, followed by a verbal form that is either unique to the subjunctive paradigm or shared by the indicative and the subjunctive. Some examples are given here:[63]

(111)   a. *C(a)* el am scyza. (suppletive imperative) (Vallader)
            that s.cl me excuse
            'Excuse me!' (to male interlocutor)

        b. *K* e vegni. (suppletive imperative) (Friulian)
            that s.cl comes
            'Come (in)!' (to female interlocutor)

As in Spanish, these cases also suggest that the complementizer checks the imperative feature in C°.[64]

Other Romance varieties resemble Spanish in that they might or might not exhibit an overt complementizer, but they differ from Spanish in not exhibiting (visible) verb movement when the complementizer is missing. One example is the dialect of Ventimiglia, spoken in the northwestern Italian region of Liguria:

(112)   a. *Ch'*i vaghe fòra de chi! (suppletive imperative) (Ventimigliese)
            that's.cl goes out of here (subjunctive)
            'Get out of here!'

b. Scia vaghe föra de chi!
she goes out of here (subjunctive)
'Get out of here!'

In these examples the verb appears to occupy the same position, whether or not the complementizer is present. If further empirical research confirms this to be the case, then two possible explanations need to be investigated. The first could be that Ventimigliese is partially like Spanish, in allowing the complementizer to be present or absent; unlike Spanish, though, when the complementizer is absent the verb does not raise overtly but only covertly. That is, the difference between these two languages might be related to the fact that the feature in C° requires overt verb movement in Spanish, but covert verb movement in Ventimigliese. Alternatively, it could be that Ventimigliese is similar to Friulian and Vallader, in having the feature in C° always checked by the complementizer; unlike these varieties, though, it allows for the complementizer to be phonetically empty.[65] Questions similar to those raised by Ventimigliese are also raised by Italian with respect to polite imperatives, since they employ a form of the subjunctive and show no evidence of verb movement.[66]

Finally, some Romance varieties have polite forms of imperatives that exhibit neither verb movement nor an overt complementizer, but an overt subjunctive marker. These are the varieties spoken in southern Calabria and northeastern Sicily. Some examples are repeated here:

(113)   a. Lu focu *mu* ti   mangia. (suppletive imperative) (southern Calabrese)
        the fire   PRT you eats
        'May the fire eat you.'

        b. *Mu* scrivi.
        PRT write (3rd sg)
        'Write.' (2nd sg)

(114)   *Ma* torna subbitu. (suppletive imperative) (Catanzarese)
        PRT return immediately (3rd sg)
        'Come back right away.' (2nd sg)

In these cases, I assume that the imperative feature is checked by the subjunctive marker, raising to C°. If *lu focu* in (113)a is in subject position and has not been moved leftward by topicalization or left-dislocation, this example suggests that the movement of the subjunctive particle (or its features) takes place at LF.

4.8.2. *Negative imperatives*

The syntax of negative imperative clauses is also determined by the property common to all imperative clauses that a certain feature in C° be checked. In addition to this requirement, imperative clauses negated by a pre-verbal negative marker are also constrained by the requirement that the head of MoodP be filled, or that its features be checked. I assume here, as in chapter 2, that the negative marker that heads NegP-1 can raise to fill the head of CP. This happens when the negative marker is the head closest to C°: the features of the negative marker constitute the closest features to the head C°; hence, they are attracted:

(115)

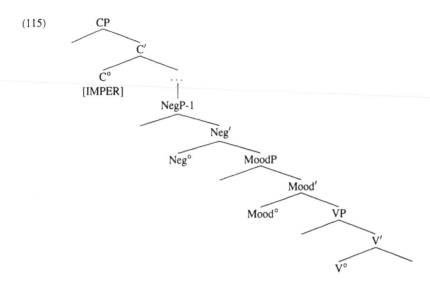

Since the negative marker satisfies the features of C°, the verb itself need not and thus cannot move to C°.

The features of Mood° also need to be checked. They will attract the verb, now the closest head. Three cases then arise, depending on the type of verb in the clause: whether the verb is (1) a true imperative auxiliary, (2) a true imperative main verb, or (3) a suppletive imperative in the indicative or the subjunctive. Let us examine them in turn.

1. As discussed in section 4.5, I take auxiliary verbs in the true imperative form to be the spell-out of the features of MoodP. Such auxiliary elements can take different forms, depending on the language; as we saw, in Paduan and Friulian they are forms of the verb 'stay', in Portuguese and Tarantino a form of 'go'. I repeat some examples here for ease of reference:

(116)   a. No *stá* parlare! (Paduan)
         neg stay to-talk
         'Don't talk!' (2nd sg)

      b. Não *vá* se afogar, moço. (Portuguese)
         neg go self drown, young man
         'Don't drown yourself, young man.'

Alternatively, the auxiliary can be null, as in Italian or Pugliese, followed by the main verb in the infinitive in the former and by the gerund in the latter. As discussed in section 4.4, the choice of verbal form that follows the phonologically null auxiliary depends on properties of the language that are independent of imperative clauses. Some examples are repeated here:

(117)   a. Non parlare! (Italian)
         neg to-talk
         'Don't talk!' (2nd sg)

b. Non facenna. (Pugliese)
neg doing
'Don't do that!' (2nd sg)

In all these cases, the features of MoodP are checked by the overt or abstract auxiliary, which can be seen either to have raised from a lower position or, more likely, to have been base generated in Mood° (or merged there, in the terminology of Chomsky 1995).

2. In contrast with the true imperative forms of auxiliary verbs just discussed, true imperative forms of main or lexical verbs give rise to ungrammaticality in the presence of a pre-verbal negative marker. In my view, this is not because the negative marker creates a minimality effect that prevents the verb from moving to C° (as in Rivero 1994b and Rivero and Terzi 1995). Rather it is because, whereas a true imperative verb can check the feature of C°, it cannot check the features of Mood°; since the pre-verbal negative marker requires that the features of MoodP be checked, this failure gives rise to ungrammaticality. I suggest that the impossibility of true imperative verbs checking the feature of Mood° is to be related to the paucity of morphological marking that characterizes their verbal forms. There are two ways to understand this relation. (a) One amounts to proposing that a true imperative verb — which consists of the verbal root, the thematic vowel, and, in some cases, an agreement morpheme — does not contain mood features that can check the feature in the head of MoodP. Therefore, the feature of Mood° remains unchecked, and ungrammaticality ensues. (b) Alternatively, one could view this impossibility as reminiscent of the one described in Pollock (1989) concerning verb movement to Infl in English and French and the difference between lexical verbs and auxiliaries.

The main points of Pollock's analysis that are relevant for such a comparison are the following. French lexical verbs, which have rich agreement, can raise to I°; on the other hand, English lexical verbs, which have poor agreement, cannot. In contrast with lexical verbs, auxiliary verbs can raise to I° in both French and English, regardless of the richness of their agreement specifications. The parallelism with the case of imperatives is most clearly seen if we interpret the presence or absence of morphological specification on a verbal form, as discussed in sections 4.3 and 4.4, to be the equivalent of Pollock's notion of rich and poor agreement. Suppletive imperative forms of lexical verbs, which have morphological specifications or rich agreement, can raise to Mood°; true imperative forms, however, which are characterized by lack of morphological specifications or poor agreement, cannot raise to Mood°. This parallels the contrast between French lexical verbs on the one hand, which have rich agreement and raise to I°, and English lexical verbs on the other, which are characterized by poor agreement and cannot raise to I°. Differing from lexical verbs, auxiliaries can always occur in Mood°, regardless of whether they are suppletive forms, which have morphological specifications, or true imperative forms, which do not. This parallels the behavior of auxiliary verbs in French and English, as they can raise to I° regardless of the richness of their agreement.

Pollock (1989) relates the difference in the behavior of lexical and auxiliary verbs to the fact that the former have thematic roles to discharge, while the latter do not. In the case examined here, it would be possible to assume something along the same lines, though some slight modification is required. Pollock's proposal was that, because lexical verbs in English lack agreement specifications, they cannot adjoin to AgrP. In this case, true imperative verbs sometimes have morphological specifications for person agreement, and moreover the projection to which they need but fail to raise is MoodP, not AgrP. Thus one would have to say that true imperative forms of lexical verbs cannot adjoin to Mood° because in these languages this projection is opaque to theta-role assignment (like AgrP is in English). Only auxiliaries can be found in this position, precisely because they do not have theta-roles to assign.

The crucial difference between verb raising to Infl of finite forms, as discussed in Pollock (1989), and verb movement of imperatives is that it is only in the presence of a pre-verbal negative marker that the latter show the previously mentioned asymmetries between true and suppletive forms and between lexical and auxiliary verbs. In my view this is because when the negative marker is not present, the head of MoodP does not have features that need to be checked. Hence the verb moves directly to C°; true imperative verbs, like suppletive imperative verbs, can check the imperative features of C°, and this projection is not opaque for theta-role assignment. It is only when the negative marker is present that the features of Mood° must be checked and that the difference among these verbs shows up.

3. Having discussed negative imperatives that employ true imperative forms of auxiliaries and main verbs, let us now turn our attention to those that employ suppletive imperative forms. We need to consider the languages that employ forms of the subjunctive (e.g., Catalan, Spanish, Sardinian, Bolognese, and the dialects of southern Calabria and northeastern Sicily) and those that employ forms of the indicative (Italian and other varieties spoken in central and southern Italy).

When a form of the subjunctive is employed, the word order is *clitic–verb*, as shown here:

(118)   No *me den* el libro! (suppletive imperative) (Spanish)
         neg me give the book (subjunctive)
         'Don't give me the book!' (2nd pl)

Depending on which one of the two proposals just outlined we subscribe to, we can analyze these examples as follows. If we think that true imperative forms of main verbs cannot left-adjoin to Mood° because their morphological specification lacks mood features, we can suggest that suppletive imperatives contrast with them in having morphological marking for mood, and therefore are able to adjoin to Mood°. Because they check the features in Mood°, the requirements imposed by the presence of the negative marker are satisfied, and no ungrammaticality ensues.

On the other hand, if we adopt the proposal outlined previously, in which MoodP is viewed as a projection opaque to theta-role assignment, then we are led to analyze these cases as having the verb in a position lower than Mood° in the syntax. We would then have to say that subjunctive verbs are associated with abstract features in Mood°, which are the null counterpart of the subjunctive particles we see in southern Calabrese, northeastern Sicilian, or Romanian. These features satisfy the requirement imposed by the presence of the negative marker, and the sentence is grammatical. In this case, a complement clitic might be left-adjoined to the head of MoodP.

When a form of the indicative is employed, as in Italian, the suppletive imperative verb can either precede or follow the clitic, as shown here:[67]

(119) a. Non *datemi* il libro! (suppletive imperative) (Italian)
           neg give-me the book (indicative)
           'Don't give me the book!'

       b. Non mi *date* il libro!
           neg me give the book
           'Don't give me the book!'

It is difficult to say exactly where the verb and the pronominal clitics are in these examples, as so many factors remain undetermined; in particular, we can analyze these examples differently, depending on where we take the complement clitic to be. In (119)a, the verb could be seen to have left-adjoined to Mood°, with the clitic in a lower position. Alternatively, if we follow the extension of Pollock's view in which Mood° is opaque to theta-role assignment, we would once again assume that indicative verbs are associated with abstract mood features in MoodP and that the verb does not move to this projection. In this case, the verb in (119)a would be in a higher structural position, and the clitic possibly left-adjoined to Mood°. I leave the issue open for the time being, as all the suggestions I could make would be relying on assumptions that are not sufficiently justified at the moment.

Similar difficulties arise with (119)b, with the additional complication of determining whether sentences of this type have the syntactic properties of imperative clauses or whether they are clauses in the indicative with the illocutionary force that is typical of imperatives. If we subscribe to the approach that all the contexts that share the same illocutionary force also share the same syntactic properties, as I have done in the preceding discussion, then two possible analyses can be given to this type of clause. One is along the lines of the analysis suggested for suppletive imperatives with the subjunctive, outlined immediately following the examples in (118): namely, an indicative form, like a subjunctive, can check the features in the head of MoodP. Another, more speculative, possibility stems from the observation that the order *clitic–verb* in these cases is *only* possible in the presence of the negative marker. Along the lines of Kayne's analysis of infinitival imperatives, it is then tempting to think that the negative marker licenses a phonologically empty auxiliary, which in turn is followed by the verbal form in the indicative. The pronominal clitic can then be seen as adjoined to the empty auxiliary, as in other cases of long clitic climbing.[68] The aspect of this proposal that is most problematic is that, whereas we know of overt verbal forms that take an infinitival complement, we are not aware of auxiliary or modal verbs that can be followed by a form of the indicative. In view of this, it is perhaps more plausible to think that the negative marker licenses a phonologically empty counterpart of the subjunctive marker (such as the one found in southern Calabria and eastern Sicily), which is a grammatical specification for mood that is compatible with indicative forms.

4.9.   Residual empirical issues

Before I conclude this chapter, let me mention two contemporary Romance varieties that differ from those examined so far in allowing the co-occurrence of a true imperative form of the verb with a pre-verbal negative marker that by itself can negate a clause.[69] One is the dialect spoken in Cortina d'Ampezzo, in the northeastern Italian region of Veneto. As reported in Apollonio (1930), this language has a form that is unique to the imperative paradigm for the second person singular imperative: while the second person singular of the indicative and of the subjunctive ends in -s, the second person singular of the imperative consists of the root plus the thematic vowel. Such a true imperative form can co-occur with the pre-verbal negative marker *no*, a negative marker that by itself can negate the clause. The second contemporary variety I have found that allows the co-occurrence of a true imperative with a pre-verbal negative marker that by itself can negate a clause is Romagnolo, spoken in the southern part of the northern Italian region Emilia Romagna. Two examples follow, from Sancisi (1995: 29) and from Jaberg and Jud (1928–40),[70] respectively, the latter also cited in Vai (1995b: 195):

(120)   a. *No* lavúra. (true imperative) (Romagnolo)
            neg work
            'Don't work!' (2nd sg)

         b. *Nu* kàska. (true imperative) (Romagnolo from Saludecio)
            neg fall
            'Don't fall!'

Since I have only a very limited amount of data from Romagnolo, let me describe the case of the variety spoken in Cortina in some detail. The second person imperative can be expressed either by means of a true imperative form of the verb or by means of a form of the verb 'have' followed by *da* and the main verb in the infinitival form. This is illustrated with a verb from the first conjugation class (all the examples are from Apollonio 1930; the presence of the subject is optional):

(121)   a. Laóra tu. (true imperative) (Cortina)
            work you (sg)
            'You work!' (2nd sg)

         b. T'as   da   lourà   tu. (form of *have*)
            s.cl'have from to-work you
            'You work!' (2nd sg)

(122)   a. Lourà vos. (true imperative)
            work you (pl)
            'You work!' (2nd pl)

         b. Aé   da   lourà   vós. (form of *have*)
            have from to-work you (pl)
            'You work!' (2nd pl)

In the presence of the negative marker, both the second person singular and the second person plural can negate the imperative with a form of 'have' and can use a form of 'stay' followed by the main verb in the infinitival form. In addition, the second person singular can also negate the true imperative form, whereas the second person plural cannot. These options are exemplified here:

(123)   a. No laóra. (true imperative) (Cortina)
            neg work
            Don't work!' (2nd sg)

        b. No t'as   da   lourà. (form of *have*)
            neg s.cl'have from to-work
            'Don't work!' (2nd sg)

        c. No   sta a lourà. (form of *stay*)
            neg s tay at to-work
            'Don't work!' (2nd sg)

(124)   a. *No lourà. (true imperative)
            neg work
            'Don't work!' (2nd pl)

        b. No louràde. (suppletive imperative)
            neg work (subj.)
            'Don't work!' (2nd pl)

        c. No aé   da   lourà. (form of *have*)
            neg have from to-work (pl)
            'Don't work!' (2nd pl)

        d. No stagéde a lourà. (form of *stay*)
            neg stay   at to-work
            'Don't work!' (2nd sg)

Note that the verbal form used in the negative imperative of the second person plural is not a true imperative but an inflected form of the subjunctive paradigm. In contrast, the second person singular differs from the other varieties we have analyzed in being compatible with the pre-verbal negative marker.

Whereas pronominal clitics follow the verb in non-negative contexts, they precede it in the presence of the negative marker (examples from Apollonio 1930: 76):

(125)   a. Vàtin. (Cortina)
            go-you-loc
            'Go away!'

        b. No tin   va.
            neg you-loc go
            'Don't go!'

If we take the relative position of clitic and verb to reflect the extent to which the verb has moved, these data suggest that, as in the other varieties examined so far, the extent to which the verb moves differs in negative and non-negative contexts.

These data are problematic for all analyses of the incompatibility of true imperatives and pre-verbal negative markers. An analysis that argues that the pre-verbal negative marker blocks movement of the verb to C°, because it creates a minimality effect, would have to argue that the verb moves to a lesser degree in this variety, at least in the case of the second person singular. An analysis that accounts for the incompatibility of true imperatives and pre-verbal negative markers by viewing them as competing for the same position would have to say that in this case the negative marker and a true imperative verb occur in different positions. Finally, in light of the analysis proposed in this chapter, I would have to say one of two things: either that the true imperative verb of second person singular can check the features of the projection MoodP, or that the language can employ the negative marker that is not sensitive to mood specifications to negate the second singular imperative. Since I have no way to relate these putative differences between the negative marker in this language, or the true imperative verb, and their counterparts in the other Romance languages we have examined, I will not pursue either of these lines any further. All such solutions appear stipulative at the moment, as we lack enough information about these languages to be able to relate them to other properties.

Vai (1995b) reports cases of true imperatives compatible with a pre-verbal negative marker from old Italian and old Milanese, two examples of which are repeated here:

(126) a. No guarda al   mee miserie. (true imperative) (old Milanese)
           neg look   at-the my   miseries
           'Don't look at my miseries.'

       b. Ma tu   non pensa e   non isdegna. (true imperative) (old Italian)
           but you neg think and neg despise
           'But don't you think and don't despise.'

In old Italian and old Milanese, as well as in Romagnolo and in the variety spoken in Cortina, in negative imperatives the pronominal clitics immediately follow the negative marker and precede the verb. This is illustrated in the following examples, which exhibit the negative marker in first position, the clitic in second position, and the verb in a position following the clitic:[71]

(127) a. No me abbandona. (old Milanese)
           neg me leave
           'Don't leave me!'

       b. Non ti   tormenta, Marcellino mio, di questo. (old Italian)
           neg you torment, Marcellino my, of this
           'Don't torment yourself with this, my Marcellino!'

Old Italian and old Milanese differ from the varieties spoken in Cortina and in Romagna in that they exhibit a second position requirement on pronominal clitics. The compatibility of true imperative verbs with a pre-verbal negative marker combined with a second position restriction on pronominal clitics are reminiscent of the cases discussed in Rivero (1994b) and Rivero and Terzi (1995). Let me mention the case of Bulgarian, discussed in Rivero (1994b). In this language, pronominal clitics cannot be first in the clause and are strictly adjacent to the verb (thus showing properties attributed to the medieval Romance languages examined in Tobler 1913 and Mussafia 1886). The paradigm for imperatives is the following:

(128) a. Četi ja! (true imperative) (Bulgarian)
          read it
          'Read it!'

       b. Ne ja četi!
          neg it read
          'Don't read it!'

As in the case of old Milanese and old Italian, here too the true imperative verb is compatible with a pre-verbal negative marker that by itself can negate the clause. Rivero (1994b) analyzes these data suggesting that the verb raises less in Bulgarian than in the languages that show incompatibility between true imperatives and pre-verbal negative markers, like Italian and Spanish. The view expressed in that work, as well as in Rivero and Terzi (1995), is that the extent of verb raising is to be related to the function of C°, which is different in the two types of languages: C° is a morphological licenser in the languages that show second position effects on clitics, like Bulgarian, whereas it is a marker of illocutionary force in the languages that lack such effects, like Italian and Spanish. The claim is that it is only in the latter case that C° has the illocutionary feature that attracts imperative verbs. Such an analysis could be extended to old Milanese and old Italian, once it is established that they also obey second position effects on pronominal clitics. The other two varieties, though, do not fall within the class of languages that exhibit second position effects on clitics; hence they cannot be accounted for by an analysis along these lines.[72]

I leave the analysis of these data open for future research.

4.10.   Summary and conclusion

In this chapter I have discussed imperative clauses and in particular the constraints that govern the distribution of negative markers in these contexts. We have seen that, whereas post-verbal negative markers can occur in imperative clauses regardless of the verbal form employed, pre-verbal negative markers cannot occur when the verbal form is a true imperative — that is, a morphological form unique to the imperative paradigm. I have examined in some detail the morphological difference between true and suppletive imperatives and then used such observations as one of the building blocks in my account of the constraints on the distribution of negative markers in imperative clauses. I have argued that all clauses with the illocutionary force of an imperative must check certain features in C°. In addition to this requirement, imperative clauses with a pre-verbal negative marker must obey another constraint, imposed by the negative marker: the features of the head of MoodP must be checked. Main verbs from the imperative paradigm cannot check mood features, due to their poor morphological specifications. In contrast, auxiliary verbs from the imperative paradigm and main verbs from the indicative or subjunctive paradigm can. I have argued that this is because the former are the spell-out of mood features, while the latter can check the mood features either by left-adjoining to it or by being associated with an overt or abstract mood marker.

   One empirical advantage of this proposal over others existing in the literature is that it accounts for why pre-verbal negative markers are incompatible with true imperative forms of main verbs but are compatible with true imperative forms of auxiliary verbs. An account in terms of a minimality effect of the negative marker would have to say that auxiliaries raise less than main verbs, a conclusion that is hard to reconcile with what we know about auxiliaries — namely, that they generally move more than lexical verbs, and not less. In contrast, this account says that true imperative forms of auxiliary verbs are compatible with pre-verbal negative markers because they are the realization of mood features.

This proposal has the conceptual advantage of offering a uniform treatment of negative and non-negative imperative clauses: in both cases, there is a feature in $C°$ that needs to be checked. In negative clauses I assume there is an additional requirement that the features of MoodP be satisfied. But the two share basic syntactic properties. This account can be extended to all clauses that share the same illocutionary force, though I have done this only very tentatively for now. The claim that the negative marker is sensitive to mood specifications finds cross-linguistic support in those languages that have two morphologically distinct types of negative markers whose distribution is determined by mood specifications.

NOTES

Chapter 1

1. In terms of language groups, Occitan belongs to the Provençal group (spoken in southern France); Valdotain to the Franco-Provençal group (spoken on the eastern part of southern France and the westernmost area of northern Italy); Piedmontese to the Gallo-Italic group (spoken in northwestern Italy); Sursilvan to the Western Rhaeto-Romantsch; and Surmeiran to the Central Rhaeto-Romantsch group (spoken in the area called Canton Grischun, in Switzerland).

2. Example (6) is from Seutin (1975: 310). The examples in (7), which represent the variety of Occitan spoken in the Perigord region, are from Miremont (1976: 145).

3. Examples (5) and (8)b are from Chenal (1986:279 and 277, respectively); example (8)d is from Spescha (1989: 498). Valdotain is a variety of Franco-Provençal spoken in the Italian region Val d'Aosta, in the northwestern corner of Italy; Milanese is a Gallo-Italic language spoken in Milan (central northern Italy); Sursilvan is one of the five different languages that belong to the Rhaeto-Romantsch group, spoken in the westernmost corner of Canton Grischun, in Switzerland.

4. Example (11)a is from Parry (1985: 232), (11)b from Signorell (1987: 125), (11)c from Remacle (1952: 266).

5. The pre-verbal negative marker *ne* is part of standard written French (cf. Milner 1982, Muller 1991: ch. 5). It is often omitted in colloquial French spoken in France and Switzerland (cf. Ashby 1976, 1981; Muller 1991: 142–3) and references therein) and is present as a stylistic variable in the French spoken in Montreal (cf. Lemieux 1985 and Sankoff and Vincent 1980).

6. Discussing the negation system for Romance, the interesting question arises of whether the creoles that have a Romance language as their superstratum retain some of its properties in their negation system. For example, among the French creoles, the one spoken in St. Thomas uses the negative marker *pa* in post-auxiliary position (cf. Highfield 1979: 102):

(i)   J'é   *pa* fèt   sa. (St. Thomas creole)
        I'have neg done that
        'I haven't done that.'

155

Haitian, on the other hand, uses the negative marker *pa* pre-verbally (cf. Lefebvre and Lumsden 1992, DeGraff 1993):

(ii)   Pèsonn *pa* vini. (Haitian creole)
        nobody neg come
        'Nobody has come.'

In this book, I will not discuss negation in creole languages, since it would require a more general discussion of the syntax of these languages, which is not immediately comparable with the syntax of Romance. For an overview of the negation system in creoles, I refer the reader to Bickerton (1981: 65), Posner (1985: 180–3), Holm (1988: 171–4), and references therein.

7. See Zanuttini (1991) and references therein for an extensive discussion of this phenomenon and of its correlation with the position of the negative marker.

8. A more detailed discussion can be found in Zanuttini (1994a).

9. I assume that the strong negative features of NegP-1 can be checked by an element in a c-commanding position because of data like the following:

(i)   *Mai* sua madre gli avrebbe   permesso di comportarsi   così! (Italian)
       never his mother him would-have allowed   of to-behave-self so
       'Never would his mother have allowed him to behave that way!'

Assuming that *sua madre* occurs in the canonical subject position in this example, it is either in the specifier of NegP-1 or of a higher functional projection. Then the topicalized negative constituent *mai* 'never' must be in a projection structurally higher than NegP-1. Since the sentence is grammatical, I conclude that *mai* can check the features of NegP-1 from such a position, or else it moves through [Spec,NegP-1].

10. Note that this view entails that all languages have a projection NegP-1, with either strong or weak features. It also opens up a different way of looking at pre-verbal negative markers: instead of being generated in the head of NegP-1, they might in fact originate in a lower structural position. The reason why they are found in NegP-1 would then be because they have to check its strong features in the syntax.

11. "The history of negative expressions in various languages makes us witness the following curious fluctuation: the original negative adverb is first weakened, then found insufficient and therefore strengthened, generally through some additional word, and this in its turn may be felt as a negative proper and may then in course of time be subject to the same development as the original word." (Jespersen 1917: 4).

12. The examples in (21) are from Lafont (1970: 84–88). Example (22) is from Pansier (1973: 262), and (23) is from Aubanel (1963: 206).

13. This diachronic development is also mentioned in Clivio (1970: 85–6), Parry (1989), Posner (1985: 176) with data from Rohlfs (1949–54: 3, 191), Ramat, Bernini and Molinelli (1986: 255–57), and Toppino (1925/6: 42–5). See also Molinelli (1988) for an in-depth discussion of the diachronic change in the strategies for marking sentential negation in Italian and in several dialects spoken in northern Italy.

14. A more detailed overview of this debate can be found in Horn (1989: 452ff). The steps of Jespersen's cycle in English are outlined in Horn's discussion and documented in Jespersen (1917), Marchand (1938), and Joly (1972).

15. As noted in Parry (1989: 9), these languages can be seen as "transitional" between the Piedmontese and the Ligurian group, but their morphological and syntactic properties make them varieties of Piedmontese.

16. It is interesting to note, as pointed out by Parry, that the cases in which this dialect employs the pre-verbal negative marker only are the same as those in French that can employ the pre-verbal negative *ne* only, as described in Grevisse (1986: 1479–81).

Chapter 2

1. Though these negative markers also precede non-finite forms of the verb, it is their distribution with respect to the finite forms that I take to be their distinctive property.

2. Such a discussion is essential to understand the patterns under investigation and of great relevance for an understanding of this part of the grammar of the languages under study. However, insofar as it concerns the characterization of pre-verbal negative markers, it will mostly confirm the results reached in the previous section and thus can be skipped by those readers who are not interested in the intricacies of the agreement system between subject and verb in Romance.

3. Example (2)b is from Surmeiran, one of the three main Rhaeto-Romantsch dialects spoken in Switzerland, and is taken from Signorell (1987: 125) (cf. Haiman and Benincà 1992 for a comprehensive description and discussion of the Rhaeto-Romantsch languages). Example (2)c is from the dialect spoken in Bondeno, in the province of Ferrara, while example (2d) is from the dialect spoken in Carpi, Modena — both in the Italian region called Emilia-Romagna. They are taken from the dialectal atlas that is being compiled at the University of Padua, Italy, and to which I will refer as ASIS (see Benincà et al. 1990–present). Finally, example (2)e is from a variety spoken on the border between the Italian regions of Liguria and Piemonte, in northwestern Italy, in the town of Cairo Montenotte, which has been studied extensively in the work of Mair Parry (see Parry 1985, 1989, 1995, in press a). (2)e is from Parry (in press a).

4. The debate about which factors favor the absence of the pre-verbal negative marker is lively also in the literature on the varieties spoken in Italy (cf. Berruto 1990, Parry 1985, Molinelli 1988, and Vai 1996, among others). Whereas some authors suggest that phonetic factors determine the absence of the pre-verbal negative marker, others argue that its presence or absence is sensitive to the syntactic, rather than the phonetic, environment.

5. I follow a well-established tradition of linguistic and philological studies and occasionally refer to some of the languages under discussion as "dialects." For example, I might call two languages like Piedmontese and Valdotain, spoken in northern Italy (the former belongs to the Gallo-Italic group and the latter to the Franco-Provençal family) "northern Italian dialects." Such terminology emphasizes the contrast between these linguistic entities, used in restricted geographical areas and mostly restricted to informal contexts, and those like Italian or French, which are used as the language of instruction and are officially adopted as the national language in Italy and France, respectively. Alongside the term "dialect" I use the term "language" since they show syntactic differences that make them different linguistic entities for our investigation, which is not concerned with their socio-political status. Finally, I use the term "variety" to refer to languages that differ minimally from one another; for example, I distinguish Torinese from Cairese by saying that the former is the variety of Piedmontese spoken in Torino and the latter the one spoken in Cairo Montenotte.

6. This description applies only to current stages of the languages I am describing. As Parry (in press a) points out, Posner (1985: 179) and Menéndez-Pidal (1962: 114) report an example from Old Leonese, where the negative marker *no* can be found between the object clitic and the verb:

(i)   Porque *lo non* veia. (Old Leonese)
       because him neg saw
       'Because he didn't see him.'

I view such cases as a consequence of the fact that, in older stages of Romance languages, pronominal clitics were subject to a second position requirement, though not to the requirement that they be adjacent to the verb (cf. Wanner 1987, Fontana 1993, Benincà 1994, and Rivero 1994c, among others). No second position requirement on pronominal clitics is attested in the Romance languages examined in this book. Cases of interpolation parallel to the one in (i) are attested in certain contemporary varieties spoken in northern Portugal (cf. Alvarez et al. 1986, and Rouveret 1992: 110). I will not discuss them here.

7. The situation is more complex with respect to subject clitics, where at first sight it appears that some precede and some follow the pre-verbal negative markers that can negate a clause by themselves. As I will show in section 2.3, though, such cases in fact should not be interpreted as an example of re-ordering of the subject clitics and the negative marker; rather, they stem from the fact that different types of subject clitics occupy different positions in the structure, some higher and some lower than the pre-verbal negative marker.

8. Parry (in press a) mentions the dialects of Cairo Montenotte, Saliceto, Cengio, Dego, S. Giulia, Scaletta Uzzone, Piana Crixia, Merana, Motaldo di Spigno, Giusvalla, Pontivrea, and Montenotte.

9. Throughout this book, I gloss all subject clitics with the label s.cl, leaving aside gender, number, and person distinctions. The examples in (5)a–c are from Parry (1985: 232); (5)d is from Parry (in press a).

10. I am grateful to Mair Parry for kindly providing me with these data.

11. A.I.S., chart 1678, point 132.

12. An analysis along these lines is also hinted at in Kayne (1994: 135 fn).

13. I am grateful to G. Cinque (person communication) for alerting me to the relevance of these data. In this brief discussion, I will not address the issue of the relative ordering of the pronominal clitics that appear on either side of the negative marker, for example, the ordering of first or second person clitic in co-occurrence with a reflexive, or the ordering of two third person clitics. I am also collapsing all distinctions among third person non-reflexive clitics, the locative, and the genitive clitic. My tables reflect these simplifications, by grouping these clitics without further distinctions.

14. Unfortunately, I lack examples showing the co-occurrence of a negative marker, followed by first or second person clitic, another negative marker and a third person clitic, in this sequence (i.e., neg CL-1 neg CL-2). I assume that this is simply due to the paucity of data at my disposal and that such examples can be found.

15. This proposal is in agreement with the spirit of several recent proposals on the position of pre-verbal negative markers that can negate the clause by themselves (cf. Laka 1990; Ouhalla 1991; Zanuttini 1990, 1991; Rivero 1994a; among others), though these works do not focus on the relative position of negative markers and complement clitics.

16. Note that I am not making any claim about the structural position where sentential negation is interpreted. Brugger and D'Angelo (1994) argue that the position where negation is interpreted is a functional projection lower than Infl. My data do not allow me to provide clear arguments for or against such a proposal.

17. As pointed out to me by S. Anderson (personal communication), the data concerning the pre-verbal negative markers that cannot negate a clause by themselves could be analyzed in a radically different way if we considered them a kind of agreement marker. That is, instead of treating them as syntactic elements, they could be viewed as morphological elements that express negative agreement with a post-verbal negative marker. Although such a solution is appealing, I will not pursue it here, since I view my task in this work as that of exploring the power and the limitations of a purely syntactic analysis.

18. For arguments against extending Kayne's proposal to pre-verbal clitics, see Cinque (1996b).

19. We could think of the functional heads to which the negative markers of French and Cairese adjoin as negative phrases or polarity phrases. At first sight this might seem implausible, in view of the fact that these negative markers cannot negate a clause by themselves; however several considerations, which will become apparent as the book unfolds, cast doubt on the feasibility of a one-to-one mapping between the presence of a negative/polarity phrase in the

syntactic representation and an instance of sentential negation contributed to the interpretation of the clause. Thus, it is in principle possible to assume that even the negative markers that cannot negate a clause by themselves are (left-adjoined to or even base-generated in) the head of a negative or a polarity phrase. Since we are discussing three distinct positions for the pre-verbal negative markers, under this view one would then argue for the existence of three negative phrases, all of them structurally higher than the position occupied by the finite verb: (a) one for those negative markers that can negate the clause by themselves (e.g., Italian *non*); (b) one for those that cannot negate the clause by themselves and that precede all pronominal clitics (e.g., French *ne*); (c) one for those that cannot negate the clause by themselves and that follow the first cluster of pronominal clitics, CL-1 (e.g., Cairese *n*). Alternatively, in a similar vein, it would be possible to postulate the existence of two negative/polarity phrases only, collapsing the position of Italian *non* and of French *ne*, and expressing their difference in terms of strength of features. Either one of these views might prove helpful in accounting for the diachronc data, which witness the gradual loss of the ability of certain pre-verbal negative markers to negate a clause by themselves. I will not explore these possibilities here.

20. This view has been extended to Italian *non* in Belletti (1990, 1994).

21. A difficulty for this proposal is raised by examples where two pre-verbal negative markers appear, in co-occurrence with one post-verbal one, as in example (17). If one pre-verbal negative marker originated as the head of the phrase of which postverbal *nent* is the specifier, where does the other pre-verbal negative marker come from? I would have to say that the leftmost negative marker is base-generated in the position in which it occurs, similarly to the negative markers which can negate a clause by themselves, whereas the other one has moved from post-verbal position. These data would be more easily handled by proposals such as the ones sketched in notes 17 and 19.

22. Zanuttini (1994a) investigates the possibility that all pre-verbal negative markers might originate in a functional projection lower than Infl and then raise to adjoin to the head of a functional projection equivalent to what I am labeling NegP (labeled "TruthP" in that work). For the advantages of such a proposal (which I am not adopting here), I refer the reader to the work cited.

23. I assume that both the pronominal clitics in pre-verbal position and the pre-verbal negative markers are heads.

24. I am leaving aside the question of why Cairese and French have different options for the adjunction of the negative markers. As pointed out to me by N. Munaro, the solution sketched in (23) for French raises the question of why *ne* can skip the lower head, H-2, and target the higher one, H-1. In the absence of a precise characterization of what determines the possible landing site of *ne*, it is difficult to say whether and why it should be possible for it to do so. This sort of problem seems to militate against the solution in (23) and in favor of the one in (22).

25. Example (33)a is from Chenal (1986: 401), cited in Roberts (1993), and example (33)b is from Poletto (1993a).

26. For detailed descriptions and discussions of the system of subject clitics in the northern Italian dialects, see, among others, Benincà (1983), Benincà and Vanelli (1984), Benincà, Renzi and Vanelli (1985/6), Brandi and Cordin (1981, 1989), Burzio (1986), Campos (1986), Haiman and Benincà (1992), Jaeggli (1982), Napoli (1981), Poletto (1991, 1993a, 1993b), Renzi and Vanelli (1983), Roberts (1993), Saccon (1993), Safir (1983), and Vanelli (1987).

27. Although subject clitics are attested in the dialects spoken across northern Italy, I will focus my attention on those that also have a pre-verbal negative marker. This means that I will concentrate on the dialects spoken in northeastern Italy, in particular in the regions of Veneto, Trentino, Friuli; then, in section 2.3.2, I will also examine some dialects spoken in the region of Liguria.

28. In contrast, Sportiche (in press b) suggests that the differences between subject clitics in French and in northern Italian dialects can be handled without appealing to categorial differences, and proposes that all subject clitics should be consistently analyzed as the head of a projection NomP, Nominative Phrase. I refer the reader to the cited work for further details.

29. For arguments showing that the difference between agreement and vocalic clitics is a syntactic phenomenon and not the result of a phonological constraint, I refer the reader to Poletto (1993a) and Poletto (in press).

30. Example (37) is from Poletto (1993a: 18), (38) from Brandi and Cordin (1989: 120), and (39) from Rizzi (1986: 398).

31. Benincà (1983: 30, fn. 4) mentions the diachronic development of the subject clitics in Paduan, the variety of Veneto spoken in Padua. While in the 16th century subject clitics preceded the negative element, a century later all subject clitics followed the negative marker with the exception of the clitic *a*, which remained where it was. The author takes this as evidence that the clitic *a*, from this point on, was characterized by different properties than the other subject clitics.

32. As already mentioned, in some cases vocalic clitics distinguish between first and second person on the one hand and third person on the other. In Poletto (in press) this kind of morphological marking is taken not to express person distinctions, but rather to mark the speaker and the hearer, in opposition to a third party. I refer the reader to that work for a more detailed description of the data and the analysis.

33. The examples in (41) are from Poletto (1993a: 24). Note that in (41)b the vocalic clitic *a* co-occurs with the agreement clitic *te*.

34. This is also the pattern found in Basso Polesano with respect to the morpheme *co* 'when' (though it does not have WH-features, parallel to French *lorsque*), analyzed in Poletto (1993b) as occurring in C°.

35. The existence of a projection ModP is motivated in the work of Rivero (1994a), Kayne (1991), Calabrese (1993), Dobrovie-Sorin (1993), and Terzi (1992), among others.

36. As mentioned, Poletto further groups agreement clitics in five sub-classes, depending on their function. The classes are: (a) subject clitics that absorb the subject theta-role, (b) subject clitics that license a null pronominal subject (pro), (c) subject clitics that contribute (with verbal inflection) to assigning nominative case to an overt pre-verbal subject, (d) expletive subject clitics, and (e) subject clitics that appear only with auxiliaries.

37. Poletto (1993a) proposes that a "morphologically complex" head consists of a head and a specifier, and that the agreement clitic occupies the specifier position. The analysis of the examples here is not intended to imply that *all* agreement clitics should be in the same identical structural position. As documented in many of the works cited in note 26 and as we will see in section 2.3.2, agreement clitics change their structural position as they undergo diachronic change. Moreover, in some varieties agreement clitics differ according to person specification (the second person singular often differing from the others).

38. Given the assumption that vocalic clitics are in the head of the modal projection, the question arises concerning the position of full NP subjects. Poletto (personal communication) reports that in Basso Polesano NP subjects co-occur with a vocalic clitic only when they are left-dislocated (thus they occur in a position structurally higher than the one occupied by the vocalic clitics). When they are focalized, the vocalic clitic does not appear.

39. See also Vai (1995a: 160) for similar data from Milanese of the early 1600s.

40. Pre-verbal negative markers that cannot negate the clause by themselves precede only two types of subject clitics: the equivalent of Italian impersonal *si*, exemplified below, and those subject clitics that occur only with auxiliaries, of which two examples are given in (33) (cf. Poletto 1993a):

(i)   a. U   *n'* **se** diz   nent parëg.   (Carcare)
       s.cl neg *si* says neg like-that
       'One doesn't say it like that.'

(ii)   b. A*n*   '**sa** dis   mia achsé.   (Carpi — Emiliano)
       s.cl-neg *si* says neg like-that
       'One doesn't say it like that.'

Because both kinds of pre-verbal negative markers precede these clitics, I have not included them in my discussion, as they do not help me discriminate between the two classes I am investigating. I assume that such clitics occur in a position lower than the one of agreement clitics.

41. Consistent with the proposal of section 2.2, I have represented the negative markers that cannot negate a clause by themselves as left-adjoined to a functional head.

42. I am omitting from this discussion other kinds of subject clitics whose distribution does not interfere with that of the negative marker, such as the clitic *l'*, which appears with auxiliaries and with verbs beginning with a vowel, the pronoun *scia*, used in the polite form; and the expletive *a*. The examples in (51) are from Azaretti (1982: 180).

43. Examples (52)a and (52)b are from Azaretti (1982: 237); (52)c is from Azaretti (1982: 181).

44. All these examples are from ASIS (see Benincà et al. 1990–present).

45. Examples from Azaretti (1982: 237).

46. This is not the case for the dialect of Novi Ligure, though, where the subject clitic of second person singular precedes the negative marker (examples from ASIS — Benincà et al. 1990–present):

(i)   a. Ti la kati o ti-*n*   la kati? (Novi Ligure)
       s.cl it buy or s.cl-neg it buy
       'Do you buy it or don't you buy it?'
       b. T'è   ti   ke ti*n*   vö   capì.
       s.cl-is you that s.cl-neg wants to-understand
       'It's you who doesn't want to understand.'

Note that *ti* is the subject clitic, even though it is homophonous with the tonic pronoun (*Tí, ti la kati?* 'You, do you buy it?'). Parry (in press b) reports that the order *clitic–neg* for the second person is still common in Liguria, though many dialects exhibit the same order as that exhibited by Ventimigliese.

47. For example, Vai's (1996) diachronic study shows that already in the 15th century Milanese had a subject clitic for second person singular, *te*, distinct from the tonic pronoun for the same person, *tu*. In this period, the negative marker *non* follows the subject clitic, as shown in (i):

(i)   S' *te*   *non* tax.   (Milanese from the 15th century)
       if s.cl neg keep-quiet
       'If you don't keep quiet.'

By the end of the 17th century, the subject clitic appears after the negative marker, as shown in (ii):

(ii)   *No t'*hé   nagott de bon domà la scianscia. (Milanese from the 17th century)
       neg s.cl'have nothing of good except the tongue
       'You have nothing good except the tongue.'

48. As pointed out to me by B. Santorini (personal communication) this difference between second person on the one hand, and first and third person on the other, is reminiscent of a difference observed in pro-drop phenomena in Bavarian, Yiddish, and German (and

perhaps other Germanic languages as well). In these varieties, second person singular subjects are often dropped, whereas other persons are dropped only under more specialized discourse conditions (cf. Prince 1994 for Yiddish) or not at all.

49. The examples in (56) and (57) are from Antelmi (1993). This work also points out that the impersonal subject clitic *si* follows the negative marker. However, as already mentioned in note 40, I take this element to occur in a structural position lower than that of agreement clitics, and thus not to be relevant to the present discussion.

50. One variety of Fiorentino that allows both the word order *neg–subject clitic* and *subject clitic–neg*, at least for some speakers, is that spoken in Incisa Val d'Arno, discussed in Poletto (in press). The variation depends on whether the clause is declarative or interrogative/exclamative. In this variety, in matrix declarative clauses the only possible order is *neg–subject clitic*, as shown in (i):

(i)   a. Te *un tu* mangi. (Fiorentino from Incisa Val d'Arno)
          you neg s.cl eat
          'You are not eating.'
       b. *Te *tu un* mangi.

But the opposite word order is possible in yes/no questions and exclamative clauses, as shown in (ii):

(ii)   a. Te *tu un* mangi? (Fiorentino from Incisa Val d'Arno)
          you s.cl neg eat
          'You are not eating?'
       b. Te *tu un* mangi!
          you s.cl neg eat
          'You are not eating!'

I refer the reader to Poletto's work for a possible analysis in terms of features in CP that attract the subject clitic to a position higher than the one it occupies in matrix declarative clauses.

51. Parry (in press a) discusses two examples of pre-verbal negative markers that cannot negate the clause by themselves which do not follow, but rather precede, agreement subject clitics. These are from varieties of Emiliano spoken near the border with Piedmont and Liguria (from Zörner 1986: 105, 1994). Note the position of the pre-verbal negative markers, *en* and *ne*, with respect to the agreement subject clitics, *te* and *t*, respectively:

(i)   *En* **te** m'ö mia dit k *en* **te** saris   stat mia a ka.   (Varzi)
          neg s.cl me   neg said that neg s.cl would-be been neg at home
          'You didn't tell me that you wouldn't be at home.'

(ii)   *Ne* **t**   i   kuñusi míga. (Gambaro)
          neg s.cl them know   neg
          'You don't know them.'

Note that in both examples the subject clitic is the one of second person singular, the one most often found to be reanalyzed as verbal agreement. I thus suggest that in this case, as well as in those discussed before, the data that deviate from the general pattern are not to be explained by appealing to a different position for the negative marker, but rather to the fact that the subject clitic can occupy different positions in the structure. In this case, I have to say that the subject clitic of second person singular is even lower than the other agreement clitics and closer to the verb.

52. The examples are taken from Benincà and Vanelli (1982: 18) and Poletto (1993b: 211).

53. The examples in (67) are from Benincà and Vanelli (1982: 18), those in (68) from Poletto (1993b: 242). In (68)b, *nol* is taken to be a contracted form of the negative marker *no* plus the (non-interrogative) subject clitic *el*; sometimes this sequence of elements is also spelled *no (e)l*.

54. The idea that questions have an abstract operator in sentence initial position goes back to Katz and Postal (1964: 104) and Baker (1970). In the discussion of languages that show verb second effects, it is a common assumption that yes/no questions have the verb in second position, contrary to appearance, and that the first position is occupied by an abstract yes/no operator. For a recent discussion, see Haegeman (1995: §2.2.4).

55. The intuition that operators must occur in the specifer of a functional projection is frequently found in the literature. In particular, discussing related issues, Grimshaw (in press b) explicitly encodes this requirement in her system.

56. This requirement can be seen as a more general version of one of the two requirements expressed for individual functional categories under the labels of "criteria" (see the WH-Criterion in May 1985, reformulated in Rizzi's work; the Neg-Criterion in Haegeman and Zanuttini 1991, 1995 and Haegeman 1991, 1992a, 1992b, 1994, 1995; and the Clitic Criterion in Sportiche in press a, among others). Haegeman (1992a, 1995) generalizes the common phenomena involving WH- and negative phrases and formulates the more general "AFFECT-Criterion," which covers both:

(i)   An affective operator must be in a Spec-head configuration with an [AFFECTIVE] X°.

(ii)   An [AFFECTIVE] X° must be in a Spec-head configuration with an AFFECTIVE operator.

The requirement I am adopting can be seen to correspond to the first half of the AFFECT Criterion: it requires that an operator be in a Spec-head configuration with a head having compatible features.

57. One question that could be raised with respect to this proposal concerns the nature and the function of those subject clitics that appear in interrogative contexts only, to which we have been referring as interrogative subject clitics. If they appear in interrogative clauses in the absence of *no*, why don't they also appear in interrogative clauses in the presence of *no*? One possible answer to this question consists in saying that interrogative clitics do not appear in the presence of *no* because their morphological requirements are not met. If we assume that they must encliticize to a verb and cannot be hosted by elements of any other syntactic category, then their failure to appear with the negative marker could be accounted for by invoking the impossibility of the enclitic pronoun to be hosted by the negative marker. Another answer can be given in terms of the function of interrogative clitics. Poletto (1993b) argues that interrogative clitics in Paduan are present in interrogative clauses for all person specifications because (argumental) *pro* is not otherwise licensed in these contexts. That is, while the subject clitics in non-interrogative clauses co-occur with a *pro* in subject position, the subject clitics of the interrogative series occur instead of *pro*. Poletto's analysis assumes that *pro* can only be licensed in this language in a configuration of Spec-head agreement with the inflected verb and takes movement of the verb to C° to destroy such a configuration. More precisely, when the inflected verb moves to C° and thus is not in a configuration of Spec-head agreement with argumental *pro*, it cannot identify its person and number features. Hence, in these cases, an overt pronoun must be present instead of *pro* — namely, an interrogative clitic. Roberts (1993) adopts essentially the same analysis for the obligatory presence of interrogative subject clitics in Valdotain. If this reasoning is on the right track, we have a way to interpret the absence of interrogative clitics in yes/no questions in which the verb has not moved and *no* is the head whose features match those of the interrogative operator: Given that the verb has not moved to a position structurally higher than the one in which it occurs in non-interrogative contexts, the

configuration for the licensing of *pro* has not been altered. Therefore an interrogative subject clitic is not necessary: the finite verb can license *pro*, as it does in non-interrogative clauses.

58. All examples are taken from Jones (1993).

59. My analysis differs from the proposal in Chomsky (1995), which assumes, at least for WH-questions, that the features in C° can be checked by the operator in the specifier position.

60. The examples are taken both from Chen (1996) and from Cheng, Huang, and Tang (in press).

61. Mandarin has two negative markers, *bu* and *meiyou*, whose distribution is roughly the following: the former occurs with bare verbs and modals; the latter with certain aspect markers and accomplishment verbs (cf. Wang 1965; Chao 1968; Li and Thompson 1981; Chen 1996; Cheng, Huang, and Tang in press). Both appear in pre-verbal position, as shown here:

(i)   Ta *bu* lai.   (Mandarin)
       he neg come
       'He's not coming.'

(ii)   Hufei *meiyou* qu xuexiao.
       Hufei neg   go school
       'Hufei did not go to school.'

They occur in sentence final position only in yes/no questions of the type we are discussing.

62. Chen (1996) and Cheng, Huang, and Tang (in press) disagree on whether the negative marker *bu* can also occur in sentence final position in yes/no questions. Whereas the former find (i) to be grammatical, the latter does not:

(i)   Hufei hui qu *bu*? (Mandarin)
       Hufei will go neg
       'Will Hufei go?'

These two pieces of work also seem to disagree on whether or not a yes/no question with a negative marker in sentence final position is negative. Hence, they translate them into English as negative and as non-negative questions, respectively. I will report the translation given in the paper from which the example is taken.

63. Cheng, Huang, and Tang (in press) propose this analysis for Mandarin; in contrast, they argue that the negative markers are base-generated in C° in the case of Taiwanese and Cantonese, which I haven't discussed here. I refer the reader to their article for a discussion of these cases.

64. Cheng, Huang, and Tang (in press) in particular suggest that the negative markers *bu* and *meiyou* have an unspecified value for the negation feature: they are marked [+ Neg] when they remain in Neg°, whereas they are specified as [−Neg] when they move to C°.

65. I am grateful to H. Haider (personal communication) for pointing out the relevance of this question.

66. See Rizzi and Roberts (1989) for a discussion of selected clauses that do not allow I to C movement even in the absence of a complementizer (whereas they allow I to C movement in main clauses).

67. The same pattern for *cossa* also holds with *chi* 'who':

(i)   *Chi *no* ga-*lo*   visto? (Paduan)
       who neg has-s.cl seen
       'Who hasn't he seen?'

(ii)   *Chi *nol*   ga visto?
       who neg-s.cl has seen
       'Who hasn't he seen?'

68. In this respect as well the WH-word *chi* 'who' exhibits the same pattern as *cossa*:

(i)   Chi ze che *nol*   ga invità? (Paduan)
       who is that neg-s.cl has invited
       'Who is it that he hasn't invited?'

69. See Benincà and Vanelli (1982: 33), Poletto (1993b: 237), and Munaro (1995, 1996).

70. Dealing with partially similar data in a different empirical domain, Watanabe (1992) suggests that in the case of WH-phrases in situ an abstract operator moves to CP in the syntax.

71. Poletto (1993b) and Roberts (1993) also argue that non-interrogative and interrogative subject clitics occupy structurally different positions, though they view the latter as being higher than the former, contrary to what we are proposing. For example, Roberts (1993), basing his analysis on the phrase structure proposed in Cardinaletti and Roberts (in press), argues that the interrogative subject clitic is in the specifier of AgrP-2, whereas the non-interrogative subject clitic is the head of AgrP-2.

72. It might be possible to argue that the verb left-adjoins to the interrogative subject clitic in order to reach a position from which its features can then raise to the relevant head ($C°$). This view would suggest that, whereas complement clitics can occur between the finite verb and $C°$ without blocking movement of the verbal features to $C°$, interrogative subject clitics cannot. This might be due to the fact that complement clitics do not have features that can be attracted by $C°$, whereas interrogative subject clitics do. But if this were so, then we would need to ask why the features of interrogative subject clitics cannot raise to $C°$ themselves, always obviating the need for verb movement. This problem would be avoided by adopting Sportiche's (in press b) proposal, which, as mentioned, views the sequence of the verb and the interrogative subject as a morphological unit, licensed by LF-movement of the verb to $C°$.

73. Example (87)a is from Poletto (1993a: 119), (87)b–d from Poletto (1995). It should be noted that, in all these examples, the non-interrogative subject clitic is a vocalic clitic, *a*, and never an agreement clitic. Recall from the discussion in section 2.3 that vocalic clitics are structurally higher than agreement clitics. Examples (87)e–f are from Roberts (1993); here the subject clitic that precedes the verb belongs to the class of subject clitics that only appear with auxiliaries.

74. The subject clitic *l* in (88)b is an example of a subject clitic of the class that only co-occurs with auxiliaries.

75. I hesitate to view such a position as part of CP because I see it as lower than the one occupied by complement clitics. Poletto (1995), in contrast, argues that all the positions that make up CP are higher than the position where complement clitics occur. One set of data discussed in that work that is problematic for the view I am exploring here comes from a (non-V2) Rhaeto-Romantsch dialect, Fassano. In this variety, a WH-phrase can be immediately followed by the question marker *pa* and no verb movement around the subject clitic, as in (i)a. The contrast with (i)b suggests that *pa* is higher than a non-interrogative subject clitic:

(i)   a. Olà *pa* tu vas? (Fassano)
          where pa s.cl go
          'Where are you going?'
       b. *Olà tu vas *pa*?
          where s.cl go pa

If the verb appears on the left of an interrogative subject clitic, it must precede the question marker *pa*, as shown in (ii):

(ii)   a. Olà   vas-to *pa*? (Fassano)
          where go-s.cl pa
          'Where are you going?'

b. *Olà *pa* vas-to?
    where pa go-s.cl

Poletto (1995) takes *pa* to be a question marker in the specifier of one of the positions of a split CP and assumes that it only occurs in one structural position. Then she concludes from (ii)a that the verb and the interrogative subject clitic have raised to a position higher than the one occupied by *pa*. Such a position is higher than the one in which a non-interrogative subject clitic occurs (cf. the position of *tu* in (i)a), a conclusion in contrast to what my analysis has led me to propose. At the moment, I do not have a proposal on how to accommodate these data within my analysis.

76. Sportiche (in press b) argues that the finite verb and the subject clitic that follows it in cases of inversion are a morphological complex and do not result from the verb having syntactically adjoined to the subject clitic. However, the proposal that the verb does not move to C° in the syntax is independent from this particular assumption. As is stated explicitly in Sportiche's work, it could be maintained even if the verb were taken to move overtly to left-adjoin to the subject clitic — that is, under an analysis similar to the one I am advocating here.

77. Among the northern Italian dialects, complex inversion is attested in Valdotain, as discussed in Roberts (1993).

78. This is what Rizzi and Roberts (1989) call the "landing site problem." I refer the reader to their paper for a solution to the problem radically different from the one proposed by Sportiche.

79. As mentioned in note 76, Sportiche (in press b) assumes that the sequence consisting of the verb and the subject clitic (e.g., *est-il* in our examples) is the result of a morphological operation. In order to limit the presence of such a unit to the right set of root clauses, he crucially assumes that the subject clitic must be licensed in the head of the projection NomP (Nominative Phrase) by verb movement to C° triggered by the presence of an operator. Though Sportiche's work assumes that the verb moves from AgrS° through Nom° to C° at LF, the analysis would also be compatible with the view that the verb moves to Nom° overtly and then to C° at LF (as long as movement to C° remains crucial for the licensing of the subject clitic in Nom°).

80. The Walloon examples are from Remacle (1952: 375–77).

81. Note that this also contrasts with WH-questions. In matrix WH-questions, the complementizer is never present and the sentence exhibits inversion of the verb around the interrogative subject clitic (cf. (77)). In negative WH-questions, the WH-phrase cannot be adjacent to the negative marker and a cleft-construction must be used (cf. (80)).

82. I thank N. Munaro (personal communication) for providing me with these data. Note that the counterpart of (96)a without the negative marker is grammatical but has a different reading, where *cossa* is interpreted as specific (cf. (i)). The counterpart of (96)b without the negative marker is ungrammatical, as shown in (ii):

(i)   Cossa *che* l'ha   fat! (Bellunese)
      what that s.cl'has done
      'That thing he has done!'

(ii) *Cossa ha-*lo*   fat!
      what   has-s.cl done
      'That thing he has done!'

The Bellunese counterpart of these exclamatives with the WH-word *che*, which remains in situ, does not differ from the case of interrogatives:

(iii) Ghe dis-lo   che! (Bellunese)
      him says-s.cl what
      'What things he's telling him!'

83. Italian has a parallel construction, exemplified here:

(i)   Cosa *non* ha fatto, per ottenere quel posto!   (Italian)
       what neg has done for to-obtain that position
       'What things he has done in order to obtain that position!'

(ii)   Cosa non farebbero, pur   di vederli   contenti!
       what neg would-do, emph of to-see-them happy
       'What things they'd be willing to do, just to see them happy!'

In the absence of subject clitics, though, it is impossible to say whether the verb has moved further in these contexts than in others.

84. The counterpart of (98) without subject clitic inversion is available as well, as shown in (i), but only as an echo-question:

(i)   Parcossa *no* te   ve anca ti? (Paduan)
       why   neg s.cl. go also you
       'Why aren't you going as well?'

It is interesting to note the different behavior exhibited by *parcossa* and by another WH-element with related meaning, *parché* 'why'. *Parché* differs both from *parcossa* and from other WH-phrases in not requiring a cleft construction in the presence of *no*. Moreover, it does not exhibit subject clitic inversion:

(ii)   a. Parché *no* te   ve anca ti? (Paduan)
          why   neg s.cl go also you
          'Why aren't you going also?'

       b. *Parché *no* ve-to   anca ti?
          why   neg go-s.cl also you
          'Why aren't you going also?'

On the difference between *parcossa* and *parchè*, Poletto (1993b: §3.3) suggests that while the former is an unanalyzable WH-word in [Spec,CP], the latter consists of *par* 'for' plus the complementizer *che* 'that'. If this analysis is on the right track, I can interpret the contrast between *parchè* and *parcossa* in light of my proposal. *Parché* differs from *parcossa* in that the XP already has a head with which it shares features: *par* occurs in the specifier of *che*. Hence, neither verb movement nor the use of a cleft is necessary.

85. The distribution of the post-verbal negative marker *miga* will be discussed at length in the next chapter, where I will examine its counterpart in several Romance varieties.

86. P. Benincà (personal communication) pointed out another context in which the pre-verbal negative marker co-occurs with movement of the verb to the left of the subject clitic, discussed in Benincà (1996). It is that of non-WH-exclamative clauses. Imagine a context in which there is a child who does not usually eat much; one day, surprisingly, he eats everything. In such a context, the following sentence is felicitous:

(i)   *No* ga-*lo*   magnà tuto!   (Paduan)
       neg has-s.cl eaten   everything
       'He's eaten everything!'

It conveys that the fact that he ate everything is very surprising. This context is discussed to some extent in Portner and Zanuttini (1996).

87. A second negative marker, *miga*, is present only in the case of (99).

88. I am grateful to C. Poletto for providing me with these data.

Chapter 3

1. It is important to bear in mind that because of the different degrees to which the past participle can move, Cinque's delimitation of the syntactic space does not always correspond to a surface word order in which the participle is the left-most element. This can be illustrated with the contrast we observe comparing northern and southern varieties of standard Italian. While in central and southern varieties the most natural word order has the past participle before the lower adverbs *già* 'already' (cf. (i)), in the northern varieties the most natural word order has the participle after such adverb (cf. (ii)):

(i)   Ho **mangiato** *già*.   (central and southern varieties of standard Italian)
       have eaten   already
       'I have already eaten.'

(ii)   Ho *già*   **mangiato**. (northern variety of standard Italian)
       have already eaten
       'I have already eaten.'

The syntactic space defined in Cinque's work is delimited on the left by the position the past participle occupies in (i). The word order in (ii) is taken to result from the fact that the past participle has raised to a lesser extent than it has in (i).

2. Moreover, the class of adverbs ending in *-mente* or *-ment* in Italian and French, respectively, does not find an exact counterpart in many of the Romance varieties I examined.

3. All the examples in this section are taken from Cinque's work.

4. Cinque's work also shows that in each case the opposite order is not possible. I will not report the examples here, but simply refer the reader to the work cited.

5. Cinque convincingly argues that the lack of co-occurrence of *pas* and *plus* should not be taken to show that they occur in the same position. First, while *pas* precedes *déjà*, *plus* follows it, as we have seen. Second, while a main verb in the infinitival form can precede *plus*, it can never precede *pas*, as pointed out in Pollock (1989: 413). We will return to these data in section 3.3.2. (Incidentally, *pas* and *plus* can co-occur when the latter is not an aspectual adverb, but a degree element; however, this is irrelevant to our discussion.)

6. Cinque derives further support for this view from the ordering among functional morphemes. Under a view of morphological composition like that pursued in Baker (1988), Cinque demonstrates that the cross-linguistically uniform ordering among such morphemes is directly derivable from the same hierarchy of functional projections that host the adverbial elements.

7. Cinque's (1994, 1996a) work addresses some of the criticisms moved to Pollock's (1989) approach in Iatridou (1990), in particular concerning the characterization of "short Verb Movement." It is also in agreement with Iatridou's claim that different adverbs have different base generated positions, following Jackendoff (1972, 1977) and Travis (1988).

8. Since I am not interested in the different phonetic realizations of the negative markers, unless they correspond to syntactic differences, I will always write the second of the two negative markers of Piedmontese as *nen*. In the varieties of Piedmontese spoken in Canavese, though, this negative marker is pronounced with a palatalized initial consonant and a higher vowel, [ñin], or else as [nin].

9. On the use of *nen* and *pa* in Piedmontese, see Aly-Belfàdel (1890: 75), Berruto (1974: 34), and Albin (1984).

10. French *tout* and Italian *tutto* 'all', when they are not modified, coordinated, or focused, occur in a position preceding all complements of the participle (cf. Kayne 1975: Ch. 1; Sportiche 1988: 433; Belletti 1990; and Cinque 1994, 1995b: Ch. 9). I verified that this property is shared by the counterpart of *tout* in the varieties examined in this chapter.

11. As Paola Benincà points out to me, standard Italian also allows both a pre- and a post-participial position for *sempre* 'always'. These two positions are associated with two different interpretations. Let us see how:

(i)   Ho *sempre* pagato le tasse. (Italian)
       have always paid   the taxes
       'I have always paid taxes.'

(ii)   Ho pagato *sempre* le tasse.
       have paid   always the taxes
       'I have paid taxes always.'

The pre-participial position, exemplified in (i), is interpreted as asserting that I have paid taxes from the beginning, since the day I was supposed to. It can be used even if I have occasionally failed to pay an individual tax. On the other hand, the post-participial position, exemplified in (ii), is interpreted as asserting that, at every instance in which I was supposed to pay a tax, I have paid it; it would be false if I had in fact occasionally failed to pay. I am not in a position to judge whether parallel differences are associated with the two positions in Piedmontese as well.

12. The question then arises of what sort of process gives rise to the unit *pi nen*. It could be a process that takes place before the words enter the syntactic component or a process that takes place in the syntax. I will not elaborate on this issue here.

13. Parry (1985) notes that in Cairese, the variety of Piedmontese spoken in Cairo Montenotte, in the presence of infinitives it is possible to find residual instances of an earlier form *nun*, besides the more common *nen*:

(i)   U m dispjaz tant   ed *nun* puraeime ferme. (Cairese)
       s.cl. me pains   much of neg to-can   stay
       'I am very sorry about not being able to stay.'

(ii)   Cerkuma d *nun* spurkese.
       try (1st,pl) of neg to-dirty-self
       'Let's try not to get dirty.'

This negative marker, like *nen*, precedes a lexical verb in the infinitival form.

14. Berruto (1990) describes infinitival verbs as occurring to the right of *nen*, but reports an example with the opposite word order:

(i)   Pudèj *nen* fé   gnente! (Piedmontese)
       to-can neg to-do nothing
       'Not to be able to do anything!

In this example, the infinitival form that precedes *nen* is a modal verb, an element of a class that (like auxiliaries) tends to raise higher than lexical verbs.

15. Their co-occurrence is not readily accepted by my informants from the variety of Torino, who tend to judge examples like (46)a as "redundant."

16. Berruto (1990) also reports as grammatical an example identical to the one given in (46)a except for some phonetic details.

17. *Propi* can modify the adverb *pi* alone, as in (i), in a variety where *pi* need not co-occur with *nen*. Note that *propi* cannot modify the negative marker *pa* alone, as in (ii):

(i)   A'm   pias   *propi*   *pi*.   (Piedmontese from Broglina)
       s.cl'me pleases absolutely no more
       'I absolutely don't like it anymore.'

(ii)   *A'm   pias   *propi*   *pa.*
s.cl'me pleases absolutely not
'I absolutely don't like it.'

Different varieties differ as to the degree to which they accept examples like (i). The discriminating factor seems to be whether or not *pi* is inherently negative in a given variety: if it is, then (i) is acceptable. Otherwise, *pi* must co-occur with a negative element. My main informant for the variety of Piedmontese from Turin, for example, has the following judgments:

(iii)   a. *A'm   pias   *propi*   *pi.*   (Piedmontese from Torino)
s.cl'me please absolutely no more
'I absolutely don't like it anymore.'

b. A'm   pias   *propi*   *pi nen.*
s.cl'me please absolutely no more
'I absolutely don't like it anymore.'

c. A'm   cunta *propi*   *pi*   *gnente.*
s.cl-me tells   absolutely no more nothing
'He doesn't tell me absolutely anything anymore.'

The sequence in which *pa* precedes *propi pi*, as in (iv), is ungrammatical for speakers of all varieties:

(iv)   *A'm pias *pa propi pi.* (Piedmontese)

This ungrammaticality parallels that of the corresponding sequence in Italian:

(v)   *Non mi piace *mica proprio più.* (Italian)

18. Standard Italian as well provides an interesting set of data in this respect. *Più* 'no more' cannot precede the negative marker *non* (which is a pre-verbal negative marker); it can follow it, though, and the two can occur in isolation, for example, as an answer to a question:

(i)   Lo fai ancora? *Non più.* (Italian)
it do still   neg more
'Are you still doing that? Not anymore.'

On the other hand, *più* can precede as well as follow a negative indefinite like *nessuno* 'nobody' (also *mai* 'never' and *niente* 'nothing', but less freely):

(ii)   a. *Più   nessuno* mi ha cercato. (Italian)
more nobody me has seeked
'Nobody has looked for me anymore.'

b. *Nessuno più* mi ha cercato.
nobody more me has seeked
'Nobody has looked for me anymore.'

Given that *più* is a negative polarity item (cf. English 'anymore'), we must analyze example (ii)a as having *più* in the same constituent as the negative marker and not in one that is structurally higher (where the negative marker would fail to c-command the polarity item). I thank G. Cinque for drawing my attention to the Italian data.

19. This contrast does not appear when the negative element *gnun* precedes a head noun, as in (i):

(i)   A'm   da   *(nen) gnun cunseil.* (Piedmontese)
s.cl'me gives (neg) no   advice
'S/he doesn't give me any advice.'

20. I have simplified Parry's phonetic transcription.

21. My informants accept the order *past participle–tot* only if *tot* receives emphatic stress, or if it is 'heavy', as in (i):

(i)   Giani l'a   pa **compré**   *tot* cen que d'ei   deulle.   (Cognen)
       Giani s.cl'has neg understood all that that s.cl'have told-him
       'John didn't understand everything I told him.'

In such cases, *tot* might have remained inside of VP.

22. As for the case of *pi nen*, the question then arises of whether such a unit is the result of a syntactic process or of a process that takes place pre-syntactically.

23. See Rowlett (1993a, 1993b) for some interesting proposals on the syntax of French *pas*.

24. As pointed out to me by N. Munaro (personal communication), in Italian as well the co-occurrence of *già* 'already' and the sentential negative marker *non* is more freely available in interrogative than in declarative clauses. That is, while (i) is the natural way of asking a question in which the proposition that Gianni has already arrived is assumed in the discourse, (ii) is awkward:

(i)   Gianni non è già   arrivato? (Italian)
       Gianni neg is already arrived
       '@Hasn't Gianni already arrived?'

(ii)   ??Gianni non è già arrivato.

If the declarative clause in (ii) is to be given a presuppositional reading, it requires either a particular intonation (with focal stress on the sequence *non è*), or the presence of *mica*:

(iii)   a. Gianni *NON È* già arrivato.
        b. Gianni non è *mica* già   arrivato.
           Gianni neg is neg already arrived
           '@Gianni hasn't already arrived.'

Alternatively, if the declarative clause in (ii) is to be given a non-presuppositional reading, that is, it is not to be interpreted as negating a proposition assumed in the discourse, then the use of *ancora* 'yet' is preferred:

(iv)   Gianni non è *ancora* arrivato. (Italian)
       Gianni neg is yet   arrived
       'Gianni hasn't yet arrived.'

French differs from Italian, as we have discussed in the previous chapter, in that the pre-verbal negative marker *ne* by itself cannot negate the clause. Thus, given that *pas* plays both the role of *non* and of *mica* in (iii)b, the French counterpart of this clause should be something like (v):

(v)   *Jean n'est *pas* dejà   *pas* arrivé. (French)
       Jean neg'is neg already neg arrived
       '@Jean hasn't already arrived.'

In this example, the first occurrence of *pas* would correspond to Italian *mica*, conveying the presuppositional reading, and the second to Italian *non*, negating the clause. The impossibility of such a construction is to be related to the fact that French *pas* cannot co-occur with other negative elements in the clause (except for pre-verbal *ne*) yielding a single instance of negation.

25. See Beretta (1980: 170): "Milanese *nò*: particella avverbiale autonoma fortemente accentuata" 'autonomous adverbial particle, heavily stressed'.

26. See Vai (1995a, 1995b, 1996) for a study of the diachronic change of the negation system in Milanese.

27. According to Parry (in press b) post-verbal *no* derives from a structure in which a pre-verbal negative marker *no* was repeated at the end of the sentence for the purpose of emphasis. Such structures are still found in some northern Italian varieties, such as the ones described in Siller-Runggaldier (1985), where the repetition has kept its emphatic character (see also Zörner 1989).

28. The possibility of having the presuppositional negative marker in a position preceding the finite verb is somewhat limited within Romance. It is not given to those languages that lack a pre-verbal negative marker completely, such as Piedmontese. For Piedmontese *pa*, which I have analyzed as corresponding to Italian *mica*, occurrence in pre-verbal position is utterly ungrammatical. However, the impossibility of the presuppositional negative marker in pre-verbal position is not just tied to the lack of a pre-verbal negative marker in the language in which it occurs. The counterpart of *mica* is impossible in pre-verbal position also in some of the languages that have a pre-verbal negative marker, like Paduan and Venetian. I do not know at this point which factors are relevant in determining the observed variation.

29. E. Di Domenico (personal communication), a speaker from Perugia in central Italy, finds the pre-verbal position to be the only possible position for *mica*.

30. The option of occurring in a position lower than *già* 'already' is not given to Italian *mica*.

31. If *minga* is structurally ambiguous, as I suggested previously, we would expect that when it functions as a regular negative marker, it occurs in a position lower than *gemò*. Given that the participle can raise past *gemò*, we would then expect to find that it can raise past *minga* as well in these cases. Whereas my informants reject the order *participle-minga*, Vai (1995a) reports it as marginal:

(i)   a. U *minga* vist   la   tuza. (Milanese)
          have   neg   seen the   girl
          'I haven't seen the girl.'
       b. ?U vist   *minga* la   tuza.

When asked about the reading of (i)b, Vai (personal communication) stated that it is that of a regular, not a presuppositional, negative marker. Though this provides only a small amount of evidence, I suggest that the participle precedes *minga* in (i)b because the negative marker occupies a lower position than the one it occupies when it is interpreted as a presuppositional negative marker.

32. I am grateful to M. Vai (personal communication) for these examples. I only exemplify the examples corresponding to 'already' and 'always' since, as was mentioned before, *no* does not co-occur with *pü*, 'no more', in any order.

33. Pavese *no* (as well as Milanese *no*) cannot co-occur with negative indefinites in the same clause, as shown here:

(i)   *La Maria l'ha   no vist *nient*. (Pavese)
       the Maria s.cl'has neg seen nothing
       'Maria hasn't seen anything.'

This is also true of French *pas* (though not of Quebecois), while Piedmontese *nen* can occur with such elements in the same clause so long as they are not adjacent, as mentioned toward the end of section 3.3.1.

34. *No* is not an instance of constituent negation in these sentences. In (115), for example, it does not have to be adjacent to *sempar* 'always', as it would if it were a case of constituent negation. One can find lexical material intervening between the two, as shown in (i):

(i)   ??L'ha *no* dumà *sempar* vinciu cla gara chi. (Pavese)
s.cl'has neg only always won   this race here
'@He hasn't only always won this race.'

35. I will come back to this issue in section 3.5.

36. Moreover, sentences like those in (129) might be subject to some parallelism requirement.

37. See Parkinson (1988: 158), Thomas (1969: 289), and Schwegler (1991). I am grateful to H. Britto, J. da Silva Santos, C. Figueiredo-Silva, C. Galves, M. Guimarães, E. Pagotto, A.-P. Scher, and G. Silveira for sharing with me their knowledge of different varieties of Brazilian Portuguese.

38. I am leaving out of the discussion the position of the negative markers in the Trentino dialects of Cembra and Lisignago, as well as Brazilian Portuguese, mentioned briefly at the end of the previous section. They occur in a position following the VP-complements.

39. An analogous question could be asked with respect to the adverb 'no more', which occurs in the specifier of the projection $AspP_{perf}$, expressing perfective aspect. Unfortunately, though, this is very hard to answer, due to the general lack of co-occurrence of these negative markers with this adverb. In both Milanese and Pavese, the adverb *pü* 'no more' cannot co-occur with the negative marker *no* in NegP-4 (though it may co-occur with the negative marker in NegP-2, with some degree of marginality). In Piedmontese, when no other negative constituent occurs in the clause, *pi* 'no more' appears as *pi nen*, a sequence that exhibits the behavior of a syntactic unit and does not co-occur with *nen*.

40. In order to take scope over elements it does not c-command, such as the adverb for 'already', *nen* is forced to move to NegP-2, which it can do with some degree of marginality. If it does not move to NegP-2 and co-occurs with 'already', this adverb is outside its scope, as we saw in (29). Note that *nen* can (marginally) move to NegP-2, as shown in (28)a.

41. Hirschbühler and Labelle (1994) discuss the diachronic change in the position of negative markers such as *pas* and *point* in French. In particular, they argue that *pas* is first adjoined to VP and then, at a later stage, adjoined to the projection InfnP (Infinitival Phrase), which is structurally higher than VP. Both the data and the analysis they propose are in broad terms compatible with the view I outlined in the text, though I would argue that the position the negative markers occupy changes from a lower to a higher NegP.

42. In the case of Italian, Piedmontese, Valdotain, and French, I have indicated as the lowest position where the past participle may occur the one immediately below 'always' and immediately above the negative marker in NegP-4. This might turn out to be wrong, and the past participle might be even lower — that is, in a position corresponding to the one it can occupy in Pavese. Unfortunately, I have not had the opportunity to see which elements, if any, occur in NegP-4 in these languages, the necessary step to determine whether the participle has the option of occurring to their immediate right. For further examples of variation in the position of the past participle across Romance, I refer the reader to Cinque's (1995a, 1996a) work.

Chapter 4

1. Both Joseph and Philippaki-Warburton (1987) and Rivero (1994a, 1994b) use the term "surrogate" imperative rather than "suppletive" imperative. I attach no particular significance to this terminological choice.

2. A clear and thorough description of imperatives in Italian can be found in Salvi and Borgato (1995).

3. As discussed in Salvi and Borgato (1995), second person singular imperatives that are morphologically distinct from the corresponding person of the present indicative are found

only with verbs of the first class and with certain irregular verbs from other verbal classes — for example *dire* 'to say' (third conjugation class):

(i)   *Di*llo! (true imperative) (Italian)
        say-it
        'Say it!'

(ii)   Lo *dici*. (indicative)
        it say
        'You say it.'

(iii)   Lo *dica*. (subjunctive)

Usually, verbs of the second and third conjugation classes have forms for the familiar imperative that are formally identical to the corresponding form of the present indicative. As will become clear in the course of the discussion, despite the superficial similarity with the corresponding indicative forms, I will treat these imperative forms as true imperatives, in light of their behavior in the presence of negation.

4. Kayne (1992) and Graffi (1996) consider these types of sentences declarative clauses with imperative force. Other sentences that have imperative force but are syntactically indistinguishable from declarative clauses are those with third person subjects, of the type of English 'Everybody please stand up!', 'Nobody move!'. In Italian, they always employ verbal forms from the subjunctive, as illustrated here:

(i)   Nessuno si muova! (Italian)
        nobody self move (subjunctive)
        'Nobody move!'

In Zanuttini (1991) I argued that such verbal forms are not true imperative forms in English, either, but rather forms of the subjunctive used in sentences with imperative force.

5. The use of the particle *mi* in northeastern Sicily is discussed in detail in Sorrento (1912), which traces its origin to Latin *mŏdŏ*, a temporal adverb very frequently found in imperative clauses. Though this work is mainly devoted to the use of *mi* in matrix clauses — that is, in the polite form of the imperative — it also discusses its use in embedded contexts in place of the infinitive, for example:

(i)   Ci dissi *mi*   trasi. (northeastern Sicilian)
        him told PRT enter
        'I told him to come in.'

(ii)   Vi preiu *mi* mi diciti.
        you beg   PRT me tell
        'I beg you to tell me.'

6. Similar analysis is to be given to the imperative forms found in Salento (in the southern Italian region of Puglia), where *cu* in sentence initial position is followed by an inflected form of the verb (example from Rohlfs 1968: 355):

(i)   Cu ffaza cce bbòle. (Salentino)
        PRT does what wants
        'Do what you want!' (polite form)

The complementizer *cu* is the one that introduces subjunctive clauses (possibly the complementizer plus a subjunctive particle).

7. One exception seems to be the post-verbal negative marker of modern central Occitan, which will be discussed toward the end of this section.

8. In Latin as well the negative marker *non* was incompatible with imperatives. A form of the subjunctive negated by the negative marker *ne* was used instead (from Togeby 1970):

(i)   Canta! (true imperative) (Latin)
       'Sing!' (sg)

(ii)   Ne   cantes (subjunctive)
       'Don't sing!'

9. I will take a closer look at the morphological make-up of true imperatives in section 4.3.

10. Both Kayne (1990: 259, 1991: 651), following Raposo (1987), and Guasti (1991, 1992) have suggested that the morpheme *-re* can be viewed as the head of an InfP (InfinitivalPhrase). In Kayne's proposal, such a phrase is distinct from the tense projection, which has an abstract head in infinitives (to which the clitic is adjoined).

11. This conclusion is not surprising, given that certain forms used as suppletive imperatives, namely the infinitival forms in Italian, also lack any agreement specification.

12. Rivero (1994b: 93) also treats French as lacking imperative morphology.

13. The judgments given in (28) are not shared by all the native speakers of Italian I have consulted. G. Graffi (personal communication), for example, reports that when a negative constituent occurs in pre-verbal position, he must use a modal verb followed by the infinitive, as in (i):

(i)   *Niente* devi dirgli!   (Italian)
       nothing must to-tell-him
       'You must tell him nothing!'

14. The vowel *e*, instead of the expected *i*, is also found in the present participle of verbs of the third class, for example, *sentente* from *sentire* 'to hear' and *inferente* from *inferire* 'to infer'. See Napoli and Vogel (1990: 494).

15. For the sake of simplicity, I am omitting any discussion of the position of the stress in these verbs.

16. Napoli and Vogel (1990) argue that these forms use the second singular familiar imperative as the base form of the verb.

17. R. Kayne (personal communication) suggested that it might have a syntactic function: it might be required to turn a morpheme of a category lower than X° into one of type X°. Alternatively, it is possible that its function is that of making the syllable structure fit the requirements of the language. Notice that the thematic vowel never appears when the following morpheme corresponds to a simple vowel only (e.g., *parl-o*, and not **parl-a-o*, first singular present indicative). But if we view this vowel as satisfying syllabification requirements, it is difficult to explain why it also appears with roots that already end in a vowel — for example, *creare, sciare* 'to create, to ski'.

18. DiFabio (1990) suggests that the morpheme *-sc-* is added to carry stress when neither the root itself nor the verbal ending can do so.

19. While the data presented in the previous chapters were taken from a variety of sources, which include scholarly literature, work with informants, and questionnaires from ASIS (cf. Benincà et al. 1990–present), the data discussed in this section are mainly from Rohlfs (1968, 1969). Rohlfs gathered his data both from the linguistic atlas of Jaberg and Jud (1928–40), A.I.S., and from his own fieldwork. My reliance on Rohlfs means that, in many cases, I will not be able to be as specific as I would like to be on the place where the sentences were collected. Hence the reader will note that in some cases the data are classified in very broad terms with the name of the region (e.g., Sicilian, Calabrese) instead of that of the town where they were collected.

20. Besides imperatives where the verbal form precedes the pronominal clitics, such as those exemplified in (39), Italian also has sentences that exhibit the opposite word order — *clitic–verb* — and yet can be interpreted as imperative clauses, given appropriate intonation. Some examples are given here:

(i)   Non lo fate! (Italian)
       neg it do   (indicative form; 2nd pl)
       'Don't do it!'

(ii)   Non glielo dite!
       neg him-it tell   (indicative form; 2nd pl)
       'Don't tell him that!'

These examples raise the difficult question of determing whether they are imperative clauses or simply declarative clauses that are interpreted as imperatives by virtue of a particular intonational pattern. I will return to this issue in the course of the chapter.

21. All the examples in (40) are from Jaberg and Jud (1928–40), A.I.S., volume 8, chart 1621, and correspond to points 637, 632, 710, 183, and 873, respectively.

22. Cardinaletti (1995) raises some criticisms to Kayne's (1992) analysis of Italian negative infinitival imperatives, which stem from the observation that in some varieties of Italian the overt counterpart of the empty modal appears as an infinitive. One example from Cardinaletti's work is reported here, from the central Italian variety spoken in Ancona:

(i)   *Non* me sta'   a di'   ste   robe. (Italian from Ancona)
       neg me to-stay at to-tell these things
       'Don't tell me these things!'

Cardinaletti points out that Kayne's analysis leads us to analyze this example as involving an empty modal followed by the infinitival form of 'stay', in turn followed by the infinitival form of the main verb. This is seen as an undesirable conclusion because it breaks the parallelism between the empty modal and the overt element *stá* used in Paduan.

I also found examples where the counterpart of *stá* is in the infinitival form (cf. (54)b and (55)b). Moreover, such a construction exists in the northern Italian variety (from Piedmont) spoken by the author of this book. In my variety, though, this construction is not equivalent to a simple negative infinitival imperative; the difference can be roughly illustrated by the translations given to the following examples:

(ii)   a. *Non* lavarlo!   (northern Italian from Piedmont)
          neg to-wash-it
          'Don't wash it!'
       b. *Non* stare   a lavarlo!
          neg to-stay at to-wash-it
          'Don't bother to wash it!' *or*
          'Don't take the trouble to wash it!'

If interpretative differences along these lines were found also in the other varieties examined, then it seems to me that it might be desirable to analyze the constructions with an infinitival form of 'stay' differently from their counterparts with an (overt or abstract) finite form. That is, it might indeed be appropriate to analyze (ii)a as having an empty verb that takes the infinitival form of the main verb, whereas (ii)b as having an empty verb that takes an infinitival form of 'stay', which in turn takes an infinitival form of the main verb — especially if such a syntactic difference can be shown to correspond to the interpretative difference I mentioned.

23. By proposing an empty modal-like element, Kayne could draw a straightforward parallelism with cases of overt modals in Italian, which are followed by infinitival verbs and

allow long clitic climbing. If I argue for an auxiliary-like element, that parallelism might become weaker, but the semantics of this constructions becomes simpler: the imperative force of these sentences will then come from the same place it comes from in true imperatives, and not from the presence of a modal element. Note also that in Italian there are verbs other than modals that are followed by infinitival verbs and allow long clitic climbing, for example, *desiderare, preferire, cominciare* 'to wish, to prefer, to begin.' (The last one takes an infinitive preceded by *a*, as is the case in some of the contexts I am examining.)

24. Forms of the verb *stare* are used as auxiliaries in Italian as well, not in imperatives, but to express progressive aspect. In these cases, they are followed by a gerund, as shown by the following examples:

(i)   Sto scrivendo. (Italian)
       stay writing   (1st sg)
       'I am writing.'

(ii)   Stava dormendo.
       stayed sleeping (3rd sg)
       'He was sleeping.'

25. As pointed out to me by R. Frank and R. Fasold (personal communication), colloquial American English also has a construction that can be analyzed along the same lines — that is, as having an auxiliary verb that is only licensed in the presence of the negative marker of sentential negation. Such a construction is a negative imperative consisting of the verb *be* followed by the main verb with the *-ing* suffix. As exemplified in (i), this is only possible in a negative imperative:

(i)   a. Don't be mouthing off to me!
       b. *Be mouthing off to someone else!

The construction exemplified in (i) differs from the one in (ii) following, where auxiliary *be* may appear without the presence of negation:

(ii)   ??(Do) be studying for that exam when I call!

The example in (ii), though somewhat marginal, is interpreted as progressive, whereas (i) is not. I am grateful to J. Bernstein for bringing this example to my attention.

26. The diacritic ˆ over a vowel is used to indicate length.

27. I thank L. Vanelli (personal communication) for providing me with example (49)d.

28. Note that *sta* is not the only auxiliary form that is found in suppletive imperatives. Rohlfs (1968: 357) provides an example with a form of 'have' from the southern Italian region of Molise:

(i)   Nnə vv'avəssít a credərə.   (Molise)
       neg you'had   a to-believe (past subjunctive; 2nd pl)
       'Don't believe that!'

Portuguese can adopt either a form of the indicative to negate an imperative or a strategy analogous to the one of Friulian and Paduan, but with a true imperative form of the verb 'to go'. The grammar of Portuguese by Cunha and Cintra (1985: 469) reports the following examples:

(ii)   Não vá se afogar, moço.   (Portuguese)
       neg go self drown young man (true imperative)
       'Don't drown yourself, young man.'

(iii) Não vá me dizer que foi o Diabo.
       neg go me to-tell that was the devil (true imperative)
       'Don't tell me it was the devil!'

In this case as well, a form of the true imperative is compatible with the pre-verbal negative marker, if the verbal form is used as an auxiliary and not as a main verb.

29. Trentino is spoken in the homonymous region of northern Italy, around the city of Trent; Emiliano is from the northern Italian region of Emilia, which lies south of Lombardy and Veneto.

30. With either form, the pronominal clitics must follow the auxiliary and cannot precede it. Compare the examples in (56) with the following:

(i)   *No melo stá   dire! (Paduan)
      neg me-i t stay to-say
      'Don't tell me that!'

(ii) *No melo star   dire!
      neg me-it to-stay to-say
      'Don't tell me that!'

In other words, the pronominal clitics do not appear to be able to raise and left-adjoin to the auxiliary. It should be noted that clitic climbing is not commonly found in Paduan in general.

31. I am grateful to M. Picciarelli (personal communication) for providing me the data from Tarantino.

32. According to my informant, in the more modern part of the city of Taranto, where the dialect is more in contact with standard Italian, it is possible to negate the second singular by means of an infinitive, on the model of Italian:

(i)   No scé! (Tarantino)
      neg to-go
      'Don't go!' (2nd sg)

(ii) No 'u pigghjà(rə)!
      neg it to-take
      'Don't take it!' (2nd sg)

33. Mancarella (1975: 21), describing the dialects of Salento in general (and not Tarantino in particular), mentions the preference for a modal followed by a finite clause, though also providing a few examples of a modal followed by an infinitive (without specifying which variety they are from).

34. Note that a form of the verb 'go' can be used as an auxiliary in standard Italian as well, not in imperatives, but in finite clauses:

(i)   Questo va   detto subito!   (Italian)
      this   goes said immediately
      'This must be said right away!'

(ii) Quel ragazzo va   rimproverato!
      that boy   goes scolded
      'That boy must be scolded!'

(iii) Quella faccenda andrebbe risolta il più   presto possibile.
      that   issue   should-go solved the more soon   possible
      'That issue should be resolved as soon as possible!'

As pointed out in Benincà and Poletto (1994: §2.2), in addition to the deontic reading, this form used as an auxiliary can also have simply the reading of a passive. A sentence like (iv) illustrates this ambiguity:

(iv) La sterpaglia   andava bruciata tutti gli anni.   (Italian)
      the brushwood went   burnt   all   the years
      'The brushwood was burnt every year' *or*
      'The brushwood had to be burnt every year.'

35. The time lag between these two pieces of work is accidental; the article that appeared in 1996 was written in 1990, one year before the dissertation was completed.

36. Admittedly, the observations in section 4.3 provide only partial support for the assumption that true imperatives lack mood specification. They show that they consist of the stem, the thematic vowel, and, in some cases, an agreement morpheme. I have to hypothesize that, among the morphological marking that is missing, mood is the one that plays a role in the distribution of the true imperatives in clauses negated by a pre-verbal negative marker.

37. For the case of modern central Occitan, see note 7 and the discussion at the end of section 4.2.

38. The grammaticality of example (69) suggests that, if the preposed negative constituent licenses a phonetically empty negative head (as suggested in Haegeman 1995), such a head differs from its overt counterpart in being compatible with a true imperative. The grammaticality judgment of (69) contrasts with that of what appears to be a similar example found in Rivero (1994b: 103):

(i)   *A ningún sitio id vosotros sin   abrigo! (Spanish)
      to no   place go you   without coat
      'Don't you go anywhere without a coat!'

I am not sure whether this contrast is to be related to the fact that these examples might have been given a different intonation in the two cases, or to the fact that even in Italian such examples are not accepted by all speakers, as mentioned in note 13.

39. In Italian, for example, the opposite word order — that is *infinitive–clitic* — is obligatory in every context other than a negative imperative. An example is given in (i):

(i)   Preferisco non **far***lo*.   (Italian)
      prefer   neg to-do-it
      'I prefer not to do it.'

(ii) *Preferisco non *lo* **fare**.

40. The examples in (70) are from Rivero (1994a: 103–4), those in (71) from Rivero (1994b: 97–98).

41. The examples in (72) are from Rivero (1994a: 105), those in (73) from Rivero (1994b: 101).

42. The claim that imperative verbs move to C° is not new. For Romance imperatives, it is also found in Rooryck (1992) and more recently in Graffi (1996). In Rooryck's proposal, the verb adjoins to C° after excorporating from the cluster *verb–clitic*. His article does not address the issue of the incompatibility of pre-verbal negative markers with true imperatives.

43. The presence of an imperative feature on the verb itself is used in Rivero (1994b) to account for examples like (i), which contrasts with (ii):

(i)   *Que escribid! (true imperative) (Spanish)
      that write
      'Write!'

(ii)   Que escribáis! (suppletive imperative)
    that write   (present subj, 2nd pl)
    'Write!'

The complementizer *que*, in C°, blocks raising of the true imperative verb to that position. Ungrammaticality is taken to arise from the fact that the imperative feature on the verb does not get checked.

    44. Rivero provides a different analysis for the polite forms of the imperative in Spanish, which employ forms of the subjunctives both in the presence and in the absence of negation. In such cases, when nothing intervenes on the path to C°, the verb must raise to check the imperative feature, as shown in (i) (the C° position is available and no intervening head blocks movement of the verb):

(i)   a. *Den*-me el libro! (suppletive imperative) (Spanish)
      give-me the book (subj, 2nd pl)
      'Give me the book!'
    b. *Me *den* el libro!

On the other hand, the verb can fail to raise when something occupies C° or intervenes on the path to C°, as in (ii)a and (ii)b, respectively:

(ii)   a. Que me *den* el libro! (Spanish)
      that me give the book
      'Give me the book!'
    b. No me *den* el libro!
      neg me give the book
      'Don't give me the book!'

The analysis suggested for these cases is that "the combination of (subject) Agreement (Person and Number) and Mood with 'operator' properties (Subjunctive) successfully checks the abstract Imperative feature in C°, when 'true' imperative morphology is unavailable" (Rivero 1994b: 105).

    45. See section 4.4 for a discussion of these cases.

    46. The view that imperatives cannot be embedded is also expressed in Platzack and Rosengren (1994: 27). Some examples of what appear to be embedded imperatives in old Italian are reported in Vai (1995b).

    47. See section 3.2 for a more thorough summary of Cinque's analysis of the syntax of adverbs.

    48. The examples in (82), (83), and (84) are from Cinque (1995a).

    49. The position of TP-1 described here does not correspond to the one in Cinque (1995a) but to the one in Cinque (1996a).

    50. Interesting insights and observations concerning the adverb classes in imperative clauses are found in Bosque (1994), a study that analyzes degree quantifiers denoting excess in Spanish — for example: *demasiado(s)* 'too much, too many', *excesivo* 'excessive', *desmesurado* 'disproportionate'. These adverbs cannot occur in imperative clauses, as shown in the following examples from Bosque (1994):

(i)   a. *Por favor, trabaja *demasiado*. (Spanish)
      'Please, work too much.'
    b. *Ayúdale *excesivamente*.
      'Help him excessively.'

    Bosque attributes this restriction on the distribution of the class of degree quantifiers to the lack of a projection MP (a "modal estimative phrase") from imperative clauses. Since this projection is necessary for the licensing of the adverbs, they are excluded from these contexts. On the contrary, they can occur in so-called conditional imperatives, where this projection is argued to be present (examples again from Bosque 1994):

(ii)   a. Trabaja demasiado y moriràs joven. (Spanish)
          'Work too much and you'll die young.'

It is interesting to note that the presence or absence of these adverbs is not sensitive to the distinction between true and suppletive imperatives: the contexts where the degree quantifiers are excluded are the same regardless of the verb employed. I will show this using examples from Italian, which uses a true imperative for the second person singular and a suppletive imperative for the second plural. As shown in the following examples, both true and suppletive imperatives are incompatible with adverbs denoting excess:

(iii)   a. *Per favore lavora *troppo*! (true imperative) (Italian)
           'Please work too much.' (2nd sg)
        b. *Aiutatelo *troppo*. (suppletive imperative)
           'Help him excessively.' (2nd pl)

However, both true and suppletive imperatives can co-occur with this class of adverbs in conditional imperatives, as shown in the following examples:

(iv)   a. Lavora *troppo* e finirai con l'ammalarti! (true imperative) (Italian)
           'Work too much and you'll end up getting sick.' (2nd sg)
       b. Lavorate *troppo* e finirete con l'ammalarvi. (suppletive imperative)
           'Work to much and you'll end up getting sick.' (2nd pl)

Following Bosque's reasoning, this suggests that the functional projection that is unavailable in true imperatives is also unavailable in suppletive imperatives.

51. The subject-oriented adverbs, argued to be in the specifier of a modal phrase (e.g., *intelligentemente* 'intelligently') can occur in imperative clauses, but only with a different interpretation, namely that of manner adverbs. With such an interpretation, they must follow the verb as well as the object, as shown in the examples below:

(i)   a. ?Dagli la notizia intelligentemente! (true imperative) (Italian)
           'Give him the news intelligently!' (2nd sg)
       b. Dategli la notizia intelligentemente! (suppletive imperative)
           'Give him the news intelligently!' (2nd pl)

This suggests that in such cases the adverbs occur in a projection that is lower in the clause.

52. The parallelism between imperatives on the one hand and infinitivals and gerunds on the other is limited to their (lack of) co-occurrence with the adverb classes just mentioned. Crucially, it does not extend to co-occurrence with the pre-verbal negative markers: infinitives and gerunds differ from true imperatives, and they pattern like suppletive imperatives in being able to co-occur with the pre-verbal negative marker *non*. Some examples of such co-occurrence are given here:

(i)   *Non* andare al cinema è un vero peccato. (Italian)
       'Not to go to the movies is a real shame.'

(ii)   *Non* andando al cinema, non conosceva Massimo Troisi.
       'Not going to the movies, he did not know Massimo Troisi.'

53. The presence of a pause can best be detected by comparing these examples with others in which the adverb follows the verb but not any complement, as in (i) and (ii) here:

(i)   Io parto adesso. (Italian)
       I leave now
       'I am leaving now.'

(ii)   Lui era stato assunto allora.
       he was been hired   then
       'He had been hired then.'

In (i) and (ii), no pause separates the adverb from the rest of the clause. I thank G. Cinque for discussing these data with me.

54. Infinitives and gerunds differ from imperatives in that they cannot follow these adverbs but can only precede them. This is exemplified here for the case of infinitives:

(i)   a. Ho   deciso di (*adesso) andare (adesso) a Roma (adesso). (Italian)
          have decided of (*now)   to-go (now)   to Rome (now)
          'I have decided to go to Rome now.'
       b. Vorrei (*adesso) dirti   (adesso) il   mio segreto (adesso)
          want (*now)   to-tell-you (now)   the my secret (now)
          'I would like to tell you my secret now.'
       c. (*Adesso) andare (adesso) in montagna (adesso) sarebbe   molto bello.
          (*now)   to-go (now)   in mountain (now)   would be very   nice
          'To go to the mountains now would be very nice.'

55. The other interpretation, the one that seems to contrast the present moment of time with another one ('now [as opposed to later] you go/tell him'), is also possible, though less favored. It seems to be available only if the adverb is stressed, as if it were topicalized. I am grateful for these observations to the audience of the colloquium series of the University of Padua, where a preliminary version of this work was presented in November 1994.

56. The tree in (106) contains only the functional projections of the higher part of the clause. If we consider also the functional projections of the lower part of the clause, we obtain the following sequence (from Cinque 1996a, with the addition of NegP-1):

(i) $ModP_{eval}-ModP_{epist}-TP-1-NegP-1-MoodP-ModP_{root}-AspP_{habit}-NegP-2-TP-2-$
       $AspP_{perf}-AspP_{gen/prog}-AspPO_{compl}-AspPS_{compl}-VoiceP-VP$

57. In a view of clausal structure where CP is split into several components, this claim would have to be made more precise. Note that it is also compatible with the proposal in Platzack and Rosengren (1994) that imperative features are in a projection that expresses sentence type, as long as this projection were to occupy a structural position higher than TP-1.

58. A straightforward account of the incompatibility between true imperatives and pre-verbal negative markers in terms of verb movement might consist in arguing that the true imperative verb and the negative marker compete for the same structural position. This has been proposed in the literature, on the basis of different observations and assumptions, in Laka (1990) and Zanuttini (1994b). In this view, the difference between true and suppletive imperatives can be captured as follows. True imperative verbs move to the structural position in which the pre-verbal negative marker occurs, namely the head of NegP-1; in the absence of a negative marker they can left-adjoin to Neg°, whereas when a negative marker is present this option is blocked. Suppletive imperatives, on the other hand, move to a head position that is structurally lower than the head of NegP-1; consequently, they are not sensitive to the presence or absence of a negative marker in the head of NegP-1. The different extent to which true and suppletive imperatives move can be related to the different amount of morphological specification exhibited by their verbal forms, as suggested in Zanuttini (1994b). A true imperative verb can be said to move higher than a suppletive imperative because,

whereas it cannot raise to any of the functional projections that carry information associated with verbal morphology, it can raise to a projection whose features are not related to verbal morphology, such as NegP-1.

This proposal constitutes a good first approximation, but it is not sufficient to account for the range of data discussed in this chapter. First, our examination of several Romance varieties has revealed a split between main verbs and auxiliary verbs: while true imperative forms of main verbs are (in most varieties) incompatible with a pre-verbal negative marker that by itself can negate the clause, true imperative forms of auxiliary verbs do not exhibit the same incompatibility. To illustrate this contrast, I will repeat an example from Friulian already discussed in section 4.4:

(i)   a. *No sta donge il fûc! (*sta* as a main verb) (Friulian)
         neg stay near the fire (2nd sg)
         'Don't stay near the fire!'
    b. *No stàit donge il fûc! (*sta* as a main verb)
         neg stay near the fire (2nd pl)
         'Don't stay near the fire!'
(ii)   a. No sta (a) crodi!   (*sta* as an auxiliary) (Friulian)
         neg stay *a* to-believe
         'Don't believe that!' (2nd sg)
    b. No stàit a crodi.   (*sta* as an auxiliary)
         neg stay *a* to-believe
         'Don't believe that!' (2nd pl)

Second, while some suppletive imperatives raise less than true imperatives, others raise to the same extent at least in non-negative clauses, judging from their position with respect to adverb classes. For example, Italian suppletive imperatives that employ a form of the indicative have the same distribution as true imperatives with respect to the adverb classes examined in section 4.7. A proposal that argues true imperatives occur in the same structural position as the negative marker, whereas suppletive imperatives occur in a lower structural position, fails to account for both the facts just mentioned: that is, that true imperative forms of auxiliary verbs can co-occur with a negative marker and that certain suppletive imperatives appear to be in the same structural position as true imperatives.

59. The postulation of an imperative feature can be dated back to Katz and Postal (1964). It is also found in much recent literature on the subject, which relates it to verb movement. For example, the proposals in Rivero (1994b) and Rivero and Terzi (1995) assume that the verb moves to C° in imperatives to check an imperative feature. Laenzlinger (1994) assumes the presence of an imperative feature on I° and views verb movement to C° as triggered by the need to instantiate a specifier-head configuration with an imperative operator in the specifier of CP. Platzack and Rosengren (1994: fn. 6) suggest that imperative verbs move to a functional projection that expresses sentence type. According to the definition of sentence type given in Sadock and Zwicky (1985), which these authors follow, three sentence types exist and are mutually exclusive: imperative, declarative, and interrogative. Laka (1990) argues that the position to which both the pre-verbal negative marker and a true imperative move is the head of a functional projection, labelled ΣP, which can be specified for one of three values: negation, emphatic affirmation, or imperative.

60. Recall that, in chapter 2, we argued that the pre-verbal negative marker can satisfy the feature in C° of interrogative clauses.

61. In Chomsky's (1995) terms, true imperatives could also be viewed as being merged directly in C°, as long as theta-role assignment were possible in that position.

62. Admittedly, I am at fault here for talking about the illocutionary force of imperatives without defining it. I refer the reader to Hamblin (1987) and references therein.

63. The examples in (111) are from Haiman and Benincà (1992); those in (112) are from Azaretti (1982: 226).

64. This raises the question whether the complementizer of subjunctive clauses is the same or different from that of indicative clauses (despite their phonological similarity), an issue that will not be discussed here.

65. One could then wonder why such an abstract complementizer cannot be present in the case of a true imperative as well, thus making verb movement unnecessary. I think that this is related to the fact that true imperatives are non-finite forms and therefore incompatible with this kind of complementizer. That true imperatives should be viewed as non-finite forms is suggested by their being incompatible with subject clitics (in the Romance varieties that exhibit subject clitics) and with those classes of adverbs that are also incompatible with infinitives and gerunds, discussed in section 4.7.

66. Italian suppletive imperatives with a form of the subjunctive do not exhibit the diagnostics we have taken to indicate verb movement when they are in the third person, either as polite imperatives (cf. (i)) or as imperatives with a third person subject (cf. (ii)). As shown in these examples, the verb follows the subject:

(i)   Lei stia fermo! (suppletive imperative) (Italian)
       she stay still   (subjunctive)
       'You stand still!'

(ii)   Nessuno si   muova!
       nobody self move   (subjunctive)
       'Nobody move!'

An overt complementizer is possible in (ii) (*Che nessuno si muova!*). This provides some support for the hypothesis that, even in the absence of an overt complementizer, a phonologically null one can check the imperative feature in C°. An overt complementizer is less acceptable in (i), though, for reasons that are unclear. Note that in previous analyses, these cases have been set aside and treated as regular subjunctive clauses with the illocutionary force of imperatives; see Kayne (1992), Zanuttini (1991, 1994b), and Graffi (1996).

67. Speakers from northern Italy find (119)b not to be part of their grammar, but recognize it as acceptable in the grammar of central and southern Italian varieties.

68. This would provide an account of why northern Italian speakers find examples like (119)b not to be integral part of their grammar: long clitic climbing is less common in northern than in central and southern Italy, as pointed out in Kayne (1992) in relation to the discussion of negative infinitival imperatives.

69. I thank C. Poletto and G. Cinque (personal communication) for drawing my attention to these data. See also Vai (1995b) for a discussion of these data.

70. Jaberg and Jud (1928), volume 8, chart 1621, point 499, which corresponds to the town of Saludecio.

71. Examples (127)a and (127)b from Vai (1995b).

72. Rivero (1994b) and Rivero and Terzi (1995) also discuss the case of Serbo-Croatian, where imperatives can be negated, as shown here:

(i)   Ne čitajte je! (Serbo-Croatian)
       neg read   it
       'Don't read it!'

Since the pronominal clitics appear in strict second position in the clause in this language, both articles analyze examples like (i) as having the negative marker and the verb count as a syntactic unit.

BIBLIOGRAPHY

Acquaviva, P. (1992). The representation of negative 'quantifiers'. *Rivista di Linguistica*, 4:319–81.

Acquaviva, P. (1993). The logical form of negation. A study of operator-variable structures in syntax. Ph.D. thesis, Scuola Normale Superiore, Pisa.

Acquaviva, P. (1994). The representation of operator-variable dependencies in sentential negation. *Studia Linguistica*, 48(2):91–132.

Acquaviva, P. (1995). Operator composition and the derivation of negative concord. Unpublished manuscript, University College Dublin.

Agouraki, Y. (1993). Spec/Head Licensing: The cases of foci, clitic constructions and polarity items. A study of Modern Greek. Ph.D. thesis, University College London.

Albin, T. J. (1984). Syntactic peculiarities of Piedmontese. Ph.D. thesis, University of Michigan, Ann Arbor.

Alvarez, R., Regueira, X. L., and Monteagudo, H. (1986). *Gramatica Galega*. Galaxia, Vigo.

Aly-Belfàdel, A. (1890). *Conoscere il Piemontese*. Viglongo, Turin.

Antelmi, D. (1993). La negazione in fiorentino. *Quaderni Patavini di Linguistica*, 12:3–30.

Aoun, J. and Li, A. (1993). Wh-elements in situ: Syntax or LF? *Linguistic Inquiry*, 24(2):199–238.

Apollonio, B. (1930). *Grammatica del Dialetto Ampezzano*. Arti Grafiche Tridentum, Trent. Reprinted in 1987 by Cooperativa di Consumo di Cortina d'Ampezzo.

Ashby, W. J. (1976). The loss of the negative morpheme, *ne*, in Parisian French. *Lingua*, 39:119–37.

Ashby, W. J. (1981). The loss of the negative particle *ne* in French. *Language*, 57:674–87.

Aubanel, T. (1963). *Le pain du péché, le rapt, le patre*. E. Aubanel.

Azaretti, E. (1982). *L'evoluzione dei dialetti liguri, esaminata attraverso la grammatica storica del ventimigliese*. 2nd ed. Casabianca, San Remo.

Baker, C. L. (1970). Notes on the description of English questions: The role of an abstract question morpheme. *Foundations of Language*, 6:197–219.

Baker, M. (1988). *Incorporation: A Theory of Grammatical Function Changing.* University of Chicago Press, Chicago.

Belletti, A. (1990). *Generalized Verb Movement.* Rosenberg and Sellier, Turin.

Belletti, A. (1994). Verb positions; NP positions. Evidence from Italian. In Lightfoot, D. and Hornstein, N., eds., *Verb Movement.* Cambridge University Press, Cambridge.

Benincà, P. (1983). Il clitico "a" nel dialetto padovano. In *Scritti linguistici in onore di Giovan Battista Pellegrini,* pages 25–35. Pacini, Pisa. Reprinted in Benincà (1994).

Benincà, P. (1986). Punti di sintassi comparata dei dialetti italiani settentrionali. In Holtus, G. and Ringger, K., eds., *Raetia Antiqua et Moderna: W.Th. Elwert zum 80. Geburtstag,* pages 457–79. Niemeyer, Tübingen. Reprinted in Benincà (1994).

Benincà, P. (1994). *La Variazione Sintattica.* Il Mulino, Bologna.

Benincà, P. (1996). La struttura della frase esclamativa alla luce del dialetto padovano. In Benincà, P., Cinque, G., De Mauro, T., and Vincent, N., eds., *Italiano e dialetti nel tempo: Saggi di grammatica per Giulio C. Lepschy,* pages 23–43. Bulzoni, Rome.

Benincà, P., Kayne, R. S., Poletto, C., and Vanelli, L. (1990–present). Atlante sintattico dell'Italia settentrionale (ASIS). Unpublished manuscript, Centro di Dialettologia, Università degli Studi di Padova.

Benincà, P. and Poletto, C. (1994). Bisogna and its companions: The verbs of necessity. In Cinque, G., Koster, J., Pollock, J.-Y., Rizzi, L., and Zanuttini, R., eds., *Paths towards Universal Grammar: Studies in Honor of Richard S. Kayne,* pages 35–57. Georgetown University Press, Washington, D.C.

Benincà, P., Renzi, L., and Vanelli, L. (1985/6). Tipologia dei pronomi soggetto nelle lingue romanze. *Quaderni Patavini di Linguistica,* 5:49–66. Reprinted in Benincà (1994).

Benincà, P. and Vanelli, L. (1982). Appunti di sintassi veneta. In Cortelazzo, M., ed., *Guida ai dialetti veneti,* vol. 4, pages 7–38. CLEUP, Padua. Reprinted in Benincà (1994).

Benincà, P. and Vanelli, L. (1984). Ricerche sul parametro del soggetto nelle varietà italiane settentrionali. In *Scienza e Cultura.* Edizioni Universitarie Patavine, Padua.

Beretta, C. (1980). *Contributo per una grammatica del milanese contemporaneo.* Virgilio, Milan.

Berruto, G. (1974). *Piemonte e Valle d'Aosta.* Pacini, Pisa.

Berruto, G. (1990). Note tipologiche di un non tipologo sul dialetto piemontese. In Berruto, G. and Sobrero, A. A., eds., *Studi di sociolinguistica e dialettologia italiana offerti a Corrado Grassi,* pages 3–24. Congedo, Galatina, Italy.

Besio, G. B. N. and Buzzano, A. E. (1979). *Amü de scheuggiu, rèixe de nasciùn.* Editrice Liguria, Savona, Italy.

Bickerton, D. (1981). *Roots of Language.* Karoma, Ann Arbor.

Borer, H. (1983). *Parametric Syntax: Case Studies in Semitic and Romance Languages.* Foris, Dordrecht.

Bosque, I. (1994). Degree quantification and modal operators in Spanish. In *24th Linguistics Symposium on Romance Languages — Abstracts,* pages 7a–7b. University of Southern California and University of California, Los Angeles.

Brandi, L. and Cordin, P. (1981). Dialetto e italiano: un confronto sul parametro del soggetto nullo. *Rivista di Grammatica Generativa,* 6:33–87.

Brandi, L. and Cordin, P. (1989). Two Italian dialects and the null subject parameter. In Jaeggli, O. and Safir, K., eds., *The Null Subject Parameter,* pages 111–42. Kluwer, Dordrecht.

Brero, C. (1988). *Grammatica della lingua piemontese.* Edizione Piemont/Europa, Turin.

Brody, M. (1990). Some remarks on the Focus Field in Hungarian. In Harris, J., ed., *UCL Working Papers in Linguistics,* vol. 2, pages 201–25. Department of Linguistics, University College London.

Brugger, G. and D'Angelo, M. (1994). Tempo, modo e la posizione di NegP. In Borgato, G., ed., *Teoria del linguaggio e analisi linguistica — XX Incontro di Grammatica Generativa*, pages 109–23. Unipress, Padua.

Burzio, L. (1986). *Italian Syntax*. Reidel, Dordrecht.

Butz, B. (1981). *Morphosyntax der Mundart von Vermes (Val Terbi)*. Francke, Bern.

Calabrese, A. (1993). The sentential complementation of Salentino: A study of a language without infinitival clauses. In Belletti, A., ed., *Syntactic Theory and the Dialects of Italy*, pages 28–98. Rosenberg and Sellier, Turin.

Campos, H. (1986). Inflectional elements in Romance. Ph.D. thesis, University of California, Los Angeles.

Cardinaletti, A. (1995). Clitic placement with imperatives: Evidence from Italian varieties. Unpublished manuscript, University of Venice.

Cardinaletti, A. and Roberts, I. G. (in press). Clause structure and X-second. In Chao, W. and Horrocks, G., eds., *Levels, Principles and Processes: The Structure of Grammatical Representation*. Foris, Dordrecht.

Cardinaletti, A. and Starke, M. (in press). The typology of structural deficiency: On the three grammatical classes. In van Riemsdijk, H., ed., *Clitics in the Languages of Europe*, vol. 8 of *Empirical Approaches to Language Typology*. Mouton de Gruyter, Berlin.

Chao, Y.-R. (1968). *A Grammar of Spoken Chinese*. University of California Press, Berkeley.

Chen, L.-P. (1996). Negation in Mandarin Chinese. Unpublished manuscript, Georgetown University, Washington, D.C.

Chenal, A. (1986). *Le Franco-Provençal Valdotain: Morphologie et Syntaxe*. Musumeci, Aosta.

Cheng, L. L.-S., Huang, C.-T. J., and Tang, C.-C. J. (in press). Negative particle questions: A dialectal comparison. In Black, J. and Motapanyane, V., eds., *Micro-Parametric Syntax: Dialectal Variation in Syntax*. John Benjamins, Philadelphia.

Chomsky, N. (1991). Some notes on economy of derivation and representation. In Freidin, R., ed., *Principles and Parameters in Comparative Grammar*. MIT Press, Cambridge.

Chomsky, N. (1993). A minimalist program for linguistic theory. In Hale, K. and Keyser, S. J., eds., *The View from Building 20*. MIT Press, Cambridge.

Chomsky, N. (1995). *The Minimalist Program*. MIT Press, Cambridge.

Cinque, G. (1976). Mica. *Annali della Facoltà di Lettere e Filosofia, Università di Padova*, 1:101–12. Reprinted in Cinque (1991). *Teoria Linguistica e Sintassi Italiana*. Il Mulino, Bologna.

Cinque, G. (1990). *Types of A-bar Dependencies*, vol. 17 of *Linguistic Inquiry Monographs*. MIT Press, Cambridge.

Cinque, G. (1994). Sull'ordine relativo di alcune classi di avverbi in italiano e in francese. In Borgato, G., ed., *Teoria del linguaggio e analisi linguistica — XX Incontro di Grammatica Generativa*, pages 163–77. Unipress, Padua.

Cinque, G. (1995a). Adverbs and the universal hierarchy of functional projections. *GLOW Newsletter*, 31:14–15.

Cinque, G. (1995b). *Italian Syntax and Universal Grammar*. Cambridge University Press, Cambridge.

Cinque, G. (1996a). Adverbs and the universal hierarchy of functional projections. Unpublished book manuscript, University of Venice.

Cinque, G. (1996b). The 'antisymmetric' program: Theoretical and typological implications. *Journal of Linguistics*, 32(2).

Clivio, G. P. (1970). Osservazioni sulla varietà rustica del piemontese settecentesco. In *El nodar onorà, commedia piemontese italiana del secondo Settecento*. Centro Studi Piemontesi, Turin.

Culicover, P. W. (1992). Polarity, inversion, and focus in English. In Westphal, G., Ao, B., and Chae, H.-R., eds., *Proceeedings of ESCOL '91*, pages 46–68. Ohio State University, Columbus.

Cunha, C. and Cintra, L. F. L. (1985). *Nova Gramática do Português Contemporâneo*. Nova Fronteira, Rio de Janeiro.

DeGraff, M. (1993). A riddle on negation in Haitian. *Probus*, 5(1–2):63–93.

Déprez, V. (in press). The roots of negative concord in French and French-based creoles. In DeGraff, M., ed., *Creolization, Language Change and Language Acquisition*. MIT Press, Cambridge.

Diesing, M. (1992). *Indefinites*, vol. 20 of *Linguistic Inquiry Monographs*. MIT Press, Cambridge.

DiFabio, E. (1990). The morphology of the verbal infix /-Isk/ in Italian and in Romance. Ph.D. thesis, Harvard University, Cambridge.

Dobrovie-Sorin, C. (1993). *The Syntax of Romanian: Comparative Studies in Romance*. Mouton de Gruyter, Berlin.

Emonds, J. E. (1978). The verbal complex V'-V in French. *Linguistic Inquiry*, 9:151–75.

Fontana, J. M. (1993). Phrase structure and the syntax of clitics in the history of Spanish. Ph.D. thesis, University of Pennsylvania, Philadelphia.

Giorgi, A. and Pianesi, F. (1991). Toward a syntax of temporal representations. *Probus*, 2(3):187–213.

Graffi, G. (1996). Alcune riflessioni sugli imperativi italiani. In Benincà, P., Cinque, G., De Mauro, T., and Vincent, N., eds., *Italiano e dialetti nel tempo: Studi di grammatica per Giulio Lepschy*, pages 143–48. Bulzoni, Rome.

Grevisse, M. (1986). *Le bon usage*. Duculot, Gembloux.

Grimshaw, J. (in press a). Extended projection and locality. In Coopmans, P., Everaert, M., and Grimshaw, J., eds., *Lexical Structure*. Lawrence Erlbaum Associates, Newark, N.J.

Grimshaw, J. (in press b). Projection, heads, and optimality. *Linguistic Inquiry*.

Guasti, M. T. (1991). The *faire-par* construction in Romance and in Germanic. In *Proceedings of WCCFL 9*, pages 205–18. University of Chicago Press, Chicago.

Guasti, M. T. (1992). Causative and perception verbs. Ph.D. thesis, Université de Genève.

Haegeman, L. (1991). Negative concord, negative heads. In Delfitto, D., Everaert, M., Evers, A., and Stuurman, F., eds., *Going Romance and Beyond*, pages 46–81. OTS Working Papers, Utrecht.

Haegeman, L. (1992a). Negation in West Flemish and the Neg-Criterion. In Broderick, K., ed., *Proceedings of NELS XXII*. GLSA, University of Massachusetts, Amherst.

Haegeman, L. (1992b). Sentential negation in Italian and the Neg-Criterion. In *Geneva Generative Papers*. University of Geneva.

Haegeman, L. (1994). Negative heads and negative operators: The NEG-criterion. In Lust, B., Suñer, M., and Whitman, J., eds., *Syntactic Theory and First Language Acquisition*. Vol. 1: *Heads, Projections, and Learnability*. Lawrence Erlbaum Associates, Newark, N.J.

Haegeman, L. (1995). *The Syntax of Negation*. Cambridge University Press, Cambridge.

Haegeman, L. and Zanuttini, R. (1991). Negative heads and the Neg-Criterion. *Linguistic Review*, 8:233–51.

Haegeman, L. and Zanuttini, R. (1996). Negative concord in West Flemish. In Belletti, A. and Rizzi, L., eds., *Parameters and Functional Heads. Essays in Comparative Syntax*, pages 117–79. Oxford University Press, New York.

Haiman, J. and Benincà, P. (1992). *The Rhaeto-Romance Languages*. Routledge, London.

Hamblin, C. L. (1987). *Imperatives*. Basil Blackwell, Oxford.

Harris, J. W. (1991). The exponence of gender in Spanish. *Linguistic Inquiry*, 22(1):27–62.

Harris, M. (1976). *Romance Syntax: Synchronic and Diachronic Perspectives*. University of Salford, England.

Harris, M. (1978a). *The Evolution of French Syntax*. Longman, London.

Harris, M. (1978b). The inter-relationship between phonological and grammatical change. In Fisiak, J., ed., *Recent Developments in Historical Phonology*, pages 159–72. Mouton, The Hague.

Highfield, A. R. (1979). *The French Dialects of St. Thomas, U.S. Virgin Islands*. Karoma, Ann Arbor.

Hirschbühler, P. and Labelle, M. (1994). Changes in verb position in French negative infinitival clauses. *Language Variation and Change*, 6(2):149–78.

Holm, J. A. (1988). *Pidgins and Creoles*, vol. 1. Cambridge University Press, Cambridge.

Horn, L. (1989). *A Natural History of Negation*. University of Chicago Press, Chicago.

Huang, C.-T. J. (1982). Logical relations in Chinese and the theory of grammar. Ph.D. thesis, MIT, Cambridge.

Iatridou, S. (1990). About Agr(P). *Linguistic Inquiry*, 21(4):551–77.

Iordan, I. and Manoliu, M. (1972). *Manuale de lingüistica románica*, vol. 1. Gredos, Madrid.

Jaberg, K. and Jud, J. (1928–40). *Sprach- und Sachatlas Italiens und der Südschweiz (A.I.S.)*. Ringier, Zofingen, Switzerland.

Jackendoff, R. (1972). *Semantic Interpretation in Generative Grammar*. MIT Press, Cambridge.

Jackendoff, R. (1977). $\overline{X}$ *Syntax: A Study of Phrase Structure*. MIT Press, Cambridge.

Jaeggli, O. (1982). *Topics in Romance Syntax*. Foris, Dordrecht.

Jespersen, O. (1917). *Negation in English and Other Languages*. A. F. Host, Copenhagen.

Jespersen, O. (1924/1965). *The Philosophy of Grammar*. Norton, New York.

Joly, A. (1972). La négation dite 'explétive' en vieil anglais et dans d'autres langues indo-européennes. *Études Anglaises*, 25:30–44.

Jones, M. (1988). Sardinian. In Harris, M. and Vincent, N., eds., *The Romance Languages*, pages 314–50. Croom Helm, London.

Jones, M. (1993). *Sardinian Syntax*. Routledge, London.

Joseph, B. and Philippaki-Warburton, I. (1987). *Modern Greek*. Croom Helm, London.

Karttunen, L. and Peters, S. (1979). Conventional implicature. In Oh, C.-K. and Dinneen, D. A., eds., *Presupposition*, vol. 11 of *Syntax and Semantics*, pages 1–56. Academic Press, New York.

Katz, J. J. and Postal, P. M. (1964). *An Integrated Theory of Linguistic Descriptions*. MIT Press, Cambridge.

Kayne, R. S. (1975). *French Syntax*. MIT Press, Cambridge.

Kayne, R. S. (1989). Notes on English agreement. *CIEFL Bulletin*, 1:40–67.

Kayne, R. S. (1990). Romance clitics and PRO. In *Proceedings of NELS XX*, vol. 2, pages 255–302. GLSA, University of Massachusetts, Amherst.

Kayne, R. S. (1991). Romance clitics, verb movement and PRO. *Linguistic Inquiry*, 22(4):647–86.

Kayne, R. S. (1992). Italian negative infinitival imperatives and clitic climbing. In Tasmowsky, L. and Zribi-Hertz, A., eds., *Hommages à Nicolas Ruwet*, pages 300–12. Communication and Cognition, Ghent.

Kayne, R. S. (1994). *The Antisymmetry of Syntax*, vol. 25 of *Linguistic Inquiry Monographs*. MIT Press, Cambridge.

Klima, E. S. (1964). Negation in English. In Fodor, J. A. and Katz, J. J., eds., *The Structure of Language*. Prentice Hall, Englewood Cliffs, N.J.

Ladusaw, W. A. (1992). Expressing negation. In Barker, C. and Dowty, D., eds., *Proceedings of the Conference on Semantics and Linguistic Theory 2*, pages 237–59. Ohio State University, Columbus.

Laenzlinger, C. (1994). Enclitic clustering: The case of French positive imperatives. *Rivista di Grammatica Generativa*, 19:71–104.

Lafont, R. (1970). *Renaissance du Sud*. Gallimard, Paris.

Laka, I. (1990). Negation in syntax: On the nature of functional categories and projections. Ph.D. thesis, MIT, Cambridge.

Lefebvre, C. and Lumsden, J. S. (1992). On word order in relexification. Travaux de Recherche sur le Créole Haïtien. Université du Québec à Montréal.

Lemieux, M. (1985). Pas rien. In Lemieux, M. and Cedergren, H., eds., *Les tendances dynamiques du français parlé à Montréal*, vol. 2. Gouvernement du Québec, Office de la Langue Française, Quebec.

Li, C. and Thompson, S. A. (1981). *Mandarin Chinese: A Functional Reference Grammar*. University of California Press, Berkeley.

Lockwood, W. (1968). *Historical German Syntax*. Clarendon, Oxford.

Longobardi, G. (1991). In defense of the correspondence hypothesis: Island effects and parasitic constructions in LF. In Huang, C.-T. J. and May, R., eds., *Logical Structure and Linguistic Structure*, pages 149–96. Reidel, Dordrecht.

Mancarella, G. B. (1975). I dialetti del Salento. In Cortelazzo, M., ed., *Profilo dei dialetti italiani*, vol. 5/16, pages 6–52. Pacini, Pisa.

Marchand, H. (1938). Remarks about English negative sentences. *American Studies*, 20:198–204.

Marchetti, G. (1952). *Lineamenti di grammatica friulana*. Società Filologica Friulana, Udine, Italy.

Matalon, Z. N. (1977). *Mari Lenghe: Gramatiche furlane*. Institû di Studis Furlans, Udine, Italy.

May, R. (1985). *Logical Form: Its Structure and Derivation*, vol. 12 of *Linguistic Inquiry Monographs*. MIT Press, Cambridge.

Menéndez-Pidal, R. (1962). *El dialecto leonés*. La Cruz, Orviedo, Spain.

Milner, J.-C. (1982). *Ordres et raisons de langue*. Le Seuil, Paris.

Miremont, P. (1976). *La syntaxe occitane du Périgord*. Gerbert, Orlhac, France.

Molinelli, P. (1988). *Fenomeni della Negazione dal Latino all'Italiano*. La Nuova Italia, Florence.

Muller, C. (1991). *La Négation en Français*. Droz, Geneva.

Munaro, N. (1995). On nominal WH-phrases in some north eastern Italian dialects. *Rivista di Grammatica Generativa*, 20:69–110.

Munaro, N. (1996). Proprietà distribuzionali e strutturali dei sintagmi interrogativi in Bellunese. Unpublished manuscript, Universities of Padua and Venice.

Mussafia, A. (1886). Una particolarità sintattica della lingua italiana dei primi secoli. In *Miscellanea di filologia e linguistica in memoria di N. Caix e U.A. Canello*, pages 255–61. Le Monnier, Florence.

Napoli, D. J. (1981). Semantic interpretation vs. lexical governance: Clitic climbing in Italian. *Language*, 57:841–87.

Napoli, D. J. and Vogel, I. (1990). The conjugations of Italian. *Italica*, 67(4):479–502.

Nicoli, F. (1983). *Grammatica milanese*. Bramante, Busto Arsizio, Italy.

Ouhalla, J. (1991). *Functional Categories and Parametric Variation*. Theoretical Linguistics Series. Routledge, London.

Ouhalla, J. (1993). Negation, focus and tense: The Arabic *maa* and *laa*. *Rivista di Linguistica*, 5(2):275–300. L. Haegeman, guest ed.

Pansier, P. (1973). *Le théâtre Provençal à Avignon au XVIIème siècle*. Laffitte, Marseille.

Parkinson, S. (1988). Portuguese. In Harris, M. and Vincent, N., eds., *The Romance Languages*, pages 131–69. Croom Helm, London.

Parry, M. M. (1985). The dialect of Cairo Montenotte. Ph.D. thesis, University of Wales.

Parry, M. M. (1989). Strutture negative nei dialetti piemontesi. In *At dël V Rëscontr internassional dë studi an sla lenga e la literatura piemontèisa, Alba*. Famija Albèisa. Alba.

Parry, M. M. (1995). Some observations on the syntax of clitic pronouns in Piedmontese. In Smith, J. C. and Maiden, M., eds., *Linguistic Theory and the Romance Languages*, pages, 133–60. John Benjamins, Amsterdam.

Parry, M. M. (in press a). Preverbal negation and clitic ordering, with particular reference to a group of North-West Italian dialects. *Zeitschrift für Romanische Philologie*.

Parry, M. M. (in press b). Negation. In Maiden, M. and Parry, M. M., eds., *The Dialects of Italy*. Routledge, London.

Platzack, C. and Rosengren, I. (1994). On the subject of imperatives: A minimalist account of the imperative pronoun and negated imperatives. *Sprache und Pragmatik*, 34:26–67.

Poletto, C. (1991). Three kinds of subject clitics in Basso Polesano and the theory of *pro*. In *Clitics and Their Hosts*, Eurotyp Working Papers, Theme Group 8: Clitics, pages 269–302. European Science Foundation, Tilburg, The Netherlands. Reprinted in Belletti, A. and Rizzi, L., eds., *Parameters and Functional Heads. Essays in Comparative Syntax*, pages 269–300. Oxford University Press, New York.

Poletto, C. (1992). La sintassi del soggetto nei dialetti italiani settentrionali. Ph.D. thesis, University of Padua.

Poletto, C. (1993a). *La sintassi del soggetto nei dialetti italiani settentrionali*, vol. 12 of *Monografie*. Unipress, Padua.

Poletto, C. (1993b). Subject clitic–verb inversion in north eastern Italian dialects. In Belletti, A., ed., *Syntactic Theory and the Dialects of Italy*, pages 204–51. Rosenberg and Sellier, Turin.

Poletto, C. (1995). Interrogative structures in the northern Italian dialects. Handout of talk given at the Workshop on Clausal Architecture, University of Bergamo, Italy.

Poletto, C. (in press). The internal structure of AgrS and subject clitics. In van Riemsdijk, H., ed., *Clitics in the Languages of Europe*, Empirical Approaches to Language Typology. Mouton de Gruyter, Berlin.

Pollock, J.-Y. (1989). Verb movement, Universal Grammar and the structure of IP. *Linguistic Inquiry*, 20(3):365–424.

Portner, P. and Zanuttini, R. (1996). The syntax and semantics of scalar negation: Evidence from Paduan. In Kusumoto, K., ed., *Proceedings of NELS XXVI*, pages 257–71. GLSA, University of Massachusetts, Amherst.

Posner, R. (1985). Post-verbal negation in non-standard French: A historical and comparative view. *Romance Philology*, 39(2):170–97.

Prince, E. (1994). Subject pro-drop in Yiddish. Unpublished manuscript, University of Pennsylvania.

Puskás, G. (1994). Sentential negation in Hungarian. *Rivista di Linguistica*, 6(1):57–90. L. Haegeman, guest ed.

Ramat, P., Bernini, G., and Molinelli, P. (1986). La sintassi della negazione germanica e romanza. In Lichem, K., Mara, E., and Knaller, S., eds., *Parallela II. Aspetti della sintassi dell'italiano contemporaneo*, pages 237–70. Gunter Narr, Tübingen.

Raposo, E. (1987). Case theory and Infl-to-Comp: The inflected infinitive in European Portuguese. *Linguistic Inquiry*, 18(1):85–109.

Remacle, L. (1952). *Syntaxe du parler Wallon de La Gleize*. Société d'Édition Les Belles Lettres, Paris.

Renzi, L. and Vanelli, L. (1983). I pronomi soggetto in alcune varietà romanze. In *Scritti linguistici in onore di Giovan Battista Pellegrini*, pages 121–45. Pacini, Pisa.

Rivero, M. L. (1994a). Clause structure and V-movement in the languages of the Balkans. *Natural Language and Linguistic Theory*, 12(1):63–120.

Rivero, M. L. (1994b). Negation, imperatives and Wackernagel effects. *Rivista di Linguistica*, 6(1):39–66. L. Haegeman, guest ed.

Rivero, M. L. (1994c). On two locations for complement clitic pronouns: Serbo/Croatian, Bulgarian and Old Spanish. Paper presented at the Third Diachronic Generative Syntax Conference, Vrije Universiteit, Amsterdam.

Rivero, M. L. and Terzi, A. (1995). Imperatives, V-movement and logical mood. *Journal of Linguistics*, 31:301–32.

Rizzi, L. (1986). On the status of subject clitics in Romance. In Jaeggli, O. and Silva-Corvalan, C., eds., *Studies in Romance Linguistics*, pages 137–52. Foris, Dordrecht.

Rizzi, L. (1990). Speculations on Verb Second. In Mascaró, J. and Nespor, M., eds., *Grammar in Progress: GLOW Essays for Henk van Riemsdijk*, pages 375–86. Foris, Dordrecht.

Rizzi, L. (1996). Residual Verb Second and the Wh-criterion. In and Belletti, A. and Rizzi, L., eds., *Parameters and Functional Heads: Essays in Comparative Syntax*, pages 63–90. Oxford University Press, New York.

Rizzi, L. and Roberts, I. G. (1989). Complex inversion in French. *Probus*, 1:1–30. Reprinted in Belletti, A. and Rizzi, L., eds., *Parameters and Functional Heads: Essays in Comparative Syntax*, pages 91–116. Oxford University Press, New York.

Roberts, I. G. (1993). The nature of subject clitics in Franco-Provençal Valdôtain. In Belletti, A., ed., *Syntactic Theory and the Dialects of Italy*, pages 319–353. Rosenberg and Sellier, Turin.

Rohlfs, G. (1949). *Historische Grammatik der italienischen Sprache und ihrer Mundarten*. Vol. 2: *Formenlehre und Syntax*. A. Francke, Bern.

Rohlfs, G. (1968). *Grammatica storica della lingua italiana e dei suoi dialetti — Morfologia*, vol. 2. Einaudi, Turin. Translation (with author's updating) of Rohlfs (1949).

Rohlfs, G. (1969). *Grammatica storica della lingua italiana e dei suoi dialetti — Sintassi e formazione delle parole*, vol. 3. Einaudi, Turin.

Ronjat, J. (1980). *Grammaire historique des parlers provençaux modernes*. Slatkine Reprints, Laffitte Reprints, Geneva.

Rooryck, J. (1992). Romance enclitic ordering and Universal Grammar. *Linguistic Review*, 9(3):219–50.

Rooth, M. (1985). Association with focus. Ph.D. thesis, University of Massachusetts, Amherst.

Rouveret, A. (1992). Clitic placement, focus and the Wackernagel position in European Portuguese. In Rizzi, L., ed., *Clitics in Romance and Germanic*, vol. 3 of Eurotyp Working Papers, Theme Group 8: Clitics, pages 103–39. European Science Foundation, Tilburg, The Netherlands.

Rowlett, P. (1993a). On the syntactic derivation of negative sentence adverbials. *French Language Studies*, 3:39–69.

Rowlett, P. (1993b). Remarks on sentential negation in French. *Catalan Woking Papers in Linguistics*, 3(1):153–69.

Saccon, G. (1993). Post-verbal subjects: A study based on Italian and its dialects. Ph.D. thesis, Harvard University, Cambridge.

Sadock, J. and Zwicky, A. (1985). Speech act distinctions in syntax. In Shopen, T., ed., *Language Typology and Syntactic Description*, pages 155–96. Cambridge University Press, Cambridge.

Safir, K. (1983). On Small Clauses as constituents. *Linguistic Inquiry*, 4:730–35.

Salvi, G. and Borgato, G. (1995). Il tipo iussivo. In Renzi, L., Salvi, G., and Cardinaletti, A., eds., *Grande grammatica italiana di consultazione*, vol. 3, pages 152–59. Il Mulino, Bologna.

Sancisi, A. (1995). *Il dialetto nella scuola*. Fara, Santarcangelo, Italy.

Sankoff, G. and Vincent, D. (1980). The productive use of *ne* in spoken Montréal French. In Sankoff, G., ed., *The Social Life of Language*, pages 295–310. University of Pennsylvania Press, Philadelphia.

Schwegler, A. (1983). Predicate negation and word-order change: A problem of multiple causation. *Lingua*, 61(4):297–334.

Schwegler, A. (1991). Predicate negation in contemporary Brazilian Portuguese — A change in progress. *Orbis*, 34(1/2):187–214.

Schwegler, A. (1988). Word-order change in predicate negation strategies in Romance. *Diachronica*, 5(1/2):21–58.

Seutin, E. (1975). *Description grammaticale du parler de l'Ile-aux-Coudres*. Les Presses de l'Université de Montréal, Montreal.

Signorell, F. (1987). *Normas Surmiranas: Grammatica rumantscha digl idiom da Sur- e Sotses*. Tgesa Editoura Cantounala, Chur, Switzerland.

Siller-Runggaldier, H. (1985). La negazione nel ladino centrale. *Revue de Linguistique Romane*, 49(193–194):71–85.

Sorrento, L. (1912). *Lat.* mŏdŏ *nel dialetto siciliano*. Madrid. Reprinted in *Revue d. dialect. rom.*, 1912.

Spescha, A. (1989). *Grammatica Sursilvana*. Casa Editura per Mieds d'Instrucziun, Chur, Switzerland.

Spiess, F. (1977). Di un'innovazione morfologica nel sistema dei pronomi personali oggetto nel dialetto della Collina d'Oro. In *Problemi di morfosintassi dialettale. Atti dell'XI Convegno del C.S.D.I.*, pages 203–12, Pacini, Pisa.

Sportiche, D. (1988). A theory of floating quantifiers and its corollaries for constituent structure. *Linguistic Inquiry*, 19:425–49.

Sportiche, D. (in press a). Clitic constructions. In Zaring, L. and Rooryck, J., eds., *Phrase Structure and the Lexicon*. Kluwer, Dordrecht.

Sportiche, D. (in press b). Subject clitics in French and Romance: Complex inversion and clitic doubling. In Johnson, K. and Roberts, I., eds., *Studies in Comparative Romance Syntax*. Kluwer, Dordrecht.

Tang, T.-C. (1989). *Studies on Chinese Morphology and Syntax*, vol. 2. Student Book Co., Taipei.

Terzi, A. (1992). PRO in finite clauses: A study of the inflectional heads of the Balkan languages. Ph.D. thesis, City University of New York.

Thomas, E. W. (1969). *The syntax of spoken Brazilian Portuguese*. Vanderbilt University Press, Nashville.

Tobler, A. (1912). Review of J. Le Coultre's 'De l'ordre des mots dans Chrétien de Troyes'. *Vermischte Beiträge zur französischen Grammatik*, pages 395–414. Hirzel, Leipzig.

Togeby, K. (1970). L'impératif roman et l'impératif roumain. In Iordan, I. and Rosenstand Hansen, A., eds., *Problèmes de linguistique roumaine*, pages 74–83. Akademisk Forlag, Copenhagen.

Toppino, G. (1925,6). Il dialetto di Castellinaldo, note di sintassi. *Italia Dialettale*, 2:1–49.

Travis, L. (1988). The syntax of adverbs. In *McGill Working Papers in Linguistics. Special Issue on Comparative Germanic Syntax*. McGill University, Montreal.

Tsimpli, I.-M. (1990). The clause structure and word order of Modern Greek. In Harris, J., ed., *UCL Working Papers in Linguistics*, vol. 2. Department of Linguistics, University College London.

Vai, M. (1995a). Alcuni aspetti della negazione in milanese da Bonvesin ad oggi. In Banfi, E., Bonfandini, G., Cordin, P., and Iliescu, M., eds., *Italia Settentrionale: Crocevia di idiomi romanzi*. Atti del convegno internazionale di studi, Trento, 21–23 Ottobre 1993, pages 159–69, Niemeyer, Tübingen.

Vai, M. (1995b). Sintassi della negazione: Appunti di grammatica comparata indoeuropea e romanza. Tesi di laurea, Università di Milano.

Vai, M. (1996). Per una storia della negazione in Milanese in comparazione con altre varietà altoitaliane. *Acme*, 49(1):57–98.

Valente, V. (1975). I dialetti della Puglia. In Cortelazzo, M., ed., *Profilo dei dialetti italiani*, vol. 5/15, pages 5–78. Pacini, Pisa.

Vanelli, L. (1987). I pronomi soggetto nei dialetti italiani settentrionali dal Medio Evo ad oggi. *Medioevo Romanzo*, 13:173–211.

Vennemann, T. (1974). Topics, subjects and word order: From SXV to SVX via TVX. In Anderson, J. M. and Jones, C., eds., *Historical Linguistics: Proceedings of the First International Conference, Edinburgh, 1973*, pages 339–76, North Holland, Amsterdam.

Wang, W. (1965). Two aspect markers in Mandarin. *Language*, 41(3):457–70.

Wanner, D. (1987). *The Development of Romance Clitic Pronouns: From Latin to Old Romance*. Mouton de Gruyter, Berlin.

Watanabe, A. (1992). Subjacency and S-Structure movement of WH-in-situ. *Journal of East Asian Linguistics*, 1:255–91.

Zanuttini, R. (1990). Two types of negative markers. In *Proceedings of NELS XX*, vol. 2, pages 517–30. GLSA, University of Massachusetts, Amherst.

Zanuttini, R. (1991). Syntactic properties of sentential negation: A comparative study of Romance languages. Ph.D. thesis, University of Pennsylvania, Philadelphia.

Zanuttini, R. (1994a). Re-examining negative clauses. In Cinque, G., Koster, J., Pollock, J.-Y., Rizzi, L., and Zanuttini, R., eds., *Paths towards Universal Grammar: Studies in Honor of Richard S. Kayne*, pages 427–51. Georgetown University Press, Washington, D.C.

Zanuttini, R. (1994b). Speculations on negative imperatives. *Rivista di Linguistica*, 6(1):119–42. L. Haegeman, guest editor.

Zanuttini, R. (1996). On the relevance of tense for sentential negation. In Belletti, A. and Rizzi, L., eds., *Parameters and Functional Heads: Essays in Comparative Syntax*, pages 181–207. Oxford University Press, New York.

Zörner, L. (1986). Caratteristiche liguri nei dialetti di montagna della provincia di Piacenza. *Revue de Linguistique Romane*, 50(197–198):67–117.

Zörner, L. (1989). *Il dialetto di Cembra e dei suoi dintorni. Descrizione fonologica, storico-fonetica e morfosintattica*. Annali di S. Michele n. 2, Museo degli usi e costumi della gente trentina, San Michele all'Adige, Italy.

Zörner, L. (1994). I dialetti dell'Oltrepò pavese tra il lombardo, l'emiliano e il ligure. *Rivista Italiana di Dialettologia*, 17:55–98.

INDEX

Printed in the United States
135353LV00006B/82/A

3062910R00115

Printed in Great Britain
by Amazon.co.uk, Ltd.,
Marston Gate.